DOMESTIC NATIONALISM

Domestic Nationalism

Muslim Women, Health, and Modernity in Indonesia

CHIARA FORMICHI

STANFORD UNIVERSITY PRESS
Stanford, California

Stanford University Press
Stanford, California

This book has been partially underwritten by the Susan Groag Bell Publication Fund in Women's History. For more information on the fund, please see www.sup.org/bellfund.

Library of Congress Cataloging-in-Publication Data

Names: Formichi, Chiara, 1982- author.
Title: Domestic nationalism : Muslim women, health, and modernity in
    Indonesia / Chiara Formichi.
Description: Stanford, California : Stanford University Press, 2025. |
    Includes bibliographical references and index.
Identifiers: LCCN 2025027507 (print) | LCCN 2025027508 (ebook) | ISBN
    9781503635241 (cloth) | ISBN 9781503644427 (paperback) | ISBN
    9781503644434 (ebook)
Subjects: LCSH: Muslim women—Indonesia—History—20th century. |
    Homemakers—Indonesia—History—20th century. |
    Motherhood—Indonesia—History—20th century. | Public
    health—Indonesia—History—20th century. |
    Nationalism—Indonesia—History—20th century. | Sex
    role—Indonesia—History—20th century.
Classification: LCC HQ1170 .F676 2025 (print) | LCC HQ1170 (ebook) | DDC
    305.409598/09041—dc23/eng/20250614
LC record available at https://lccn.loc.gov/2025027507
LC ebook record available at https://lccn.loc.gov/2025027508

Cover design: Susan Zucker
Cover art: *Indonesia is my homeland . . . which I love.* Poster, National
Archives of the Netherlands, Creative Commons
Typeset by Newgen in 10/14.4

The authorized representative in the EU for product safety and compliance is: Mare Nostrum Group B.V. | Mauritskade 21D | 1091 GC Amsterdam | The Netherlands | Email address: gpsr@mare-nostrum.co.uk | KVK chamber of commerce number: 96249943

To all those who labor unseen

Contents

Illustrations

Acknowledgments

This book carries my name on the cover, and will be recognized as the product of my professional labor, but it also stands on the shoulders of those who have stepped up and stepped in with their everyday practices of care and expressions of love, as family, friends, and colleagues.

Its making was largely possible because of the sustained, quotidian support of my family. Some books might be the outcome of diligent nine-to-five, Monday-to-Friday work that reliably pauses on schools' closures. This book was not. I was able to research, think, read, write, discuss, freak out, rewrite, and complete this book thanks to the endless availability and patience of my family.

My mother, Anna, joined our household at various stages of the process, starting with the first round of fieldwork in the Netherlands, then again in what was meant to be a "brainstorming semester" in Singapore (which became lockdown), and lastly joining our extended pandemic lifestyle in North America. It is only thanks to her that I was able to write the first pages of this book in those early months, and eventually finish it. Her presence didn't just prevent disaster; it made our life richer. During the year of emergency remote teaching, it was my in-laws who took up the baton. The garret they built over the woodshed provided the oasis of calm and quiet I needed to work unaffected by school closures and parental guilt, as grandparents and aunts and uncle cared for our daughter. This project has existed for the entire duration of my daughter's conscious life, and she has thus been the unwitting force behind finishing it! Eli, my partner in life, has been the harshest reader, most constructive editor, and steadfastly loving supporter. Without his unwavering intellectual and emotional support, and daily material enabling of my work, this book would not be a reality.

I collected far too many debts, as colleagues showed generosity of time and spirit, reading, commenting, and discussing the ideas presented here. Some even found sources for me in places I could not reach, making apparent their commitment to fostering discourse, enhancing scholarship, expanding our intellectual horizons, and pushing me to do better. I list them in alphabetical order, and only hope to be able to return their kindness: Barbara Watson Andaya, Tom Hoogervorst, Kirsten Kamphuis, David Kloos, Mas Reza Maulana, Arnout van der Meer, Eva Nisa, Hans Pols, Rachel Rinaldo, Henk Schulte Nordholt, Guo-Quan Seng, Naoko Shimazu, Charles Sullivan, Evi Sutrisno, and Taomo Zhou. The support of librarians at Cornell's Kroch Library and Mann Library, Harvard University's Countway Library, Rockefeller Foundation Archives in Sleepy Hollow, NY, Yale University Library, Monash University (Melbourne, Australia), Leiden University Library, Amsterdam University Library, and the International Institute for Social History (in the Netherlands), Jakarta's National Library, Singapore's National Library, and the Food and Agriculture Organization's Library and Archives (located in Rome, Italy) was crucial to this book.

For being unafraid of choppy prose and incomplete thoughts, I extend my special appreciation to Tamara Loos, and to the members of the Society for the Humanities' Interdisciplinary Monograph Writing Groups in 2022–2023 (Suyoung Son, Peidong Sun, Oren Falk, and Natasha Raheja) and 2023–2024 (Ben Anderson, Shirley Samuels, Casey Schmitt, and Maria Fernandez). To Suyoung Son I am indebted for reading multiple chapters over the years, and being a stimulating conversation partner; co-organizing the conference "Transforming Asia with Food: Women and Everyday Life" was most exhilarating—heartfelt gratitude goes to our panelists and guests too.

My deepest appreciation for reading, engaging, and commenting on the entire manuscript goes to Christina Firpo, Shenila Khoja-Moolji, Ruth Rogaski, and Jean Gelman Taylor, who participated in a book manuscript development workshop supported by Cornell's Arts and Science Rosenthal Award for the Advancement of Women in the Sciences and Humanities, as well as to Chie Ikeya and another reader for Stanford University Press who remained anonymous. Their commitment to improving this book was extraordinary and inspiring. My two doctoral students whose committee I chair, Tsuguta Yamashita and Joshua Kam, have been a gracious captive audience for several years, and I am thankful for their patience and stimulating conversations. A particular note of thanks goes to *Ibu* Jolanda Pandin for painstakingly going over some Malay sources with me, and to Thari Zweers, who read Dutch materials with me for hours on end—all mistakes remain nonetheless mine. Writing books can be a fairly solitary and isolating process, but the solidarity of friends near and far has been a source of strength. Empathic smiles in the department hallway and long walks around Beebe Lake; late-night calls to Denver, Singapore and Hong Kong; and unplanned visits in Leiden; all made the process more humane.

Ideas underpinning this book were presented in talks, conferences, and workshops between 2019 and 2024. I am thankful for the opportunities I was given to share my work-in-progress at the following venues: Gadjah Mada University Summer School, AAS Annual Conference in Seattle, the University of Hong Kong, University of California at Berkeley, National University of Singapore, the Royal Netherlands Institute of Southeast Asian and Caribbean Studies in Leiden, the Abdallah S. Kamel Center for the Study of Islamic Law and Civilization at Yale Law School, the conference "Re-evaluating Methodological Trajectories in the Academic Study of Islam" held by the Department for the Study of Religion at the University of Toronto, and the "Transforming Asia with Food" conference that we hosted here at Cornell. Some of the ideas and sources featured here have already appeared, in different form, in the *Journal of Modern Asian Studies* (2022, vol. 56, no. 6) and *History of Religions* (2023, vol. 62, no. 4); I appreciate the work of the editors and anonymous reviewers who sharpened my analyses there.

While I recognize that financial support for research is funneled through institutions, here I wish to acknowledge the labor that enables its allocation, which is mostly executed by scholars who receive little to no recognition for it. I thus express my gratitude to the colleagues who read and selected proposals, awarded grants, and sat on budget committees at the following units at Cornell: the Society for the Humanities, the Mario Einaudi Center for International Studies, the Southeast Asia Program, the Department of Asian Studies, and the College of Arts and Science. Outside of my own university, I am grateful to colleagues at the Royal Netherlands

Institute of Southeast Asian and Caribbean Studies (KITLV) in Leiden and the Middle East Institute at the National University of Singapore, as each hosted me for a semester in 2019–2020, as I pursued early fieldwork and started generating ideas for this project.

Warmest gratitude goes to my editor at Stanford University Press, Dylan White, who kindly accommodated shifting deadlines and endless questions; Justine Sargent made production possible; and Mike Priehs and Emily Zingers at Cornell supported me as I navigated the treacherous waters of copyright permissions and fair use—final decisions rested with me only. This book features over thirty illustrations. Thanks go to Monash University Library, Yale University Library, Cornell Rare and Manuscript Collection, Cornell DCAPS, the Rockefeller Archive Center, the Wereldmuseum Collection, Leiden University, the National Archives of the Netherlands, and the National Library of the Netherlands, for providing image reproductions and permissions as needed.

Abbreviations

BPMD	Balai Pendidikan Masjarakat Desa (Village Education Center)
DVG	Dienst der Volksgezondheid (previously Gezondheidsdienst), Public Health Services
EHTINI	Eerste Hygiëne Tentoonstelling in Nederlandsch-Indië (First Hygiene Exhibition in the Netherlands Indies)
ELS	Europeesche Lagere School (European Primary Schools)
FAO	Food and Agriculture Organization of the United Nations
GERWANI	Gerakan Wanita Indonesia (Indonesian Women's Movement)
HIS	Hollandsch-Inlandsche School (Dutch Schools for Natives)
ICA	International Cooperation Administration
IHD	International Health Division (Rockefeller Foundation)
KOWANI	Kongres Wanita Indonesia (Indonesian Women's Congress)
LMR	Lembaga Makanan Rakjat (Institute for People's Nutrition)
MCH	maternal and child health
NIAS	Nederlandsch-Indische Artsen School (Indies Medical School)
Nj. / Ny.	Mrs.
Perwari	Persatuan Wanita Republik Indonesia (Women's Union of the Indonesian Republic)
PNI	Partai Nasional Indonesia (Indonesian National Party)
PPK	Kementerian Pendidikan, Pengadjaran dan Kebudajaan (Ministry of Education, Teaching, and Culture)

SGKP	Sekolah Guru Kepandaian Puteri (Schools for Teachers of Girls' Domestic Schools)
SKP	Sekolah Kepandaian Puteri (Girls' Domestic Schools)
STOVIA	School tot Opleiding van Inlandsche Artsen (School for the Training of Native Doctors)
TCA	Technical Cooperation Administration
WHO	World Health Organization

Note on Spelling

This book cuts across several spelling conventions of the Indonesian language. A core word to this book, "progress," would, then, have appeared in the original sources as: *kemadjoean* ["dj" for "j" and "oe" for "u"], *kemadjuan* ["dj" for "j" but "u"], and *kemajuan* ["j" and "u"].

For ease of use and consistency, this book uses the modern (post-1972) Indonesian spelling (hence, *kemajuan, rakyat*), unless in a direct citation, and the glossary includes variations for reference. The spelling of organizations and personal names follows the most common spelling (for instance, Muhammadiyah but Lembaga Makanan Rakjat). After Indonesian independence it was not uncommon for an individual's name to be spelled variously (Soewardjo/Suwardjo, Soekarno/Sukarno, Poorwo Soedarmo/Purwo Sudarmo). Indonesian personal names follow the use preferred by individuals, unless in citations.

Place names use modern spelling, unless in direct citation.

All direct citations are reproduced in their original spelling.

All translations, unless differently stated, are my own.

DOMESTIC NATIONALISM

INTRODUCTION

WE KNOW NOTHING ELSE ABOUT Soekarmi: only her name and her writing, found in a 1931 issue of the Indonesian-language women's magazine *Isteri* ("Wife"). She argued that "women should know about nutrition," so she explained the role of carbohydrates, proteins, fats, and vitamins. While characterizing it as a "very new" and "important" field of scientific knowledge, Soekarmi used this elucidation of nutrition as an opportunity to validate how "the habits of our women in the villages, or of old-fashioned women, are not so wrong and are, in fact, most correct. . . . In Indonesia, we know we need not fear vitamin deficiency." Eating bran, Soekarmi continued, was a common village practice that limited the presence of beriberi disease; being exposed to sunshine, Indonesians needed not be concerned with rickets; feeding bananas to small children boosted their vitamin intake, preventing xerophthalmia; and extended breastfeeding ensured the best nutrition possible.[1] Women writing in other vernacular magazines embraced ideals of scientific mothering (such as scheduled feeding, separation of mother and child, etc.)[2] while at the same time expressing a preference for breastfeeding and against bottles and formulas: mothers' milk was presented as a practice mandated by the Qur'an, as well as being more hygienic and nutritious.

———

In the early decades of the twentieth century, the colonized population of Java and Sumatra, in the Dutch East Indies, began to be exposed to "new" notions of scientific cleanliness and nutrition. If in the earliest days of health propaganda the colonial establishment had shaped a dominant discursive space that promoted the idea of physical health as an economic asset,[3] primarily engaging men as interlocutors, in the 1920s to 1930s indigenous women too entered these conversations, leveraging their "womanly" duties.[4] Mirroring dynamics already in motion across imperial metropoles, women were held responsible for the "production" of healthy (male) workers, with hygienic reforms and the "cult of domesticity" advancing together to glorify at once scientific cleanliness and women's domestic labor.[5]

In the context of emergent capitalism and aspirations to modernization, disease prevention and infant care were promoted to mitigate epidemics and mortality rates, and reinforce the superiority of Europe. In the Indies, colonial discourses redefined the parameters of mothering to comply with science; regardless of their literacy levels, women were expected to perform their duties according to the evolving principles of biomedical hygiene as defined by Europeans, rejecting practices that did not conform. Such transformations, then, marginalized indigenous women's traditional roles and religious approaches to healing.

But indigenous women advanced the idea that modern mothering could take a different approach; it could be scientific while also conforming to religious values and "traditional" practices (Ind. 'adat).[6] The published words of Soekarmi and her peers show that Indonesian women in the late colonial period actively engaged with scientific knowledge, absorbing it and rearticulating it as Islam and 'adat came to operate as alternate sources of knowledge. Through this process of epistemological resistance, indigenous women reformulated modern mothering, at once selectively pushing against and embracing aspects of it. In its 1919 opening editorial, the magazine *Perempoean Bergerak* ("Woman on the Move") argued that women were defined by "the house, infant-feeding, child-rearing, hygiene, religion, and 'native' feminism."[7] Placed in the broader context of articles on the advancement of women's education and participation in public debates and activities, including anti-colonial nationalism, this women's magazine approached the discursive and physical space of the home as a point of departure for women to strive for emancipation through modern scientific knowledge, indigeneity, and religious piety.

In these voices and images, I recover the roles of indigenous women in moving Indonesia forward, in their own terms, as they shaped a distinct discourse of progress at the intersection of gender, Islam, care work, and nationalism. *Domestic Nationalism* presents a social history of Indonesian nation-building through decades and across regimes that privileges Muslim women's social, political, and economic contribution through their quotidian activities as home-based caregivers and professional health workers, as they blurred the boundaries of biomedicine and tradition, of domestic and public engagement.

The framework of *Domestic Nationalism* proposes that indigenous women re-conceptualized modern mothering and hygienic practices, turning them into forces of counter-imperialism and nation-building, and that in this way they contributed to the emergence of Indonesia as a modern nation-state. This process unfolded across different historical phases: from the late Dutch colonial era (1901–1942) to the Japanese occupation (1942–1945), the National revolution (1945–1949), and the early years of the Indonesian republic (1949–1959). Through the chapters, I follow women's engagements with multiple projects of hygienic modernity to show that whereas they operated within their ascribed gendered role as mothers/wives, and their self-fashioned identities as indigenous and Muslim, through the decades they claimed spaces of agency and opportunity to advance a nationalist political agenda.

Analytically, I deploy the double meaning of "domestic"—pertaining to the home and to national-level politics too. I show that the two meanings are mutually reliant, as women's activities of care work had political implications, and political goals (domestic and international) were achieved through policies pertaining to care work. I leverage Amy Kaplan's observation that both domesticities, home and nation, are shaped by "everything outside the[ir] geographic and conceptual border,"[8] in a relationship that is not only oppositional, but also symbiotic. This allows me to explore tensions between the various meanings of domesticity.

Throughout, I address the first such dynamic, between the household and that immediately outside it; that is, between women's home roles and an evolving public arena, initially in the scientific field of biomedicine, and then in politics. In the first three chapters I detail how some women came to recognize the political ramifications of hygienic mothering as early as the 1920s to 1930s; and yet (as discussed in Chapter 4, "War"), it would only be in the 1940s, under sustained conditions of conflict, that a redefined "domestic arena" would become publicly visible as a political space, encompassing at once the discursive domains of home and nation.

Similarly, the second such theme, addressed primarily in the last chapter, is revealed as the domestic politics of Indonesia took form in opposition to, and yet in connection with, the international political system from which it claimed to seek independence. In Chapter 5, "Prosperity," I show that the international sphere affected both national-level and home-level domesticity, often speaking directly to the (domestic) household as a way of exerting pressure on the (domestic) government's economic and political policy. As home-based practices harnessing maternal and child health (MCH) and nutrition were, in the 1950s, seen by the government as crucial to the project of material nation-building and strengthening, Indonesian homes—and therefore the nation—received American and other forms of international aid, even despite Cold War-era political ideological frictions.

———

My gendered analysis of hygienic modernity is rooted in Ruth Rogaski's work on treaty-port China,[9] which highlights the connection made by ruling administrators between the "health of individuals" and the "health of the nation." Moving to Indonesia, I take into account the interplay of class, education, race, and religion in the colonial and postcolonial contexts. This enables me to show and explain how, while European and American women were promptly identified as necessary agents of change as home-based sanitarians,[10] when rural health and hygiene propaganda activities were launched in the Dutch East Indies in the 1910s to 1920s, these were led by white men who engaged local men in explanations of daily domestic chores usually pursued by women.

This endeavor enriches conversations about social reproduction, maternalism, and nationalism; the history of rural hygiene, health and nutrition; and the role of Islam therein. More specifically, I aim to fill a triple lacuna in the study of Indonesia. Women have been excluded first from most explorations of nationalism and nation-building[11] (with the notable exceptions of Mary Steedly and Jean Gelman Taylor),[12] and second from studies of public health and rural hygiene.[13]

Thirdly, scholars of women's activism in Indonesia have been hesitant to claim an agentive and political role for those who operated primarily within the realm of "womanly matters." Such activities have been discussed as "social" or "charitable" contributions, *in opposition to* the political activism that antagonized and challenged the state by advocating for women's rights and marriage reform.[14]

Domestic Nationalism examines how Indonesian Muslim women claimed and asserted their right to take the initiative, seize opportunities as they emerged, and contribute to Indonesia's political life through activities that leveraged their gendered identities and expertise. I focus on their agentive contributions in spite of—and sometimes as framed by—multiple patriarchal orders: colonial, nationalist, and religious. While operating within a patriarchal society that circumscribed them by the domestic sphere, regardless of socio-economic status and literacy levels, Indonesian women pushed the boundaries of that sphere, sometimes with words, at other times with actions. Throughout the book I navigate the challenge of identifying when this labor was exploitative and when it was enabling, agentive, and possibly emancipatory; I recognize that it was often both things at once.

Feminist scholars such as Judith Butler, bell hooks, and Nancy Fraser have established that racializing, patriarchal, and classist regimes always condition women's agency, as do colonization and religion. During the five decades under examination in this book, spanning at least three distinct political regimes (Dutch colonialism, Japanese occupation, and the Indonesian Revolution and republic), Indonesian women were subject to multiple sources of oppression. Reliably called upon for their "domestic" and "motherly" nature, like women in other regions—such as Europe, America and across Asia, from Egypt and Iran to India and China—their biological and caregiving capabilities were regarded as tools for the production and socialization of future laborers, soldiers, and citizens.[15]

I pursue an analysis that acknowledges the limits faced by women in Java and Sumatra, but at the same time I refuse to efface women's endeavors and desires to effect change, thus embracing Padma Anagol's idea of agency as "conscious, goal-driven activities . . . that embrace the *possibility* of change."[16] I find traces of indigenous women aspiring toward a different future, carving out niches of opportunities and expanding their footprint, asserting their epistemological authority and their own agency; leveraging opportunities in times of crises; and ultimately acting as agents of Indonesia's economic, social, and political advancement (*kemajuan*), through their gendered mothering roles.

As Afsaneh Najmabadi has pointed out for Iran, "the well-known argument for women's education—that educated women made better mothers and wives—sounds very traditional," eliciting "disappointment" on the part of those who observe the past from today's vantage point. Hence, she continues, such feelings would be better understood as "perhaps aris[ing] from lack of attention to what important shifts in 'mother' and 'wife'" came with the opportunity for education at the time.[17] Jasamin Rostam-Kolayi identifies scientific domesticity and household-management education as sites of expanding opportunities for Iranian women in the early twentieth century, noting that such education "opened the door for women to go outside the domestic sphere and enter new professions."[18] A similar argument has been advanced by scholars such as Beth Baron, Laura Bier, and Lisa Pollard for modern Egypt;[19] Mary Hancock for the Madras Presidency in colonial India;[20] and Helen Schneider for Republican China.[21] In 1910s Japan, housewives were "a recognized professional identity,"[22] and several more scholars have reclaimed the role of home economics in American women's social and political emancipation at the turn of the twentieth century, shifting away from a narrative of domestication.[23]

The discursive space of modern mothering was an upper- and middle-class one. Literate women were educated and enculturated, gaining the ability and access to engage with these conversations, rearticulating ideas of scientific care through traditional and religious knowledge,[24] and possibly escape domesticity through professionalization.[25] Many others had no choice but to pursue care work as a chore, received no formal education,[26] had no opportunities to lead, and might be seen as stuck in a static, oppressive, society.

As I theorize "care work" to be the collective labor carried out by women tending to their communities, extending from the family to the nation, the analysis I pursue crosses the class and education barrier. In this book, care work constitutes a variety of activities, those pursued inside the house for one's own family, or outside of it for neighbors or strangers; physical, intellectual, or emotional; paid or unpaid; requiring professional skills or no skill at all.[27] Because of the gendered expectations that have sustained care work through time and space, I often refer to it as "mothering." Here, mothering also appears as a variation of Rima Apple's "motherhood" when intending to dislodge infant care from the biological reproductive expectations inherent to motherhood.

This multifaceted manifestation of social reproductive labor emerges as a form of everyday public and political action, enabling me to decouple domestic work from the domestication of women. I envision this approach to care work as one that operates as a discursive equalizer that enables a cross-class analysis of women's public roles, where the voices of a (privileged) few do not conceal the silenced (disenfranchised) majority. Nor do I ignore socio-economic differences. Rather, the quasi-universal all-encompassing expectation for women to participate in care work and social reproduction creates a common understanding of political change as driven by quotidian actions. I am indebted to Paula Baker's "broad" definition of politics "to include any action, formal or informal, taken to affect the course or behavior of government or the community."[28] Hence, I reclaim and make visible the role played by Muslim women in Java and Sumatra in propelling the nation's project of modernity, as everyday guardians and promoters of health, and as producers of knowledge.

Three concepts are interwoven to craft this argument: progress, gender, and Islam. Progress—sometimes glossed as "modernity" (this usually with a "foreign" Euro-American connotation) or "advancement" (when most closely translating the Malay term *kemajuan*, with *maju* identifying forward movement)—was imagined in a variety of ways, from building bridges and owning a radio to wearing a miniskirt or a headscarf. Similar contestations were alive in the political imagination of a *maju* postcolonial Indonesia—should it be a democracy, an Islamic state, or an authoritarian regime? One point of convergence was that the people of this nation-state—whether as *rakyat* (the physical masses) or *bangsa* (the abstract nation, Benedict Anderson's "imagined community")—needed to be strong, healthy, and productive to ensure national prosperity. As I show, this is what Dutch colonizers, Japanese occupiers, and American philanthropists strived for as well, as they saw the Indonesian archipelago as a pool of resources (human and natural) ripe for exploitation.

Another aspect of progress, as promoted by imperialist forces, was the centuries-old underlying racist assumption of civilizational difference, which in the late 1920s was further reinforced by the emergence of eugenicist discourses.[29] A "native" population, then, could be shepherded "forward," but might not in fact be able to actually achieve "modernity" because of its "primitive" conditions. This attitude was common across Europe, as the intertwining of racism (Caucasian races being superior) and civilizationism (with Christianity as the only path to salvation, and the only religion-*cum*-culture that endorsed reason and could therefore lead others towards "progress") had supported European expansionism in the Middle East, South Asia, and eventually Southeast Asia.[30]

Women were especially useful in colonial reflections on Muslims' backwardness. This was exemplified by: the French "de-veiling" campaigns in North Africa;[31] British missionaries' comments that Muslim Indian women were in a "[even] more degraded, humiliating position" than their Hindu counterparts;[32] and by Dutch observers in the Indies, who dismissed altogether the possibility of Muslim women's emancipation unless they rejected their piety.[33]

This approach was reflected in the public health effort. Compared with other places, in Indonesia women were included slowly and late. Whereas, in the Global North, Christianity played an important role in the project of hygienic modernity, and in women's appropriation of it, Islam was specifically marked by the colonial establishment as a source of backwardness. And Muslim women—by European definition oppressed, subjugated and uneducated because of their religion—were among the last individuals to be targeted by hygienic propaganda. Religious and traditional practices were reliably pointed at as the source of mistrust for science and biomedicine in the early 1900s, but in fact, Indonesian women had found echoes of the Qur'an and their ancestors' practices in the precepts of modern mothering.

Demographically, the majority of the people I encountered in the sources were Muslim (Sunni Shafi'i, to be specific), an identity reflected in the history and culture of the western part of the Indonesian archipelago. This identity is central to the analysis, as their writings, images, and characterizations show that these women inhabited and experienced the world *as Muslim women*—even as they expressed themselves on secular platforms of activism, as Elora Shehabuddin has elegantly done in her own narrative of intertwining and cross-pollinating of emancipationist and feminist ideas.[34]

In this book, Islam is neither consistently apparent in explicit ways, nor always at the forefront as the primary lens of analysis. I build on Deniz Kandiyoti's reflection that Islam is neither explanatory ("all there is to know") nor marginal ("of little consequence in understanding the condition of women").[35] This approach enables us to explore Muslim women's behavior through their own voices, at the intersection of "foreign" models of modernity and "local" societal framings. In doing so, I do not intend to evoke any one world view: whether colonialists' ideas of intrinsic backwardness, unshakable rootedness in tradition, ideological rejection of colonial modernity, or the need for a secular path to emancipation. Rather, Islam sits at the center because I recognize that the sources forming the basis of this book radiate Islamic worldviews and *ethos*. I show that "Islam" is *always* present, as a framework of reference, a cultural substratum, an ancestral legacy, or an assumed boundary-marker—but strive to underline how it is not a hegemonic, deterministic force.

I address a fundamental political question—how did Muslim women, as mothers and caregivers, conceptualize the modern nation-state of Indonesia? How did they contribute to its formation? These women, from literate elites to lower-class laborers, offer new perspectives on how ideas of modernity and tradition intersected in the formation of an Indonesian identity, and on the role Islam played in that process. Extant studies of Indonesian nationalism have focused on parties or individual personalities (mostly male) who over decades of political activism and intellectual production explored abstract categories of "modernity" and "ideology" (whether secularism, Islam, communism, etc.). Often such research has overlooked how contemporaries—especially women—experienced, understood, and contributed to the making of "modern Indonesia" in the everyday.

In *Domestic Nationalism* the experiences of women expand our understanding of modernity, nationhood, and Islam from the liminal public/private space of care. Methodologically, I approach these questions through a combination of textual and visual sources. Government documents, international agencies and private foundations' reports, and the general press, all provide the socio-political discursive context for public health policies. Women's magazines reveal how middle- and upper-class women experienced, learned about, and rearticulated ideas related to "health." And visual sources—drawn from government and institutional repositories, the general press, advertisements, and other sources—render visible the "unseen world of women" excluded from or marginalized by recorded verbal archives.[36] Bringing these sources together shows the blurred areas of contact between domestic and public responsibilities; female and male spaces;

traditional and modern knowledge; the sacred and the mundane; social and political work; and women's agency and patriarchal regimes.

———

In 1910s to 1930s Java and Sumatra, both the colonial government and the aid programs of the Rockefeller Foundation promoted principles of hygiene and disease prevention, framing them as pillars of progress—whereas of course they were primarily crucial to maintain labor-intensive, exploitative capitalist practices. Hygiene work began much later than it had in British India or the American Philippines, and deployed fewer resources than the efforts of the British in neighboring Malaya. But against the backdrop of the so-called Ethical Policy, launched by Queen Wilhelmina in 1901 to putatively "repay the debt" of colonial extractionism, the Dutch fashioned themselves as educators and civilizers of the "natives."

Chapters 1 to 3 unpack the gendered approach of hygiene propaganda strategies pursued by imperialist actors, and indigenous engagements with them. Hygiene was presented as scientific, western, and therefore "modern"; and it was primarily communicated between men (this is the core of Chapter 1, "Hygiene"). But as the health and strength of colonial subjects *qua* laborers remained the responsibility of indigenous women's activities of care work, it was their (biological) reproductive function which pulled women in as interlocutors. Hygienic modernity sought to remove women from their previously acknowledged social positions as healers and producers, and instead confine them to the "domestic" sphere. But here I show that women in the late colonial period were actively engaging with scientific knowledge, absorbing it, and rearticulating it through a process that invoked indigenous practices and Islamic paradigms alongside biomedical science.

Chapter 2, "Labor," shows that women inhabited the space of colonial hygienic modernity despite institutional marginalization. Indonesian women leveraged the ideals of imperial maternalism as they labored in activities of social reproduction; rather than merely executing or mirroring them, they turned mothering into an avenue for emancipation. Some women expressed a gendered reading of anti-colonial nationalism, while others pursued professionalized employment in healthcare. This exploration is most visible in the realm of nutrition, as seen in Chapter 3, "Food." Between the 1910s and 1930s, food becomes a productive space for discussions of colonial modernity, whether as a vehicle for germs, women's domestic responsibilities and education, or pious consumption. "Food" shows that through laboratory-based knowledge production, content-creation in women's magazines, visual representation in advertisements for *halal* processed foods, and quotidian practices of food making, indigenous women emerged as the fundamental guardians and promoters of modernity in Java and Sumatra.

The second half of the book is set against the social and political impact of a decade of sustained warfare, starvation, and rampant disease, and Indonesia's emergence as a postcolonial nation. Chapter 4, "War," centers the seismic shifts of the Japanese occupation (1942–1945) and National Revolution (1945–1949). Not only did women become the bulk of the waged labor force, but they also witnessed how the home front turned into the front line of war. Women were trained as factory workers, food providers, healthcare professionals, and political campaigners—their previously ordinary tasks of care work now becoming visible as fundamental to the armed and political struggle. The Occupation was short-lived and devastating, not least for the women who were abducted, deceived, or otherwise forced into sexual slavery, sometimes through strategies of false recruitment to those same professions that created genuine opportunities for their peers. In the chapter I acknowledge the trauma, while also investigating how new paths opened for women to participate in the public realm, a trend that would continue throughout the Revolution and into the 1950s.

Indonesian women did not retreat from the frontline positions they had taken, and in fact in the early years after the transfer of sovereignty (1949) they were at the head of key strategies spearheading Indonesia's quest for socio-economic prosperity. Chapter 5, "Prosperity," centers MCH and nutrition policies. On the one hand, these were spaces of opportunity for women to expand the reach of their ascribed gendered roles, and have an effect on domestic politics. They contributed to nation-building as policymakers, outreach workers, and home-based caregivers. On the other hand, MCH and nutrition also became areas of opportunity for international aid agencies with their own agendas, even as Sukarno laid out a non-aligned political platform of political and economic self-reliance vis-à-vis the emergent Cold War. Just as the putatively separate spheres of home-domestic and national-public had become blurred in previous decades, amid polarizing global politics the putatively hard borders of national and international spheres were similarly blurred when international aid agencies came to see value in influencing those gendered home-domestic activities already linked to nationalist agendas and policies.

As I reflect on in the Epilogue, with Sukarno's declarations of Martial Law (1957) and Guided Democracy (1959) the narrative comes to full circle: the emergent hyper-masculine postcolonial military state mirrored colonial-era dynamics. It marginalized women's agency, and disregarded Islam as a potential source of progress. In the 1960s, both women and religion would be excluded from the halls of power and relegated to a clearly defined "social" sphere that by mandate had nothing to contribute to politics besides the reproduction of a patriarchal, authoritarian state.

FIGURE 1.1 "Health is a great treasure." Source: P. Peverelli and F. van Bemmel. *Blyf Gezond! = Sehatlah Selaloe*, 1933, Plate #1, Leiden University Library

1 | HYGIENE

We now live in the age of progress. Everything we see right and left, everything, seems to be moving and advancing. . . . So, if we are to move forward, we can't forget to also guard our health in a forward-thinking way. . . . If our bodies are healthy, we can work, we can choose to do this and that, whatever we please. . . . Conversely, those with sick bodies, how can they get work?[1] (Sardjito, 1930)

In the early twentieth century, the press in the Dutch East Indies connected good health and hygiene to progress, *kemajuan*—whether as technological achievement, economic uplift, personal enjoyment, or as an abstract ideal of colonial modernity. We see this role of *kemajuan* as pictured here in Figure 1.1, in a poster produced by the municipal health services of Batavia for use in local schools. We also read about *kemajuan* as articulated in the quote above, extracted from Sardjito's book "On Seeking Health," which had been printed by the government publishing house Balai Poestaka/Volkslectuur in 1930.[2]

In the poster, one young boy plays soccer with his friends, worry-free; the other, apathetic and drained of energy, leans against a tree. His father is sitting inside a thatched-roof house, reading a book—from the posture, I imagine a Qur'an or exegetical text. His mother is in the distant background; she is walking away, carrying a basket on her head. She might be going to the market, to forage, or to wash the laundry. Similarly, Sardjito speaks of good health as an enabler of a fulfilling life and a tangible source of financial benefit. It is a valuable asset that, like a treasure, needs to be "guarded."

The primary tool to achieve good health was prevention, an appealing strategy to the colonial administration as curative care was scarce and largely inaccessible to the majority of the indigenous population. When preventive care manifested as educational materials, they tied into colonial ideology in more than one way. The so-called Ethical Policy, announced in 1901, claimed to "uplift" the condition of the Indies' indigenous population through expanded educational opportunities, economic improvements, and a new public health effort.[3] But behind the drive for prevention and improvement was a darker reality: hygienic reforms were yet another discursive tool to reaffirm civilizational and racialized differences, as the colonial administration continued to operate from the position that indigenous modes of being and beliefs—including Islam—were inferior to their own.

This chapter brings to the fore colonial efforts to implement sanitary reforms in Java and Sumatra. As I analyze Dutch policies of tropical hygienic modernity at the turn of the twentieth century (placing the Indies in the broader international landscape), the focus is on how these new strategies of public health intersected with questions of gender, progress, and Islam.

Framing hygiene and health as vehicles for economic and societal progress, sources authored by the colonial establishment in the 1910s and 1920s presented a textual discourse that was scientific, secular, and primarily male-oriented. Its mirror image was the portrayal of Islam, and other traditional practices, as harmful sources of "primitive" knowledge—and of women as outsiders to public health propaganda efforts. However, women's biological reproductive function was key to the colonial project due to the very framing of health as an economic asset, in conjunction with an imperialist view of colonized territories and subjects as resources to be extracted and exploited for capitalist gains. High rates of infant mortality were blamed on mothers and traditional birth attendants. They "lacked hygienic knowledge," and thus needed instruction.[4] While in this chapter I show that this approach was intended to reinforce western, patriarchal and imperialist structures of power, I simultaneously lay the foundations of the next chapter, where I locate Muslim women's intellectual, domestic, and professionalized labor within the realm of healthcare, and trace their engagement with multiple epistemologies.

HYGIENE IN THE TROPICS

Following a flurry of scientific advances, from germ theories (Pasteur and Koch) to the discovery of parasites (Manson), sterilization (Lister) and eventually vitamins (Eijkman), hygienic reforms became a hallmark of late nineteenth-century Europe, spilling over to the United States and Japan.

The sanitary turn experienced in the European and American metropoles spurred the launch of major public health initiatives, and gave rise to a new strategy of imperial rule, with profound consequences for the colonies. The Dutch, British, and French, each in their own time, had formulated public health reforms that became "a kind of medical imperialism incorporating both the medicalization and moralization of society."[5] In the United States, the 1890s to 1930s were dubbed the "golden era" of public health, as success-ful prevention of epidemics came to the fore.[6] This was not an exclusively western phenomenon, as Japan had joined with similar efforts. The Meiji government established a Central Sanitary Board to tackle epidemics and "preserve the people's well-being throughout the nation."[7] Developing the framework of hygienic modernity, Ruth Rogaski has pointed out that "*eisei* [hygiene] was a key link in the creation of a wealthy and powerful nation," crucial to national development.[8]

Among colonial powers, the need to advance hygiene work was a shared sentiment. Persistent concerns over the health of colonizers and colonized subjects in tropical territories enabled the transfer of sanitary reforms to the imperial peripheries of Asia, where these came to be framed under the rubric of "tropical hygiene." This branch of medicine emerged as a defined field of study when Sir Patrick Manson established the London School of Tropical Hygiene in 1899. Stationed in Hong Kong, China, and Taiwan as a physician in the British colonial service, Manson had been the first to deter-mine with scientific certainty that it was parasites carried by specific animal vectors that caused filariasis and malaria.[9] The tropical climate, then, was no longer itself to be blamed for the diseases, as previous climate theories had claimed. Rather, he argued, the humid heat simply created conditions favorable to the breeding of mosquitoes and flies. In the racialized imperi-alist context, this was often translated into holding indigenous populations responsible for transmission on account of their perceived lack of personal and environmental hygiene.

As succinctly put by Manson himself, the hygienic effort was necessary because tropical diseases "burdened the revenues, interfered with the continuity of administration, repressed the energy of the population, and diverted funds which might otherwise have been invested profitably in remunerated public works."[10] The same spirit was exuded by Rockefeller Foundation administrators. As more recently argued by Richard Brown, for Frederick Gates and other early representatives of the International Health Division in the 1920s, "The *material* benefit of medicine is a healthier population and thus a healthier work force."[11] These remarks underscored the exploitative and capitalistic interests behind colonial preventive medicine.

Tropical medicine became a pillar of imperial expansion and assertion as it enabled the preservation of healthy imperialist bodies, which could conquer, colonize, and rule by focusing on the bodies who were colonized, subjected, and laboring. British India, Malaya, the Philippines, Indochina, the Dutch East Indies, Taiwan, and then treaty-port China, all witnessed intense imperial intervention in sanitation, as the authorities built public health infrastructures, and ran education programs for the "uncivilized natives"—or at least initiatives to coerce them into following western principles of sanitation.

Unfolding at the peak of tropical medicine, the US administration in the Philippines had embraced tropical hygiene as a key tool to advance the military conquest of the islands, sustain their control, and assert racialized differences. Robert Koch's discovery in German New Guinea that some individuals could be healthy carriers of diseases further exacerbated American doctors' beliefs that epidemics were caused by "natives . . . unable or unwilling to take necessary precautions against acquiring, transporting, and distributing the disease organism most virulent to whites."[12] As shown by Warwick Anderson, colonized subjects' bodily autonomy had not improved much, despite the shift from nineteenth-century coercive practices of bodily control to twentieth-century "hygienic education." The new approach had simply sidelined quarantining and forced vaccinations to favor instead a pattern of intrusive policing of behavior. Discursively, though, in the Progressive era the Americans saw the creation of public health in the Philippines as part of a civilizing project and a nation-building program aimed at transforming "subjects" into future "citizens."[13] The American

footprint in Southeast Asia was larger than their actual colonized posses-
sions, especially in terms of health propaganda, as the Rockefeller Foundation used the Philippines as a launchpad for activities in other places across
the region, including the Indies.

The dynamics of the expanding Japanese Empire were not too different.
When Japan invaded Taiwan in 1895, it considered the island's climate a
problem. But as plans developed to move further south into Southeast Asia,
the (sub)tropical ecology of Taiwan became a resource for the Empire. A
new school of medicine was established in 1936 at Taipei Imperial University, where faculty focused their efforts on researching malaria and other
tropical diseases.[14] In the late 1930s, Japanese "medical missionaries" were
sent to occupied areas of China and later in Southeast Asia for research.[15]
As articulated by Lo, "medicine laid the basis for improvement of the health
conditions and progress of society."[16] Under Japan's imperial rule, "'Hygienic modernity' became a vehicle for the expression of power, fear, and
hope in the region's [China and Taiwan] complex informal and formal colonial settings."[17] Throughout the first half of the twentieth century, then, Java
and Sumatra were similar "settings" for Dutch, American, and Japanese
projects of imperialist hygienic modernity.

In the Dutch East Indies, the earliest initiatives promoting tropical
hygiene had been advanced to ensure military victories and preserve the
health of civilian colonists. These efforts had been infrastructural; starting
in the late 1800s the Dutch had hired laborers to drain swamps, regularly
spray insecticides in yards, and set pipes to let clean water flow to the most
exclusive residences of colonial cities. An expansion of services followed
the Decentralization Act of 1903, by which the central colonial government
transferred financial and logistical responsibility for infrastructural development to the municipalities. In the following decades, local councils over-
saw roads, sewers, water supply, slaughterhouses, and covered markets,[18] as
well as street-lighting and kampung improvement programs,[19] thus shaping
the built outlook of tropical hygiene across Java and Sumatra.

By the early twentieth century, European neighborhoods across the
colony were gradually transformed into centers of public services aimed
at keeping larger—yet still affluent—sectors of the population healthy and
comfortable.[20] Whereas some of these improvements might have been
presented as an effort in concord with the so-called Ethical Policy, the
primary incentive had been the need to "support the influx of European

bodies and European capital" to the colony.[21] This had become increasingly pressing by the end of the nineteenth century, once previous practices of interracial marriages with local families came to be discouraged in favor of creating "Dutch" families.[22] As argued by Ann Stoler, both the arrival of Dutch women and the spread of discourses on European children's health were linked to "racial survival, ty[ing] increased campaigns for domestic hygiene to colonial expansion, ma[king] child-rearing an imperial and class duty, and cast[ing] white women as the bearers of a more racist imperial order and the custodians of their desire-driven, immoral men."[23] In the 1920s, young Dutch women preparing to travel to the Indies studied at the Colonial Domestic School in The Hague where they learned about the health and hygiene challenges posed by the tropics, among other subjects.[24]

The health of European bodies—as the wealth of the empire—could not be preserved in isolation from the conditions of the colonized territory and its inhabitants. The survival and welfare of the colonial family depended on the physical wellbeing of their servants, just as the metropole depended on the profitable exploitation of its colonized subject-laborers. Hence, returning to Sir Manson's and Frederick Gates' approach to public health as an investment to increase capitalist returns, the Dutch colonial government launched initiatives to address high infant mortality and rampant contagious diseases among the indigenous population.

The institutional training of birth attendants had been one of the earliest programs in the archipelago, in an unspoken recognition of the fact that biological reproduction was key to economic production. Colonial administrators had made moves to establish a midwifery school open to women of all ethnic backgrounds as early as 1850;[25] its primary goal was to "reform" traditional birth attendants' techniques, which were seen as unsanitary. Writing in 1884, the renowned Dutch physician C.L. van der Burg offered a vivid picture of the work of the traditional birth attendant—the *dukun bayi*, or in later sources *dukun beranak*. In this account, procedures during childbirth ranged from "pushing the belly" to encourage the baby's exit, to the "biting off" of the umbilical cord "for invulnerability," and the extensive use of ointments, powders, and spices. His assessment was not flattering, and concluded noting that when all remedies failed, women would either "leave it to God," or call on a European midwife or doctor.[26] Despite all this detail, Van der Burg neglected to mention that, for the majority of the population, it would have been a financial impossibility to call on professionals trained in European medicine.

Similar conclusions were reached in the late 1920s by a team of indigenous physicians. Their booklet, titled "Hygiene in Relation to the Customs ['adat], Faith, and Superstition of the Sundanese People" (printed by the Association for the Promotion of Hygiene in the Dutch East Indies), inevitably characterized the *dukun bayi* as "lack[ing] hygienic knowledge." Her "rooting around with a dirty hand" in the body of the laboring woman, with "none of the necessary instruments or disinfecting" was as harmful as the reluctance to call professionals. Attachment to tradition continued to be identified as the primary source of the problem: the fact that Muslim mothers who died in childbirth were recognized as "martyrs for the faith" (*syahid*) was seen as an additional barrier to birthing reforms.[27] This narrative would remain alive well into the 1940s. Writing in 1948, Dr. Pierre Peverelli, Director of the Municipal Health Services in Batavia, noted that: "There is no other subject about which so much has been written, with so many case reports and horror stories, as that of obstetrics."[28]

Infrastructure alone—whether in the roads and abattoirs that sprung up in many cities across Java and Sumatra, or the educational institutions aimed at training midwives—had proven insufficient. For the colonial administrators this was a reflection of the population's disinterest in reforming their behavior: "No Government can bear the burden of public health work for the whole population."[29] One might say that they did not even try, in fact, based on the selectiveness and limitations of those projects that structurally and systematically excluded the majority of the Indies' inhabitants. Piped water, for example, only reached Batavia's kampungs in the mid-1920s, and was priced as a luxury very few could afford.[30]

Hence, while the wealthier parts of larger cities were serviced with pipes, and artesian wells peppered the landscape, in the rural and peri-urban areas indigenous colonized subjects were instructed on how to build latrines and were told the importance of drinking boiled water. Life in the rural areas differed from the towns:

> The man who lives in the city can drink water from the tap without being obliged to know the details of how it has been made safe, but the man who lives in a rural area must be taught how he can make his drinking water supply safe. The city dweller uses the latrine which the

builders of his house have constructed. The man who lives in a rural district must learn how to build a satisfactory latrine, and often he must also learn how to use it.[31]

At the beginning of the twentieth century, the poor health of indigenous subjects was explained as being caused by their (perceived) lack of knowledge about hygiene. The colonial government, then, moved away from infrastructural interventions and settled on health literacy (or "propaganda," as they called it) as their primary strategy for public health improvement. While women were explicitly targeted as a key audience for matters of birthing and infant care, broader knowledge about hygienic lifestyle remained ungendered, or distributed in ways that by default primarily reached men alone.

PUBLIC HEALTH STRATEGIES IN THE INDIES

For years, or so they claimed, the Dutch had been seeking to educate the Indies' indigenous population on matters of sanitation, but had (putatively) faced the obstacle of ignorance. In this section I explore early efforts in public health in the Dutch East Indies, focusing on three key aspects, namely: whether women were seen as interlocutors and actors of change; the discursive role of Islam and tradition; and how biomedical approaches to hygiene were presented as a necessary condition for, and a facet of, European progress.

In 1884, the year Robert Koch had published the postulates providing the foundations of germ theory, the International Hygiene Congress gathered in The Hague. There, the Dutch physician N.P. van der Stok argued that the colonial government had intended to "propagat[e] hygienic knowledge among the native population of Java" since 1880,[32] but this had proven to be a particularly challenging task because of the "uncivilized" nature of the population.

Seeing the Javanese as "suspicious of anything proposed by European 'kaffirs' [sic]," he had begun to read the Qur'an, *sunna* and *fatwas* to outline an effective strategy leveraging religious commitment:

While leafing through the works on Mahometan law, I soon noticed that I could draw from them useful points for the propagation of hygienic notions among the peoples professing the Muslim religion. In fact, I have found little-known, but in any case very useful, allies in this doctrine of Islam, in its formalities and ceremonies, and in its apparently unmotivated prohibitions, most of which come only from an imperfect and distorted imitation of the laws of Moses.[33]

Van der Stok had come to the conclusion that Islam might be a productive source of legitimation. In his speech, he highlighted a handful of strategies based on Islamic scriptures that would support hygienic improvement. First, whereas colonials had been frustrated by Muslim subjects' "fatalism" (seen as stemming from an interpretation that favored predestination), van der Stok "discovered" that he could promote preventive practices, underscoring the mandate to protect health as "a gift of God." Secondly, he noted that "the fact that the native is unclean to excess . . . proves that he hardly understands the prescriptions of his religion which commands him to be very clean," as the Qur'an gave specific requirements for physical purity. Hence, van der Stok noted that hygiene propaganda should focus on its benefits for religious cleansing rituals, as Muslim subjects appeared to not see the benefits of sanitation *per se*. Lastly, van der Stok argued that similar dynamics were at play with regards to the depth of graves, the prohibition of consuming intoxicating substances (whether wine or opium), and the exhortation to postpone the *hajj* pilgrimage or to not attend the Friday communal prayer in case of health-threatening conditions (such as an epidemic). Van der Stok concluded:

It seems to me, M.M. [Messieurs], that the ally which I have spoken to you about [i.e., Islam], and which I have used . . . is not only new and perhaps useful, but also [it seems to me] that it can hardly fail to interest the hygienists of the nations that have to interact with Muslim peoples, like the English in Egypt or in India, and the French in Algeria.[34]

Contrary to van der Stok's exhortation, European physicians and hygienists employed in the Dutch East Indies government did not feel the same urge to understand and deploy Islamic beliefs and practices for the further diffusion of health propaganda. This was despite the fact that hygiene was deeply connected to morality and ideals of (Christian) religious purity in Europe itself,[35] and among Muslim physicians in Islamic Java and Sumatra.

Vernacular publications would bring Islam into conversation with health and hygiene in the 1920s and 1930s, but conversely the colonial administration in the Indies would consistently frame hygiene as exclusively western and scientific.

The Batavia Health Services ("Gezondheidsdienst," later renamed "Dienst der Volksgezondheid," DVG, to underscore the "public" dimension of these health services) was established in 1911 in the wake of the plague epidemic, and hygiene education was immediately recognized as a necessary counterpart to infrastructural interventions, as thoroughly argued by Maurits Meerwijk.[36] Alongside government initiatives—which were short-lived, especially in the 1910s—private actors were to play a key role in medical propaganda. First among them was the Rockefeller Foundation's International Health Board (later renamed "Division," IHD), which in 1915 expressed interest in doing work in the Dutch Indies.

The Rockefeller Foundation had been conducting public health campaigns in the Global South since 1913, promoting sanitation through health education campaigns and supporting local governments' own efforts toward public health. Its primary focus was hookworm eradication. On the one hand, thinking of disease prevention as enabling "the full utilization of labor," the Rockefeller Foundation had been attracted by the possibility of easing the disease's most common symptom, fatigue.[37] On the other hand, as suggested by John Ettling in his foundational work *The Germ of Laziness*, it had been the very nature of hookworm contagion, which interruption required the combination of scientific medicine and public education, that would shape the work of the Sanitary Commission for decades to come.[38]

The Foundation had taken an interest in the Dutch East Indies since the earliest days of its operations, primarily driven by the recognition of Batavia's unhealthy conditions. The American physician Victor Heiser—chief health officer in the Philippines until 1914, and then IHD director for the East—visited Java in 1915 to offer Foundation assistance in launching a hookworm survey and eradication campaign there. The report compiled in 1916 by Dr. Darling stressed the "unsanitary habits of the natives," as well as the fact that there were "not enough doctors, neither Dutch or native."[39] Possibly perceiving some criticism in Darling's statements about the lack of doctors, or about the negative impact of the irrigation system, the Dutch government suspended, without much explanation, all talks about collaboration, despite arrangements having already been drawn up.[40] While Heiser continued to prod for collaboration, the Dutch East Indies' health services embarked on their own hookworm campaign.[41]

The governor general eventually invited the Foundation back in 1921 for a survey, and in 1924 it would indeed start a hookworm eradication campaign. Under the leadership of the American physician John Lee Hydrick, this operation would lead to almost twenty years of IHD involvement in the Dutch East Indies.[42] Although officially under the umbrella of the Indies Division of Public Health, Hydrick's work was primarily in line with (and paid for by) the Rockefeller Foundation. Mirroring projects conducted in the southern United States, South America, and the Philippines, and continuing his own approach developed in several locations across those territories, Hydrick spent the first few months completing a survey in Java.[43] He then turned to hookworm eradication and education work,[44] as Heiser had intended to do a decade earlier.[45]

Hydrick's goal was "to awaken in the people a permanent interest in hygiene and to stimulate them to adopt habits and to carry out measures which will help them secure health and remain healthy."[46] Within a few months, Hydrick had branched out, launching broader educational efforts through "rural health units" in Java as well as Bali, Lombok, Sumatra, and Makassar.[47] This was not without opposition. Even with the support of the director of DVG having been secured quite promptly, and additional funding having been allocated from the Rockefeller Foundation in the late 1920s,[48] others opined differently. In 1927, for example, Dr. Rodenwaldt reportedly "disapproved of the Foundation's work to improve the living conditions of native populations of the tropics. He feels that it is a crime against civilization to help them in any way."[49] In light of these comments, it seems befitting that the same year Rodenwaldt, a German medical researcher specializing in tropical hygiene, would spearhead the establishment of the Eugenics Society of the Dutch East Indies.[50]

Despite such sporadic negative reactions, and the financial repercussions of the 1930s Depression, the Rockefeller Foundation and DVG continued to support Hydrick's work until 1940, as explored in detail in the next chapter.[51] In those fifteen years of work, Hydrick focused on what he saw as the pursuance of everyday life in a modern and sanitary environment. His primary strategy involved the establishment of health units in rural areas, where trained staff (health inspectors locally referred to as *mantri*) modeled and taught routines and patterns of behavior inspired by principles of tropical hygiene. Hydrick's empirical approach, favoring learning by watching and doing, would be impactful in a variety of ways, including an important reassessment of gender dynamics in health propaganda. In the mid-1930s, his rural hygiene work would cease privileging local men, and instead address women as primary interlocutors and agents of reform. Educated women were involved as trainees at the hygiene *mantri* school, and village women were actively sought out as participants to dedicated lectures and demonstrations. Before these innovations, however, in the earliest days of public health propaganda, women were hardly seen.

Gendering Audiences

With the halt in discussions about a possible partnership between the Rockefeller Foundation and the Dutch colonial government, in the late 1910s the colonial DVG began to engage in public health propaganda on their own terms and (limited) dime, focusing their efforts on government-sponsored publications and events. In 1918, the DVG partnered with the government printing house, Volkslectuur/Balai Poestaka, to issue the book series "Kitab Kesehatan," or "Health Books." These were primarily written in Dutch, accompanied by translations in Malay and local vernaculars (Javanese, Sundanese, and Hata Batak), either in bilingual booklets, or separate monolingual ones. The press was a branch of the Commissie voor Volkslectuur, established in 1908 by the governor general of the Indies to expand avenues of education and knowledge transmission in line with the Ethical Policy. Hence, it claimed to be a body aimed at "the production and distribution . . . of traditional literary treasures."[52] But in fact, as argued by Doris Jedamski, this publishing house was primarily "a multifunctional agency of socialization . . . of Western concepts of cognition, i.e. the designing and setting of values, models of behaviour, and new sets of social roles."[53] The "socialization" intent was certainly most evident in these "health books" and other materials produced for hygiene propaganda.

To appreciate the expected societal impact of these text-centered efforts across classes, it is first worth addressing the landscape of literacy and colonial education, and the place of women therein. The Dutch government had been slow to make basic education accessible to the non-elite, but the twentieth century experienced an "upward and downward growth" of literacy that engendered a proportionally faster and higher rate of female literacy vis-à-vis men's.[54] In 1920, over 100 thousand girls were enrolled in schools that used Malay as the primary medium across the archipelago, with half of them located in Java.[55] In 1927 the number had grown to 187 thousand,[56] and a decade later it had reached 370 thousand.[57] Numbers were smaller in terms of Dutch-language education, but did not grow any more slowly. If in 1920 there were just over 10 thousand indigenous girls enrolled in Dutch-language schools (both European Primary Schools, ELS, and Dutch Schools for Natives, HIS),[58] by 1927 that number had almost doubled.[59]

This was largely the outcome of a policy aimed at promoting Dutch-language literacy among indigenous girls as a vehicle for their uplift and "civilizing." Far from being interested in supporting girls' intellectual development *per se*, in 1917 the acting director for education and religion, K.F. Creutzberg, had argued that the goal of girls' education in the colonies was to "shape decent and civilized women and mothers." Women—as mothers and wives—were seen as able to "exert a civilizing influence on their own families,"[60] and "foster appreciation of Dutch authority and thus in time bring the Native population closer to [the colonizers]."[61] The educational system as it existed was seen as giving "too much of scholarly knowledge, and too little of what is practical knowledge for women, namely cooking, handiwork, child-rearing, hygiene, and household book-keeping." Creutzberg thought girls should not be educated too highly; just enough to support the overall "uplift of the people."[62] Dutch language and "modern" domestic skills were seen as fulfilling that goal.

The curricular gap between "native" and European schools narrowed, and non-elite pupils began to be accepted to a variety of schools. Dutch was added as a regular subject in all the Native Schools for Girls in 1924, and from the following year it was a required subject in the four-year Native Teacher Training Schools for Girls.[63] In 1930, overall female literacy in languages other than Dutch was assessed at a mere 2.17%;[64] yet, women also accounted for 25% of all indigenous literates in Dutch and 17% of all indigenous literates in any language.[65] The 1930 commentary to the census reported that it had indeed been the substantial rise in female literacy that most affected the overall increase across the indigenous population.[66]

Orality and local vernaculars, however, would remain the most impactful mediums of knowledge transmission. As argued by Jedamski, "One borrowed book would find an audience of ten to fifteen, because it was lent or read aloud to relatives, neighbours, and friends." She continues: "Especially in rural areas, whoever was literate was expected to read journals and books aloud to the village public. The Dutch had taken this fact into careful consideration."[67] This was particularly impactful among women, as their community ties were strong, enabling such indirect transmission of knowledge.[68] The contents of books were amplified through social relations, often crossing class boundaries.

Even among the literates, texts circulated further than to just those who purchased them, ensuring that DVG propaganda could expect an ever-broadening base of readers and consumers of print culture. Many borrowed books from libraries, and more still listened to them or heard about their contents from family members, neighbors, and even their employers. The inside cover of the 1934 book "Health: On Sports" included a note to borrowers: "Take care that [this book] is not lost, damaged, or soiled, because each page has great meaning for the [overall] importance of this book; return it promptly when you are done reading it, so another friend can borrow it."[69] A system of over 700 circulating public libraries had been started in the 1910s by D.A. Rinkes, a Leiden-trained Orientalist and high-ranking colonial officer.[70] Most of them were located in schools and perused by the enrolled pupils, their parents, and the teachers; but in 1925, for example, mobile libraries and sales vans were added, allowing the further diffusion of publications across the archipelago (as shown in Figure 1.2).[71] Within the scope of this chapter, I now turn to explore how publications and articles addressing hygienic concerns engaged (or did not engage) with a female audience.

The "Health Books" printed by Balai Poestaka/Volkslectuur in the late 1910s and early 1920s occasionally seemed to expect an educated audience with some foundational knowledge in biomedicine, but nonetheless most of them were didactic in spirit. They explained in simple terms how to avoid some of the most common diseases; how to tackle daily challenges; and generally illustrated ways to guard one's own health.[72]

The first three books covered, in order: beriberi disease (a vitamin B deficiency), tuberculosis, and the care of nursing infants. Later, in the early 1930s, visual representations of nutritional and contagious diseases would recognize the specific role of women audiences, as I show in the next chapter (see Figures 2.1, 2.2, and 2.3). But in these earlier texts of health literacy, only the volumes on infant care addressed women. The first one to be published, in 1919, was *Pemeliharaan Kanak-kanak jang Menjoesoe* ("Caring for Nursing Infants"),[73] followed in 1922 by *Pemimpin Bagi Mengadjar Anak-anak*

Tamoe-tamoe berdiri didepan Balai Poestaka melihat auto B. P. jang baroe datang itoe.

FIGURE 1.2   "Visitors standing in front of Balai Poestaka look at the B[alai] P[oestaka] truck that just arrived." Source: *Pandji Poestaka*, no. 37, May 19, 1925, p. 604, Leiden University Library

Disekolah dalam Hal Mengoeroes Baji ("A Guide for Teaching School Children How to Care for Infants").[74]

Both made it evident that the high rates of infant mortality were a central colonial concern, and both assigned the responsibility for keeping infants safe to their mothers and sisters, regardless of their socio-economic status. These books had been written in different styles, for audiences of different socio-economic extractions—"Caring for Nursing Infants" was bilingual in Dutch and Malay, possibly envisioned for students of the HIS, while "A Guide for Teaching" was a very basic didactic text, likely for village vernacular schools. To ensure its broad reach, this book was printed in Javanese and Hata Batak too.

The bilingual 1919 "Caring for Nursing Infants" reminded parents of the negative social effects of high mortality rates, and exhorted them to eradicate "stupidity and dirt" and save their babies' lives by embracing cleanliness and breastfeeding. The sporadic references to scientific terminology were placed in parentheses, and always accompanied by more common words.[75] Three years later, "A Guide for Teaching School Children" fit squarely within the colonial priority of establishing hygienic standards amongst the working classes. The book was a compilation of instructions for young children left in charge of their even younger siblings in their mother's absence:

> If your mother is at work or cooking in the kitchen, or if she has gone to the market, or with your father to the paddy field, you, oh eldest daughter, have to care for your sibling who is still so little![76]

Likely to be mediated by a teacher or another adult, like "Caring for Nursing Infants," this book similarly insisted on the importance of hygiene and cleanliness, but the language was even simpler. It gave absolute priority to the avoidance of "little bugs," mosquitos, and flies, as well as the careful removal of dirt from the caretaker's body and the infant's surrounding environment.[77] (I return to these two booklets when discussing infant feeding in Chapter 3.)

In 1922 the government published another booklet, this one aimed at those who helped birthing mothers in the villages. *Pemimpin Doekoen Beranak* ("A Guide for the Traditional Birth Attendant"), a manual for traditional birth attendants and those who trained them, opened with a reminder that "here in the Indies many women still die when giving birth." The primary cause was identified in the methods of the traditional birth attendants, which were "far from perfect, and need[ed] to be changed and improved."[78] The book illustrated basic principles of hygiene. While acknowledging that even in Europe it had only recently become accepted that post-partum fever and death were caused by "the dirty hands of the person helping," the colonial public health official Von Römer stressed that in the Indies things were made even harder by "ignorance." Hence, he added, "the most important thing for us to know and pay attention to when helping a woman give birth is cleanliness, cleanliness!" The booklet started with the discovery of germs, introduced Louis Pasteur and Joseph Lister, and proceeded to illustrate the process of sterilization. The authority of science had been thus asserted.[79]

In 1924 "A Guide for Teaching School Children" was the twenty-sixth most borrowed Malay-language book across the public libraries' network, surpassed only by a history of Java and a number of Javanese, Malay, and European works of literature still commonly read today.[80] In 1926 "Caring for Nursing Infants" was the most popular health book in the Javanese language.[81] This was thanks to Rinkes' expansion of the activities of the Balai Poestaka/Volkslectuur and the circulation of its publications.[82] These efforts included the printing of the annual *Volksalmanak* ("People's Almanac"), beginning in 1919, in Javanese, Malay, Sundanese, and Madurese; in its fourth year, 50,000 copies of the Almanac had been sold across the archipelago.[83] A few years later that number had doubled, reaching even more readers through the government's library system. Through the years, Balai Poestaka would also support the publication of periodicals. *Pandji Poestaka*, launched in 1923 under Rinkes' leadership, quickly became "one of the most popular journals among Indonesians," with a circulation of about 7,000 copies.[84]

These periodicals covered news about culture and politics, and had various dedicated sections, usually including one on health and another for women. Their coverage of topics often intersected, but remained clearly differentiated in the tone and words chosen. Articles on diseases endemic to the Indies, as with publications on birthing, were clear about the scientific demands for hygiene, even when the terminology was simplified because of an anticipated undereducated audience. The framing of domestic cleanliness (around the house or the kitchen), however, varied. When written for a general audience, medicalized concepts would be included. But when presented to a female audience, its language was simpler, as a mere aspect of gendered housework. We see this play out clearly on the pages of the *Volksalmanak*.

The *Volksalmanak Melajoe 1920* dedicated an entire section to health matters, covering topics that ranged from sleep habits to tuberculosis and other contagious diseases. Preventive solutions were often identified in everyday activities of care work, as the publication argued that fresh air and sunlight ought to be brought daily into every room of the house, and food needed to be kept away from flies; meals should be nutritious, and water was to be boiled. The language was consistently scientific.[85]

The subsequent section was dedicated to "Womanly Skills." The chapter shows no clear intellectual agenda, covering a great variety of topics without any evident organizational principle. At first it seemed to aim at defining the boundaries of what constituted a woman's domain. It opened with a Roman-era story, "Loyalty of a Wife," and swiftly transitioned to an article titled "On Caring for the Household." There, a woman's inability to prepare good food was presented as a character flaw that might have driven a husband away—but not as a health hazard. The cleanliness of a mother's body and clothes engendered good modeling of "tidy" behavior for the children, not a hygienic, healthy, and fulfilling life.[86] This was followed by a seemingly ill-fitting article, titled "'Couac' Becomes the Food of Many." But here, comparing the eating habits of Java and Brazil, the Almanac in fact provided detailed nutritional information about rice and cassava, including instructions on how to process the root into flour, and how to cook it to maximize its flavor and nutrition.[87]

After several pages covering various household tasks, the section returned once again to food, covering topics resembling the earlier, general section on health. There is no clear direction, and most of the language is practical and instructional, shying away from scientific explanations. But again, with a twist. On the one hand, the article made clear that the mandate of boiling water sourced from wells was necessary to prevent infections from contagious diseases.[88] On the other, the causes of cholera, dysentery, etc., were here referred to as *bibit penjakit* (literally "seeds of illness"), with sporadic adaptations like *microbe/mikrobe* and *baccil/bacil*.[89] The Almanac targeted a mixed audience.

Narrative trajectories were not linear. In 1929 another discussion of water in the *Volksalmanak*'s women's section proclaimed: "Remember, for us it is best to only drink raw water! Never drink water that is too hot or very cold because it might break the teeth." Sidestepping the issue of microbes and water-borne diseases altogether, here the concern was dental health.[90] Meanwhile, sweeping and disposing of household dust had been characterized as a disease-preventing measure,[91] and other tasks were presented as advantageous "for health,"[92] but in none of these examples were scientific explanations or details provided.

The scientific underpinning of the hygienic message was clearly presented in writings for the general readership, but articles for women oscillated between unsatisfactory explanations (conforming to an abstract concept of "hygiene"), and perpetuation of practices that would elsewhere be considered unhealthy and dangerous. This seemed to be a peculiar approach advanced by the Dutch in the Indies, as in several other places women had reliably been identified as primary drivers of reforms. In Britain, as a contemporary put it, "Long before the word sanitation was heard of, or any other word that conveyed the idea of a science of health, the good, trained, thrifty housewife was a practical sanitary reformer."[93] In Japan, "domestic matters" were turned into "domestic management studies, the discipline of a corps of specialists" made of women trained by women, in "childcare, nursing of the sick, and prevention of contagious disease." By the 1910s, Japanese housewives were "a recognized professional identity."[94] In the Dutch East Indies, this would be a later development.

Unless they were addressed as soon-to-be mothers, in the 1920s there had been no intentional effort to make local women privy to the scientific principles of hygiene. This was despite the fact that the whole project of hygienic modernity—aimed at maintaining the laboring population healthy—was designed to rest on women's own quotidian household chores.[95] While periodicals' health pages put much emphasis on medical science, tropical hygiene, and daily practices of hygiene, women were simply addressed as cooks and housekeepers.[96]

Scientific Progress

Since the discovery of germs and other scientific advances, the biomedical foundations of hygiene had been crucial to imperialist assertions of superiority over colonized subjects. Showing hints of his later sympathy to eugenics,[97] at the beginning of the century the Dutch physician J.H.F. Kohlbrugge (1865–1941) claimed that the "lesser prosperity of the natives" was caused by popular superstitions that negatively impacted hygiene and health.[98] In this last section I explore how colonial exhibitions and popular night fairs promoted public health propaganda within a narrative of progress and modernization, highlighting how its roots in imperialist discourses demanded a dismissal of non-scientific forms of knowledge.

As we are reminded by Arnout van der Meer, exhibitions held at annual fairs were, since the beginning of the Ethical Policy, tools to both assert the "benevolence" of the colonial state, and to establish its superiority through the performance of modernity.[99] Public health as a topic was a perfect match, as fairs showcased modernization and education for the benefit of a larger segment of the indigenous population. With the authorities expecting a socio-economically diverse crowd of spectators, the "pedagogical intentions" now motivating the events required an entertainment apparatus that attracted—and transmitted knowledge to—a much broader audience.[100]

Alongside publications, popular fairs emerged as attractive sites to dispel "superstition" and promote scientific ideas of health. In 1923, for example, the popular night fair at Pasar Gambir (in Batavia) hosted a DVG show of "Fruits and Vegetables."[101] After a couple of small events,[102] in 1925 the DVG held its first substantial hygiene exhibition putting infant care under the spotlight—a theme that would return with much fanfare in the 1930s.[103] For now, in 1925 the Hygiene Commission's stall modestly displayed infant mortality rates across the colony and, for comparison, in the Netherlands and other European cities.[104]

The real goal was to offer "advice for mothers and children." Echoing the same information included in the Balai Poestaka/Volkslectuur books, but now reaching a much broader audience, the booth promoted rules pertinent to everyday care (from bathing to feeding and clothing), as well as to the birthing process: the umbilical cord ought to be cut with a tool that had been boiled for at least ten minutes, and the newborn ought to be washed right after birth with warm soapy water.[105] These instructions clearly promoted scientific biomedicine and challenged traditional practices as performed by the *dukun bayi*. The intent of offering "further instruction" to people—besides merely "show[ing] to the public what has been done in the last few years in the field of hygiene"[106]—was made explicit in 1927, and it was steeped in the mindset of racialized civilizationism.

In the second half of the 1920s, as the colonial administration readied itself for the First Hygiene Exhibition (Eerste Hygiëne Tentoonstelling in Nederlandsch-Indië, EHTINI, held in Bandung in 1927), propaganda materials came to present even more explicitly "unhygienic" behavior as visual evidence of civilizational difference. Supported by an extensive government effort, the preparation of this event would provide a strong infrastructure the DVG propaganda machine could draw from for years to come, in logistical and discursive terms alike. Alongside the displays that had been crafted specifically for this event—and which subsequently travelled for years to provincial fairs, schools, health centers, etc., around the archipelago[107]—the Bandung event also instigated much racialized and civilizational discourse on scientific hygiene as progress.

As stated in its name, this was the first dedicated hygiene exhibition in the Indies, and mirrored similar endeavors across Europe and Asia, which had been sources of inspiration and materials. H.M. Neeb, professor of hygiene and primary architect of the event, had sought pamphlets, publications, and films from across the world: these came from the Public Health Services in Manila and Singapore, and the League of Nations, as well as from London, Davos, Dresden, Dusseldorf, and many cities in the Netherlands.[108] Similarly, he had reached out to the Rockefeller Foundation, resulting in the display of materials from the US National Health Council, MetLife, and the American Social Hygiene Association (ASHA) at the exhibition.[109] Considering the eugenicist affiliations of the ASHA, the use of its materials likely contributed further to the racialized undertones of the exhibition. It was at this juncture that Dr. Rodenwaldt, already the most active member of the Indies' Eugenics Society, had expressed his dismay at the hygienist efforts to educate colonized subjects at all.[110]

Professor Neeb and the secretary of the head-committee of the EHTINI, M.A.J. Kelling, however, believed in improvement through reform, and argued it was the colonizer's duty to civilize the "primitive natives." They contrasted Europe and North America with the "primitive" conditions of the Indies: many common practices were seen as "mock[ing] the most basic principles of hygiene,"[111] but improvement of the "absolutely inadequate" conditions of education and health was possible, potentially bringing "the blessings of hygiene" to a "diseased people" that was "unhealthy" in its bodies and thoughts.[112]

One of the first matters to be addressed was exactly how to deliver that message. Kelling argued that "a people still attuned to primitive circumstances" could not "be w[o]n over on the basics of hygiene by presenting them with tables, statistics!" Instead, they needed "illustrative plates, drawings, dioramas with light effects and models, set up exuberantly."[113] Kelling's disparaging approach to the Indies population influenced his strategies for health propaganda.

The space of the exhibition was divided into several areas, with multiple stands each presenting its own theme. These addressed specific diseases and concerns, from hookworms, tuberculosis, and malaria to the plague, milk hygiene, and slaughter, the latter including a cardboard model of "the modern abattoir."[114] As seen in the Official Catalogue, several of the reproduced illustrative plates contrasted European and "native" practices. Two of them, for example, showed how the "native waiter" shared his germs by placing his thumb in the soup bowl (see Figure 1.3),[115] and then cleaned his ears with the cloth meant for wiping tables and glasses.[116] Similarly, a beautifully decorated cake (a European-styled *taart*) was depicted next to a vegetable garden for which irrigation water was drawn from the proximities of a latrine.[117] Another series "educated" viewers on matters of nutrition.[118] The

FIGURE 1.3 Illustrations displayed at the EHTINI exhibition, Bandung 1927. Source: *Officieele Catalogus der 8ᵉ Ned.-Ind. Jaarbeurs en-Markt en der Eerste Hygiëne Tentoonstelling in Ned. Indië*, 1927, pp. 38–39, Yale University Library

attention to food was matched only by the dangers of malarian mosquitoes and the primacy of cleanliness and disinfectants to keep them at bay.[119]

The emphasis, then, was on individual agency to improve the conditions of one's own person and home, for the benefit of the community. The core message was that "the battle for the maintenance, and more so the achievement, of peoples' health, does not befall on a single person, it is unconditionally beholden to the purposeful collaboration of the masses."[120]

This was part of a broader strategy to improve the character of the Indies' peoples, which the colonizers saw as lacking "determination, thrift, and productivity."[121] The exhibition's goal of increasing awareness and interest in health literacy, pursued by showcasing practical applications and suggestions, was in fact intended to facilitate a long-term impact on the productive employment of "latent labor" toward "the advancement of economic, ethical and moral interests."[122] Echoing Kohlbrugge's statements from two decades earlier, Neeb's exhibition supported a colonialist and capitalist vision of the colony. Notably, Kelling and Neeb pictured a male audience: neither identified women as interlocutors; nor does it seem that women were represented in any of the visual props exhibited at the EHTINI (at least, based on the sources available).

As the Dutch colonial project of hygienic modernity could not break the strictures created by its own multifaceted hierarchal order (which saw colonized subjects as inferiors based on perceived differences in the realms of race, civilization, religion, and gender relations), indigenous women and Islamic beliefs were both excluded from sanitary reforms. This contrasted with the experience in Europe, America, and Japan, where women caregivers were identified as primary drivers of the efforts, able to receive science-based hygienic propaganda for a modernizing society. Moreover, there religious symbols and shared moral values were often part of the same diffusion of sanitary reforms in imperial metropoles and their peripheries.

In imperial formulations, though, colonized subjects were irredeemably uncivilized, and Islam had featured prominently among Christian Europeans' constructions of that difference since earlier times. For indigenous, colonized Muslim subjects, progress could only be approximated, through exposure to western (scientific) knowledge and emulation of (or at least the *attempt* and *aspiration* to emulate) western superior civilization. At best, there ought to be a point of rupture with "native" life. Women, like Islam, were seen as too distant from that (androcentric) vision of modernity. As we saw in publications and at the exhibitions, the Dutch promoted health in an exclusively secular, scientific, and western framework that interfaced almost exclusively with men.

The colonial administration dominated and controlled much of the press, but it did not retain a hegemonic discursive agency: on the one hand, Muslims in the Indies autonomously articulated ideas of health; on the other, progress and hygiene intersected in the bodies of women as birthing mothers.

At the 1924 Muhammadiyah congress, the physician Dr. Soemowidagdo argued that "Maintaining one's health is different from guarding what one eats and drinks. . . . What is truly important is diligent work, cleanliness, *hawa* [air, bodily desires] and brightness." This reflection combined biomedical science and Islamic paradigms, as Kevin Ko reminds us that purity of the *hawa* could refer to both fresh air and the purification of one's bodily desires.[123] The same word had appeared in the 1919 Malay text "Caring for Nursing Infants," where the "zuivere frissche lucht" ("pure clean air") that ought to circulate in the newborn's room was rendered as the "hawa jang soetji dan segar," thus choosing two terms with religious connotations: the layered meanings of *hawa* were here reinforced by its adjectives, one (*segar*) indexing a more material freshness, the other (*soetji*) pointing at a potentially spiritual reflection.[124]

The booklet "The Foundations of Health," printed by Balai Poestaka in 1925 and reprinted in 1926 as an insert to the well-distributed *Pandji Poestaka*, had taken the commonly promoted argument of good health as a "basis for prosperity" and infused it with Islamic references and religious terms.[125] In 1925, a writer on the *Volksalmanak Melajoe* had similarly argued that it was a religious duty to guard one's health, as life was a gift of God; rejecting colonial dichotomies, the article proposed in both secular *and* Islamic terms that "rationality" ought to be the primary source of knowledge:

> All diseases are caused by Allah *subhanahu wa ta'ala*. Similarly, various kinds of medicine have been sent down by none other than Allah *subhanahu wa ta'ala* to fight diseases. // God *al-rahman wa'l-rahim* sent down his blessings on humans, and also bestowed them with reason, knowledge, and wisdom so that they would know which medicines are good—the ones which will cure the various diseases.[126]

Whereas the colonial establishment constructed epistemological binaries, Muslim voices connected Islam to modern medicine and the concept of prosperity, and indigenous women introduced the notion—omitted from the administration's calculus—that hygienic birthing was a facet of progress, both social and political. When in 1924 Anna Sjarif reviewed "A Guide for Teaching School Children," she described the book as "useful" for young girls and adults, as by acquiring new knowledge from the medical field, they could become "modern women." Should a child fall ill, the modern mother should know how to care for them, *and* be able to assess when to seek a doctor too.[127] Sjarif was the women's section editor for *Bintang Hindia*, a widely read Malay-language bi-weekly paper supported by the government, and a promoter of its "Ethical" policies.

Indigenous women in Java and Sumatra were increasingly aware that birthing and their gendered responsibilities of care bore an impact beyond their own homes, and that their discursive agency could not be limited. In the next chapter I expand on how women were able to assert their own agency in professionalized healthcare, and the often-politicized discursive realm.

FIGURE 2.1 "Only piped water is to be trusted." Source: P. Peverelli and F. van Bemmel. *Blyf Gezond! = Sehatlah Selaloe,* 1933, Plate #13, Leiden University Library

2 | LABOR

WITH THE TITLE "ALWAYS HEALTHY!," in 1933 the Dutch East Indies' Office of Public Health Propaganda produced a series of plates illustrating, it claimed, how a hygienic lifestyle was typically experienced or ignored in a *desa*, the rural village of the Indies. Meant to be hung in classrooms—befitting of the Ethical Policy's claimed aim of educating a new generation of "natives"— the vignettes presented snapshots of hygienic and unhygienic life in the countryside. (The series was also available for purchase.) This was one of the earliest—and surely most vividly explicit— representations of women's daily activities of care work as foundational to a hygienic life.

The village reflected a blend of Orientalist inspiration and civilization-ist hubris, but not all was imagined.[1] The plates depict a rural village built along a river, where children wear a mixture of western and local clothing, and the houses are made of rattan. Health and hygiene are within reach, and are tools to obtain personal and societal success, as discussed in the opening of the previous chapter.

The social reproductive labor of women is everywhere, sometimes in the background—like women boiling water (Figure 2.1)—and at other times strikingly visible, from a mother's acumen saving a toddler from tuberculo-sis (Figure 2.2), to multiple instances of female nurses (e.g., Figure 2.3). The first plate in the series, which is reproduced in the opening to the previous

FIGURE 2.2   "The dangers of tuberculosis and the way to keep it at bay." Source:
P. Peverelli and F. van Bemmel. *Blyf Gezond! = Sehatlah Selaloe,* 1933, Plate #17,
Leiden University Library

chapter (Figure 1.1), proclaimed health to be "a great treasure," showing that
whoever falls ill can no longer enjoy the idyllic village life. Throughout, mosquitoes, flies, lice, and rats are singled out as the main culprits of many diseases, and prevention is identified as achievable through improved personal
hygiene, consumption of uncontaminated foods, and conscious sourcing of
drinking water. Much of this was a rejection of common "native" practices,
such as eating from road-side peddlers or seeking the help of a traditional
dukun (also Figure 2.3).

Most importantly, ordinary women were depicted as at once indispens-
able and marginalized. The sanitary project was shown to lean primarily on women's daily labor of social reproduction, as they were portrayed
performing those actions deemed necessary to foster a healthy domestic
environment and healthy bodies—echoing the concerns expressed in the
texts printed by the public health propaganda office. But in fact, as had also
been evident in textual sources, women were usually in the background.
The focus of Figure 2.1 is a boy drinking boiled water from a cup, but it is a
woman that is pulling the water from the well and pouring it into the kettle.
While we see a man drinking from it, no one is shown putting the kettle on
the stove. It was likely the responsibility of women to make that happen,
laying bare the invisibility of their labor.

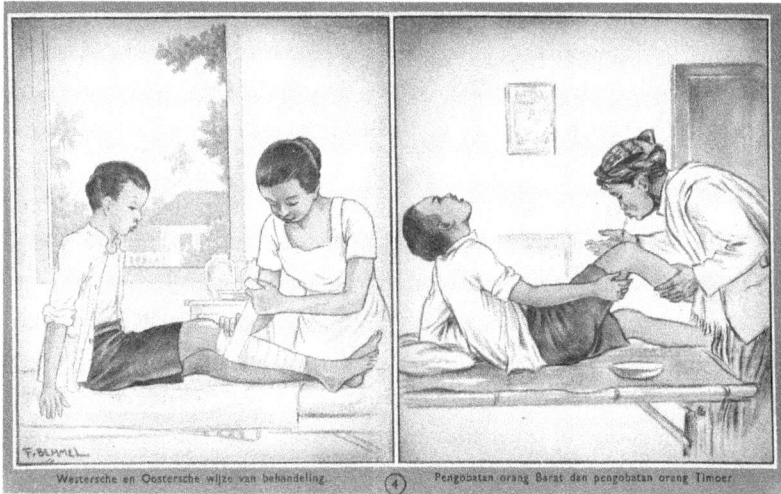

FIGURE 2.3 "Western cures and Eastern cures." Source: P. Peverelli and F. van Bemmel. *Blyf Gezond! = Sehatlah Selaloe*, 1933, Plate #4, Leiden University Library

In a twist on the previous chapter's narrative, though, the plates here show ordinary men pursuing unhygienic practices and ordinary women as attuned to biomedical concerns. In Figure 2.2 we see how it is the mother who takes the baby to the doctor after the tuberculotic father has coughed in its face; the solution presented is to place the child in a colonial sanatorium. It will be recalled that tuberculosis had been the subject of the first publication of the "Kitab Kesehatan" series issued by Balai Poestaka/Volkslectuur in 1919–1922. There had been no reference to women then, but now the mother is at the center of the action, as the man appears unaware of basic principles of disease transmission.

Depicting native men as "backward" was likely the outcome of a new focus on children as disciplined colonial subjects, rather than attempting reform of the adult population. In the early 1930s, the Indies' colonial government was ramping up political repression and censorship against nationalist expressions (domains the Dutch saw as primarily male).[2] For this reason, I suggest that women as mothers were seen as "allies" in these policies aimed at shaping new subjects.

Three other plates in this series show women among the ranks of "modern" healthcare professionals (out of six depicting biomedicine in total). If in two of these plates indigenous women were pictured as nurses assisting a racially ambiguous male doctor, in Figure 2.3 we see a young indigenous nurse sporting a neat, short-sleeved white uniform. A young child, who is beaming a confident expression while sitting up on an examination table, is getting his wound dressed in a clean room filled with light, and fresh air is streaming in from an open window. The indigenous nurse stands in for western biomedicine, in clear opposition to the traditional male *dukun* healer, who spits on the wound of a boy cringing in pain, sitting on a rickety bamboo cot, in a dark and windowless room.

These plates show that by the 1930s the previously reticent colonial administration had come to acknowledge indigenous women's involvement in various endeavors of scientifically informed social reproduction. I connect this change in representation to bigger shifts in colonial politics in the 1930s, and to how the Dutch continued to read the Indies through their European eyes, including their gendered separation of spheres. However, I also argue that the authors of these plates, Dr. Peverelli and Van Bemmel, were enabled to depict indigenous women as we see them represented because of women's self-directed participation in the public sphere.[3]

In this chapter I trace two trajectories that help us further understand these plates, and further foreshadow a trend of increasing professionalization and mobilization of women through their gendered roles. First, I analyze women's writings that engaged with hygienic mothering and maternalism as anchors for gendered and political emancipation; next, I follow the life stories of a few women from privileged backgrounds who gained access to the field of professionalized healthcare. I take both as forms of labor that reveal the quotidian intersection of gender and hygiene. Both the written word and professional work illustrate women's own awareness of their contribution to the larger project of modernization through their activities of care work. The voices and experiences of these women, then, provide the building blocks for my analysis of "domestic nationalism" as a framework that brings together gendered labor, nation-building, and religion.

———

The Dutch colonial administration had, by the time of the design of the plates, engaged with the Indies' women as mothers for decades. They had expressed concerns over women's sustained reliance on *dukuns*, the need for them to be educated, and to be ultimately trusting of doctors, foremost in supporting births.[4] But as shown in the previous chapter, the effort to educate colonized women on the scientific underpinnings of cleanliness had been short-lived. Even the seemingly superficial early references to microbes and bacilli had disappeared by the late 1920s, with a shift to simply instructing women on how to maintain a clean house. Similarly, writings on domestic matters authored by men and aimed at indigenous women did not connect care work or birthing to progress, but rather to women's gendered duties that now needed policing and reform. Nor had the colonial message incorporated the quotidian effort of social reproductive labor in which the Indies' women were involved. This all fit within a long-lasting effort to define the boundaries of women's roles and presence in education, homes, and the workplace.

The Orientalist vision that had taken shape in the second half of the nineteenth century still thrived in the 1920s, perpetuating a racialized understanding of the Indies' societies. The Dutch had merged "a Western and essentially middle-class vision of women's maternal destiny and housewifely duties . . . with respect for *adat*." This had supported patriarchal understandings of Javanese customs and the limiting of women's agency. As eloquently argued by Frances Gouda, elite Muslim women were painted as immured;[5] this despite the fact that Islamic reformism was gradually recognizing women's social roles, opening up new avenues for education and employment.[6] Similarly, the interest in expanding the framework of families as modeled on the "husband provider" and "domestic/ated housewife" dichotomy was linked to colonial needs to create a new middle class anchored to the colonial service and oriented towards consumption (which I explore in the next chapter). As suggested by Gouda, this process of turning colonized women into "housewives" was aimed at removing them from remunerative work and instead framing their activities as "domestic"—even when they were employed as nurses or midwives.[7]

This was not a process that exclusively involved elite women, as the colonial establishment also curbed opportunities for lower-class women who sought employment to make ends meet. This is evident in the debate on a bill on the regulation of women's night labor. Promoting Victorian values of housewifery on the one hand, and expressing concerns about women's mobility and employment on the other,[8] the bill was intended to limit the access of unskilled female laborers to waged work in coffee, tea, and tobacco plantations.[9] Again, domestic labor was seen as the one acceptable form of employment. Under this optic, indigenous women in the 1920s might be perceived as mostly—if not exclusively—contributing to the advancement of the Indies as biological reproducers. Yet, as shown in this chapter, they were primary contributors to this effort through a much broader engagement in social reproduction, which included intellectual and professionalized healthcare labor.

INTELLECTUAL LABOR

As illustrated in the previous chapter, literate women remained a fraction of the population, yet they were an active constituency of the publishing realm as writers as much as consumers.[10] They engaged with a variety of topics, and while they remained marginalized in official policy and propaganda, matters of health were often featured in the women's press. Here, then, I show that women made themselves an integral part of the socialization efforts of the colonial establishment in matters of hygiene, mothering, and progress, thus resisting a curated gendered public discourse intended to dictate imperialist purposes. Engaging with social and political developments in non-western settings, Muslim women fostered a dynamic intellectual environment that displayed their initiative and political awareness in interweaving birthing reforms with political reflections, and thus entered into conversations on the emergence of a "modern" nation to which they were agentive contributors.

Common domestic and bodily practices were not being presented to indigenous women as drivers of socio-economic progress, and the European "feminist" press promoted conventional patriotic commentaries on maternalism, printing articles indicating that a woman's only expected contribution was biological reproduction. This was evident, for example, in the primarily Dutch-language newsletter *De Vrouw*—a monthly "propaganda periodical for the women's movement in Indonesia" with a mixed Dutch and local editorial board. In a 1927 article, published in Malay, the author focused on the importance of educating young indigenous women in matters of pregnancy and early childhood so as to prepare them to become "earnest soldiers" as mothers, and instilling in them love for the motherland.[11]

But more nuanced approaches had already been put forward by indigenous Muslim women. In the 1919 opening editorial for the Medan-based

Perempoean Bergerak ("Woman on the Move"), already quoted in the introduction to this book, the *rédactrice* Batoet Satidja had indexed women's interests as encompassing "the house, infant-feeding, child-rearing, hygiene,
religion, and 'native' feminism."[12] Alongside these gendered concerns, for
which she deployed Dutch words, Satidja also expressed the hope that by
reading her magazine women would expand their knowledge and eventually be seen as intellectual equals by Europeans in the Indies.

While using the language of the colonizing authority, and seemingly
echoing European ideas of imperial maternalism, I suggest that putting all
of those categories of action on the same level of importance Satidja was
pursuing a project of epistemological resistance by intertwining medicalized domestic literacy, gender emancipation, and Islamic ethos through
an autonomous process of knowledge production. Autonomy was further
asserted in the process of transmission, as this was an exclusively indigenous platform that printed news about local and foreign politics and the
international women's movement—including other colonized territories
where women's emancipatory efforts were already explicitly connected to
anti-colonial nationalism.

For Satidja, the combination of literacy, worldly understanding, and
autonomous processes of knowledge production and transmission were
the threads that connected the domestic sphere of mothering and care
work to gender emancipation, public engagement, and national progress.
And she was not the only one making these connections. An article in
the Solonese Islamic reformist periodical *Isteri Soesila - Taman Moeslimah*, printed in the wake of the abolition of the Ottoman Caliphate in
March 1924, shows this point too. It might have echoed the message of *De
Vrouw* in its observation that Turkish women, who now "had a homeland,"
held as their "biggest goal to bring into this world brave children"; but she
pushed beyond a conventional reading of imperial maternalism, as Turkish women remained dedicated to Islamic clothing while, for example,
avidly reading newspapers and engaging in political matters.[13] Religious
identity, political awareness, and mothering were all interconnected in the
women's press, and as I explore in the next chapter, the Muslim identity
of female writers would come through even more strongly when writing
about food.

Disparaging the adoption of western modern trends did not mean a
fundamental rejection of all things foreign. In fact, modern women went

to college, practiced science, were politically engaged, *and* embraced their Islamic identity. They fashioned themselves as modern Muslim mothers. In 1925, an anonymous writer at *Isteri Soesila* brought birthing explicitly to the fore in relation to women's progress, noting that women in the Philippines were "very clever and very advanced. Not *madjoe* only with western-styled dresses and short hair like the women of our people, but they are *madjoe* in knowledge and ability," as many were university graduates with degrees in pharmacy and medicine.[14] As discussed in another article on infant care in the Philippines, printed that same year, women there "can already be said to be [politically] aware. Their level of *kemadjoean* can be said to be the highest if compared to that of other Eastern peoples."[15] The author, Soewarsih—possibly Soewarsih Djojopoespito (1912–1977), a Javanese teacher as well as feminist writer and nationalist activist—identified the care paid to infants as crucial to Filipina women's advancement. In Soewarsih's narrative, women were now able to care for children and the sick, and therefore "advance." This was possible thanks to the combined efforts of the American colonial administration and local elites who launched "courses on the care of infants and young children,"[16] and of the Filipina teachers who engaged in health literacy propaganda. Schools, birthing clinics, and the women's press had all been key tools for the progress of Filipina women,[17] and that could be a model for Indonesians.

Modern birthing and child-rearing, then, emerged as an important facet of indigenous women's articulations of progress, despite a lack of fostering on the part of the Indies' colonial government. This was clearly spelled out by Chan Leang Nio, as she emphasized the nationalist maternalism coming out of India and China, celebrating the mother of Shaukat Ali and the wives of Tagore and Sun Yat Sen as "the most important women in the world of *kemadjoean*" and among nationalist movements. Asserting that "Women of the East have their own way of doing things, different from others who embraced progress, bringing no little benefit to themselves," this Sino-Javanese novelist thus concluded that "the sun has already risen high enough so as to awaken the women of the East from their deep sleep."[18]

As the civilizationist discourse had ramped up in conjunction with the First Hygiene Exhibition in Bandung (EHTINI, discussed in the previous chapter), connections between mothering and progress were becoming more widespread. In 1928, the government-sponsored organization Twee Kruisen (Palang Doewa, or "Two Crosses") was setting out to train midwives and build hospitals for "modern birthing" in Batavia. The goal was to teach "modern upbringing" techniques to "the backward *boemipoet-era*." The narrative, although published in a government publication, continued to make references to other Asian contexts:

> If Chinese women were able to give birth to men like Dr. Sun Yat Sen and Chiang Kai Shek; if a Turkish woman could give birth to a man like Kemal Pasha [Ataturk]; if a Hindu woman could give birth to a man like Gandhi; if . . . [*sic*] why have Indies' women—and there are millions of them—not been able to give birth to a hero whose name would ring across the entire world? We hear this question being asked many times.[19]

This question—the article explained—could be addressed only if people began to pay attention to "how a mother who is giving birth should be taken care of, and how the baby should be cared for. If not, then the question is not worth asking."[20] Far from being a criticism of Indonesian women's "lacking," the article praised the active labor of women as crucial to the progress of any nation, as apparent in the reference to a string of nationalist (anti-colonial) leaders.

In addition to birthing, women's fashion, and education, infant competitions emerged in the 1920s Indies as the ultimate intersection for hygienic mothering, national emancipation, and economic prosperity, in religious and secular spaces alike. Originating in the United States at the beginning of the twentieth century primarily to advance a eugenicist agenda that encouraged the "breeding" of "better babies,"[21] in the transnational space these contests were thought of as an "effort to 'save children'" from high mortality rates, as argued by Margaret Mih Tillman.[22] In fact, if in the imperialist Global North baby shows promoted a Mendelian eugenic standpoint in which women's roles "further[ed] the supposed quality of the 'race'" via the biological choices they made,[23] in East Asia improvement focused on proper nurturing.[24] New ideas of infant care in the Indies appear to parallel Juliette Chung's suggestion that China's efforts to assert national "strength" can be read as "a social-control project under Jean-Baptiste Lamarck's tenet of inheritance of acquired characters." Whereas the US (and Japan) stressed genetic principles, conversations in China and the Indies invoked public health, social hygiene, and education promoting hygienic reforms—often explicitly tied to birthing and care of infants—as key strategies for a "better" people.[25]

The first competition in the Indies was advanced in 1924 by Anna Sjarif, the editor of *Bintang Hindia*'s women's column, in order to promote the centrality of children's health to national progress. Anna Sjarif encouraged her readers to participate in the competition, reminding them that "beauty, abilities and health are the result of the complete and mindful care" of infants. Parents thus had the duty to go beyond the mere act of following "nature," as their care could shape children as "healthy, educated, of good character, [and] with bright faces." In their own words, the editors of *Bintang Hindia* were initiating this contest because "it is on children that progress depends."[26] Anna Sjarif had indicated that her model was Europe's competition, but as she focused on mothering, the article explained her distancing from mainline eugenics. Sjarif was keenly aware of racialized identities—when commenting on Soewarsih's article on Filipina women she had exhorted her own peers, glossing: "The Philippines are part of Asia. Its population doesn't have white skin, but pale-yellow skin; therefore they are of the same people as us. They have been able to walk so far, doesn't it intrigue the minds of people here to take example from them?" As Soewarsih too had argued, the path to progress and awareness was forged with a commitment to modern birthing and care of children.[27]

Baby shows would soon become recurrent on a variety of occasions, and would be used to advance a diversity of viewpoints. In 1928 there would be one at the Bandung *Jaarbeurs* (the annual trade fair) and another one at the Muhammadiyah and 'Aisyiyah Congress.[28] Like similar events held in large cities across Asia, such as Shanghai, Singapore, and Manila,[29] these were to become a yearly event. Parading chubby, clean, and calm babies—demonstrating that good nutrition and hygiene reigned supreme—the stated goal was to promote "the advancement of good health and infant-care."[30]

While Anna Sjarif had seen baby contests as platforms to make explicit a connection between mothering and the "qualitative" improvement of the upcoming generation, the *Pandji Poestaka* report on the *Jaarbeurs* competition zeroed in on the economic argument—a narrative that often accompanied colonial concerns over high rates of infant death:

People in Europe pay a lot of attention to the care of babies. This care is always carried forward so as to decrease instances of infant death. That decrease in child mortality is very beneficial to the economy (wealth) of the people. If many babies, or young people, die, are weak, or are not strong enough to work, it will surely negatively affect the wealth of the people and the state.[31]

Health was placed at center stage as the goal of infant care and children's "success" in the competitions, but, in aggregate, the overall message was that paying attention—and allocating resources—to the care of infants and the advancement of their health would engender "the prosperity and progress of the people and its nation."

The colonial state (whose voice we hear in *Pandji Poestaka*) supported these endeavors within the logic of exploitative capitalism, and echoed conservative visions of maternalism. Conversely the women-directed indigenous narrative stressed nationalist goals, and lingered, perhaps, at the edges of eugenics, but stood far from patriarchal views of the nation-state. Even while anchoring their visions of womanhood to biological reproduction, women writers stressed the political importance of a positive birthing experience and children's sound upbringing, and the need for women to be involved in such politics.[32]

Satidja, Soewarsih, Chan Leang Nio, Anna Sjarif, and the many other writers who remained anonymous had identified a thread connecting women's education, hygienic modernity, and national progress. Whereas this intellectual position aligned them with elite white women in the imperial metropole—where maternalism was commonly embraced by educated women, and from where it spread to colonized territories—it was also different from some prevalent Dutch attitudes. First of all, indigenous networks of knowledge were diverse, including other Muslim and Asian contexts. Second, indigenous Muslim women could leverage a self-awareness of their ascribed role in social reproductive labor to carve a niche as guardians and drivers of hygienic modernity. Under such circumstances, modern mothering became a field of externally recognized gendered expertise, as well as an internalized framework for national emancipation. This pivot away from mainstream maternalism led to two discursive and material transformations, which are apparent in the illustrative plates I opened this chapter with. On the one hand, (lower-class) Indies women's everyday activities of care work were eventually recognized as integral to sanitary reforms. On the other, educated women gradually entered the healthcare system as professionals.

PROFESSIONAL HEALTHCARE

Becoming an indigenous healthcare professional was a male business, as public health officers did not see women as able to substitute science for long-held traditional beliefs. The Ethicist mandate notwithstanding, the overall colonial education system was lacking, and was not designed to facilitate the access of capable women to medical education. Whereas midwifery and nursing were exclusively female fields, and most practitioners were indigenous, by 1929 there were only three women appointed as Indies doctors.[33] One of them was *Roro* Soerti Tirtotenojo, the first Javanese woman to become a physician and to do so through local schooling.[34] Born in Madiun (East Java) in the early 1900s, daughter to the vice-regent of Pekalongan,[35] Soerti had graduated from an ELS in 1918, and swiftly passed the admission exam to Surabaya's Medical College (NIAS, Nederlandsch-Indische Artsen School).[36] She started her studies there in 1920.[37]

Commentators had expressed hopes that more indigenous people would enter the medical professions. In 1925 Anna Sjarif bemoaned that there were "not enough doctors, nurses and midwives" in the Indies, and connected this shortage to women's sustained reliance on *dukuns*.[38] Four years later, in 1929, an article published in the progressive East Indies Dutch-language newspaper *De Locomotief* called for a greater effort in training "native" healthcare professionals. The author, Professor J.J. van Loghem, argued that the work done on the plantations (where laborers needed to be kept healthy enough to sustain the colonial economy) and in the more affluent urban neighborhoods was not sufficient. He recognized that "native nurses and midwives" were performing "important work for the benefit of public health"; however, a larger body of local personnel trained according to the principles of western biomedicine was needed, and the colonial government ought to seek direct cooperation with the local population to increase popular confidence in western medicine.[39] Sjarif and Loghem similarly identified the double challenge of staffing and strategy.

In this section I show that the deepest impact on improving MCH, in the 1930s as in the 1950s, was yielded through grassroots programs that employed (the few) indigenous female healthcare professionals formed in the biomedical tradition to train (the much larger number of) *dukuns* and conduct (even broader) outreach activities with rural women. In the mid-1920s the colonial administration had sought to further restrict the scope of women in the public sphere, including limiting their presence in educational and professional spaces. Throughout the 1930s, then, the number of indigenous women enrolled in the territory's medical schools was still small, and most of them were members of the local aristocracy. Yet, despite still being a small portion of all admitted pupils, this was nonetheless a net improvement that would indeed make a mark on society, and lead to the increased visibility of the value of indigenous women in hygiene work.

Surabaya's NIAS enrolled nine women: J.A. Gerungan, A. Sakul, *Raden Roro* Sapartinah, *Siti* Roebiah, *Roro* Soemini, *Siti* Kasmiah, *Roro* Esmirah, *Roro* Sri Moe, and *Raden Roro* Soetirah Soeparman.[40] Another handful were enrolled at Batavia's Medical Advanced School (Hoogeschool), including *Raden Roro* Moedinem, who would become the first indigenous woman to graduate from that school.[41] While close to half of them either dropped out or never practiced, a few would go on to have fulfilling medical professional careers, mostly in the private sector. Soetirah was "admitted to the practice of medicine, surgery and obstetrics in the Dutch East Indies as *Indisch Artse*" in 1934,[42] as were *Siti* Kasmiah in 1935,[43] *Raden Roro* Sapartinah in 1936,[44] *Raden Roro* Moedinem Moedinem in 1937,[45] J.A. Gerungan in 1938,[46] and A. Sakul in 1941.[47] Sapartinah would be the only one among her female peers from NIAS to succeed in becoming employed in medicine.[48] She first held the position of assistant director, and next director, of the training school at the Rockefeller Foundation demonstration unit in Purwokerto. This had been established by John Lee Hydrick in 1933 to pursue rural hygiene work, after a decade spent in the Indies leading hookworm eradication campaigns. Another educational path was the midwifery school, from which several hundred indigenous women had graduated, according to the Rockefeller Foundation records.[49] I here mention one, *Raden Roro* Marsidah, as she would have an exceptional professional life contributing to the recognition and visibility of women's work in healthcare. Graduating from a prestigious high school in Batavia in 1935,[50] Marsidah was admitted to practice midwifery by the DVG in 1939.[51] Like Sapartinah, Marsidah too would be employed at the Purwokerto demonstration unit.[52]

Soerti, like Marsidah, Sapartinah, and their peers, was well aware of the limits of text-based channels of knowledge transmission and formal events such as lectures, and thus they often combined office-based medical practice with outreach activities. After two years of public service in social pediatrics in Malang,[53] Soerti had moved to Solo to work as palace physician at the sultan's Kraton court.[54] From the beginning, however, she had also been involved in "nurturing hygiene literacy among the local youth," collaborating with one of the city's Dutch Schools for Natives (Hollandsch-Inlandsche School, HIS),[55] and pursuing broader educational efforts, including teaching about infant care and the importance of "bathing, clothing, food and cleanliness" to local communities in the neighborhood.[56]

Medical women remained few, far between, and an overall minority. But in the very early 1930s, before the medium-term impact of the Depression stalled all new initiatives, there were expanding employment prospects for women in public health. A few had joined the broader field of healthcare as pharmacists (a rank in which Dutch women had long outnumbered men) and more as laboratory analysts. The Eijkman Institute for Nutrition would employ quite a few of them, as nutrition had taken shape as a field of research perceived as in alignment with "domestic matters." It had already created opportunities for women in Europe and America to enter the scientific world,[57] and the Indies were no exception. The Eijkman Institute, whose work focused on researching the nutritional value and bacteriological contamination of common foodstuffs, became an important site for women's employment.

The now scientifically proven importance of "food" offered women a wider avenue into the world of science through their ascribed roles as mothers and wives. Soekarmi, whom I quoted in the introduction to this book, would make that most clear to her Malay-reading peers in 1931, but that road had been opened by Dutch (possibly Eurasian) women a decade earlier. In the late 1910s, the Dutch Dr. B.C. Jansen worked alongside Miss M. Noordink (a laboratory analyst) and Miss E. Carpentier Alting (a chemist).[58] Miss Alting left her position likely in 1920,[59] and Miss Noordink in 1924;[60] but in 1929 the laboratory had appointed Ms. Ir. E.L. Triebart to conduct work on vitamins A and C. The following year Ms. Dr. van Marle was attached to the Food Commission as first-class technical officer to expand the available data on commonly consumed foods.[61]

The volume of tests run by the laboratories continued to grow,[62] necessitating an expansion of personnel. The inclusion of indigenous analysts, then, came from pure necessity, with the colonial laboratory operating on a combination of financial, elitist, and racist considerations.[63] As reminisced by the former head of the Department of Public Health, Willem De Vogel, routine work was seen as "a matter of practice" rather than "keen intellect."

Thus, in his own words, "it can therefore be left to the less skilled, cheaper workers, without compromising the accuracy of the results, by [exercising] judicious control" of their operations.[64]

Their participation had been the result of European civilizationism's reckoning with financial conservatism. Regardless of its motivations, this move opened a new path for the employment of indigenous analysts. Although just a handful in number, their presence—especially that of women—in the laboratory would have reverberations in the broader community, as the knowledge they produced circulated widely. In July 1935 ten trainees were admitted to tackle the high volume of analyses. Among them, six were young women (three Dutch, two Javanese, and one Chinese).[65] They all graduated in June 1938, and were absorbed into the Eijkman Institute. Among them, Miss C.G. Chaulan and Miss Eny Wirasasmita would continue to work as analysts until the Japanese occupation. In 1938, a Miss R.T. Risakotta was first clerk, and a Miss Dahlia Dachlan was listed as "volunteering" personnel.[66] Unfortunately, they all disappear from the record with the Japanese invasion, and their names do not resurface after independence. But as recalled by *Nyonya* Lily Gamar Sutantio, who worked at the Eijkman Institute during the Japanese occupation, "many women worked there."[67]

Purwokerto

Larger numbers of women found employment outside of the government laboratories and hospitals, as John Lee Hydrick expanded the initiatives of the Rockefeller Foundation in rural hygiene and readjusted his methods. In the early years of his appointment to the Indies, Hydrick had focused on the identification and gradual eradication of contagious diseases, primary among them the hookworm.[68] Hence, while the colonial administration focused on soil and water pollution, attempting big infrastructural plans—and often failing to make an impact on the broader population—the Rockefeller Foundation strived to establish a network of rural units where trained personnel conducted preventive medicine. Mirroring other endeavors in the Southern United States and South America, the favored method of rural hygiene propaganda had been to provide lectures to villagers, combining instruction with group administration of medicines and more entertaining activities, such as film screenings.

In the 1920s to 1930s it became clear that these activities almost exclusively reached men. They were more likely to be literate, available to attend these events, and perceived as heads of their households—and thus targeted by healthcare professionals (here called *mantris*) for instruction. Women, on the other hand, were rarely sought out as interlocutors, either because they were seen as ignorant, or because they were not at home (or even in the village). When public health officials began to see women's roles as home-based promoters of health, it seeded the idea that women health workers might be even more effective than their male peers.

For Hydrick, hygiene work ought to be centered on "*direct contact with the people,*"[69] which he saw as the foundation for teaching "practicable measures, so that the people will be able to give cooperation."[70] Establishing a rapport with villagers was the responsibility of the *mantris* ("inspectors"). Neither nurses nor doctors, these staff (both male and female) were specifically trained to deploy a variety of educational methods to teach villagers the tenets of preventive care in an accessible, relatable, and personable way. According to Hydrick, this goal could only be achieved through itinerant *mantris*, rather than expecting the people they served to travel. The *mantris*, then, travelled extensively within their regional purview. Through home visits and demonstrations, and by offering lectures, showing films, distributing booklets, etc.,[71] they strove to both educate the public, and build a rapport with communities. Within this approach, Hydrick grew increasingly skeptical of the public lectures, which by the mid-1930s were considered "not of great value."[72] Instead, "the most valuable method of carrying on health education [was] the house visit."[73] Published as captions to two illustrative plates included in his book *Intensive Rural Hygiene Work in Netherlands India*, these quotes were echoed in recurrent statements such as: "*The best results can be secured by the house visits.*"[74]

There were both male and female house visitors, but it is telling that the only explicit reference to effectiveness in Hydrick's text points at women. The first image shows one female *mantri* conferring with a mother during a house visit in a village (Figure 2.4); the second image shows another female *mantri* approaching a school to instruct the children there (Figure 2.5). While house visits had always been part of the Rockefeller Foundation's method of rural hygiene work, it was only in 1935 that Hydrick explicitly recognized its superior impact in the Indies, and he connected it to women. It was around that time that he expanded his efforts to maternal health and infant hygiene.[75]

FIGURE 2.4   "House visits by female hygiene *mantris*." Source: J. L. Hydrick. *Intensive Rural Hygiene Work in Netherlands India*, 1937, n.p., Cornell University Library

Infant and maternal health provided the best example for Hydrick to prove the stronger positive impact of his method. The Dutch had set up consultation offices (*consultatie-bureaux*) in several cities in Java, Sumatra, and Sulawesi, which expectant women and new mothers were supposed to visit regularly. But Hydrick deemed infant clinics unsuitable to "the beginning stages of [rural hygiene] work" when "*hygiene must be carried to the family house . . . so that the mothers of the infants can apply in their homes what they learn at hygiene centers*," under the watchful eye of the *mantri*, ready to correct the mother in her space.[76] Hence, whereas the general hygiene center did receive expectant and new mothers for check-ups, in Hydrick's vision visiting the health unit was a future goal, not the first point of departure—and one that still needed to be supported by *mantris'* home

FIGURE 2.5   "The *mantri*-nurse, who has been working in propaganda for two years, also regularly visits schools independently. Her means of transport for this is a cart." Source: Rockefeller Archive Center, 655 J Java, Public Health 2

visits. The *mantris* were thus able to service those women—the majority, in fact—who could not (or would not) visit the clinic.

By the mid-1930s, Hydrick had advanced basic infant care for several years, but it was with the establishment of a maternal and infant health center at Purwokerto that this specific work came to the surface as a core concern. The expansion of Hydrick's work in rural hygiene culminated in 1933 with the establishment of a central demonstration unit at Purwokerto, in Central Java,[77] This health unit replicated many of the services provided by other centers across Java and the other islands, including sending *mantris* to visit people in the surrounding villages. But Purwokerto was much more than that: it operated as a testing ground for new methods and materials, as a training base for the personnel, and an open-door laboratory that "encapsulat[ed] in utopian fashion, the ideal conditions of hygiene in the life of 'natives,' in Java and everywhere".[78]

The difference in approach between the colonial DVG and Hydrick's rural hygiene work was structural as much as philosophical, and as a direct consequence women came to be more consciously incorporated in hygiene work efforts,[79] both as audiences and as service providers. The divergence was echoed at the Pasar Gambir fair, when infant care was twice, in 1931 and 1933, the focus of the DVG booth. In 1931, the cinema showed the film "Care of the Infant" (as part of an exhibition otherwise centered on nutrition),[80] while in 1933 the fair hosted the "Exhibition for Babies." This was "the most attractive" installation at Gambir, according to one journalist.[81] Underscoring how useful it would be "for the Natives, with their very unhygienic conditions in the kampung," the exhibition promoted hygienic practices, condemned superstition and the use of amulets, and encouraged breastfeeding over "artificial feeding" as an important step to curb infant mortality.[82] At Gambir, the colonial government was interfacing with an urban audience, and once again had opted for essentially blaming mothers for their inadequacy and ignorance.

In contrast, Hydrick's strategy educated through demonstration, and focused on the rural environment. As women were to be met in their own space, the *mantris* travelled to them, offering basic knowledge through simple instructions and visual materials. The goal was to instill the idea that hygiene was paramount in everyday activities, and that in case of emergency a medical doctor was the only person one should rely on. Writing in early 1934, Hydrick commented that initially, in his hookworm eradication and hygiene education work, he had "followed the advice of those who had worked in Netherlands India for years and used in the beginning only male nurses, but later wherever possible began to use female nurses."[83] Hydrick's case reinforces what Anne-Emanuelle Birn found in the case of IHD work in Mexico in the 1920s. In her 1999 seminal article "Skirting the Issue," she has highlighted how the IHD "did not initially consider women as partners," as the initiatives were "conceived as largely masculine endeavors."[84] We see the same dynamic at play here in Indonesia.

It eventually became apparent: women health workers might be more effective in establishing a rapport with other women, especially when it came to infant care and nutrition more broadly.[85] In the mid-1930s, then, all of Hydrick's smaller rural units included several female health workers:

> [They] have been doing excellent work and we plan to use more female nurses if we can get them. // The problem involves the usual prejudices. Women have no rank in Java; it is very difficult to get women to take up work of this sort; a special training will be needed; and those who will be successful in this work must have a talent for it. // However, there is

a daughter of one of the Regents . . . who has just completed her course and secured her diploma as midwife, who is interested in health work and has applied for a position in the health unit. // When Dr. Heiser was here he said he would try to get her a fellowship to Manila [to] take the course given for Public Health Nurses. . . . She could then be given work in the unit and would, we hope, influence others of good families to take up work of this sort.[86]

The regular reports sent by Hydrick to the Rockefeller Foundation detailed the personnel employed at the Purwokerto health unit, but not in other centers. If we take Purwokerto as representative of trends, it is fair to say that indigenous women were developing an increasingly strong presence in the 1930s (Figure 2.6). The number of female *mantris* jumped from two in late 1934 to nine in mid-1935.[87] At that point there were four midwives at Purwokerto.[88] Towards the end of the decade, each unit would usually have at least one doctor and a midwife, alongside a handful of *mantris*.[89]

Hydrick had seen the many difficulties women faced in entering the health workforce, which compounded with the challenges of inserting

FIGURE 2.6   "(1738) At the weekly meeting of the *mantris* of a Health Unit, the doctor gives a lecture." Source: Rockefeller Archive Center, 655 Java circa 1905–1980, Photographs, Series 100–1000

clinically trained nurses and midwives in a rural health program. In Purwokerto and at the other health units, midwives did not merely help with de-
liveries, but rather—in the fullest spirit of preventive care that underpinned
rural hygiene work—they guided pregnant women and mothers in their
quotidian activities of care, including bathing and feeding their infants. To
underscore the importance of this more holistic vision of their profession,
nurses and midwives employed in the hygiene centers needed three months
of further training after the five years of schooling and internship.[90]

The setting up of a training center had, then, been a priority for Hydrick, who continued to raise doubts about "trained nurses . . . because they
cannot forget their technical terms and remain too far above the ordinary
village people." Hydrick was inspired by nursing work being done in the
Philippines, British India, and China.[91] In August 1935, he started to broach
the matter of additional funds to open the school for hygiene *mantri* to
the New York office.[92] Despite the multiple letters and reiterative statements
about the challenges of employing hospital-trained nurses, the Rockefeller Foundation continued to reject the request, to the point that the Dutch
Indies government eventually stepped in to bankroll Hydrick's plans.[93]

When drafting plans for a hygiene *mantri* school in 1935–1936, Hydrick
thought the director should be a professionally trained woman, rather than
a man, in order to build a rapport with patients as well as the trainees.[94]
To further encourage women to enter the profession—which appeared to
hold low social status[95]—Hydrick suggested that the IHD should support
the Dutch Indies government in increasing the *mantris'* salary.[96] These
strategies might indeed have attracted more women. Looking back on the
school's activities in 1938, Hydrick reflected how "progress has been made
in securing women candidates [for the *mantri* school] and the group regis-
tered for the last quarter of 1938 contained more women than men."[97]

At the school's opening in April 1936, Sapartinah—whom we had briefly
met earlier in the chapter—was appointed assistant director of the Hygiene
Mantri School.[98] In August 1938 she was promoted to the position of director of the school, and a few months later she took charge of the entire
Purwokerto unit in collaboration with Warsono, a male Indonesian physician who had previously been assistant director.[99] The appointment of Sapartinah at an equal rank as Warsono underscored Hydrick's conviction
that women were crucial to the work of rural hygiene. Within a few months
Sapartinah had been transferred to Yogyakarta to reorganize the rural

hygiene program there, the culmination of a distinguished career in medicine at a time when none of her peers appeared to have ever been employed.

Marsidah, another pioneering woman in the healthcare profession (as
mentioned earlier), became "the new midwife" at Purwokerto. When she
showed up for the first day of work in August 1938, Hydrick was hopeful, but
skeptical too. He recorded in his diary:

> She has had a very good school training (and is a graduate of a Hoogere
> Burger School—5 year course). Her technical training is good—she is a
> graduate of the Ziekenzorg Hospital in Solo. The midwife training there
> is given under the direction of Dr. Wendel. Marsidah is to work first in
> the village to see if she likes the work and to give us a chance to see if she
> has talent for the work. If she proves to be good, she can be given charge
> of the theoretical and practical training of midwives at Poerwokerto.[100]

Hydrick recognized the high standing of Marsidah's qualifications—like
Soerti and Sapartinah, Marsidah had similarly attended a prestigious high
school in Batavia in the early 1930s, passing the midwifery exam only days
before arriving at Purwokerto.[101] But Hydrick admitted that to be effective in
rural hygiene, one needed more than just a good degree: unlike hospital-based
nursing, the work required constant interfacing with undereducated village
women, and demanded a lifestyle different from what a representative of the
lower *priyayi* nobility like Marsidah would have been used to.

By the end of 1938, though, she had proven herself well-tailored for the
job. Hydrick noted: "Visited the center at Tjikadang [West Java] and then
went to the village to find the midwife Marsidah. Inspected her work with
Warsono. The centers are improving under her leadership."[102] Three months
later she was in charge of the Cilongok hygiene center just outside of Purwokerto, and Hydrick's plan was to appoint her as teacher at the *mantri*
school.[103] In preparation for that, Marsidah travelled extensively across
West Java, visiting various centers attached to the Bandung health unit to
study their various training courses;[104] in addition, it was decided that she
would "go to Batavia for a course in diet and food habits under de Haas,"[105]
a Dutch pediatrician with a keen interest in nutrition.

Nutrition, as a topic of outreach, had found its way to Purwokerto following a report put together by André G. van Veen for the 1937 conference
on rural hygiene held in Bandung (Van Veen was head of department of

the Chemical Division of the Batavia Medical Laboratory, and, later, in the 1950s, became an FAO adviser to Indonesia, as discussed in Chapter 5).[106] John Lee Hydrick added "work on food habit" to the portfolio of educational activities pursued by the health centers,[107] and to the program of the Purwokerto Health Unit in 1938.[108] Colored charts showing vitamin-rich local foods (such as bananas, papaya, and tomatoes) were now used in house visits, and selected *mantris* received specialized training at the Institute for Nutrition in Batavia, like Marsidah had.[109] Choosing a midwife as the resident expert on nutrition acknowledged the important intersection of mothering, infant care, and food, on which I expound in the next chapter.

After its first appearance in 1933 in formal prevention work, maternal health would feature as an important area throughout the decade. Hydrick's reports were filled with detailed information and pictures about hygiene work with mothers, infants, and children; the training of midwives for hygiene work; the importance of female *mantris*; and the training of traditional birth attendants. Much differed from the general Dutch approach that exclusively supported clinic-based "modern birthing" (like the Twee Kruisen[110]), and continued to chastise the *dukun bayi*.

Aware that the colonial government was unable to provide enough well-trained midwives, Hydrick determined that "the customs of the people will be used temporarily to help."[111] Seeing the hygiene center as a resource and a hub, he advocated its use for the training of *dukun bayi*:

> There is no training in obstetrics [for them], but the doekoens are trained in the simple hygienic measures which they themselves can carry out. They learn to wash their hands properly, to clean their nails, to care for the cord properly, etc. . . . For the present the doekoens are allowed to care for the mother and child as long as the birth is normal. As soon as they see that the labor is abnormal or too lengthy, then the doekoen must call the midwife or the doctor.[112]

The training was to be carried out in small groups and by

> midwives [who have been] very carefully trained for this work, for through the cooperation of the midwife and the doekoens it is possible to get the pregnant women to come to the hygiene-centers for examination early in their pregnancy and regularly until the delivery.[113]

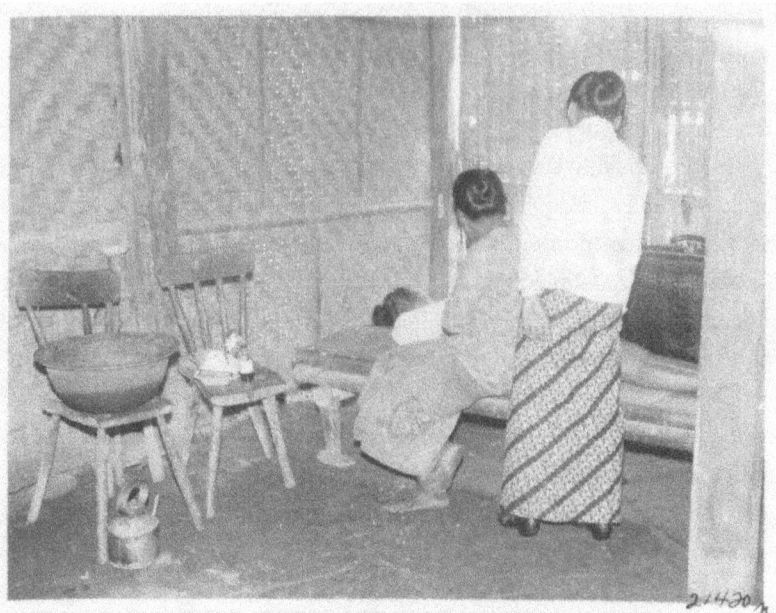

FIGURE 2.7   "Untrained village midwives attend demonstrations in hygiene and learn to work hygienically even in unfavorable conditions, 1937." Source: Rockefeller Archive Center, 655 J Java Public Health, Photographs, Series 100–1000

The core goal, besides improving health, was thus to secure the collaboration of the *dukuns* and the local population with the health units, as a way to sustain and expand their work. The rapport was built over time, with demonstrations held weekly.[114] The *dukuns* were expected to attend regularly (Figure 2.7).[115] Building on the work of Susan Smith, Margaret Charles Smith, and Linda Janet Holmes on Black midwives in the Southern United States, Birn has argued that the incorporation of traditional birth attendants in Mexico's public health ultimately caused the displacement of their knowledge, and the undermining of their authority and respect, which rested on these women's ability to navigate both healing and ritual practices.[116] In Java this might have not been the case, as the IHD presence had not been sustained enough to erase the *dukun bayi* and their traditional knowledge.

————

In the 1920s and 1930s, the efforts of indigenous women across classes and fields of expertise transformed domestic labor into a pillar of health, social improvement, and progress—so much so that in the 1950s, health-informed care work would become part of official policies in the fledgling Indonesian nation-state (as explored in Chapter 5). On a first layer, this process was shaped by three forces set into motion by colonial authorities: the hygienic reforms spearheaded by the DVG and the work of John Lee Hydrick at Purwokerto; conversations about imperial maternalism; and the framing of health as a stepping-stone for progress. But none of these processes unfolded without indigenous interventions and reshaping.

As teased out in this chapter, modern mothering came to denote a counter-imperialist discourse. In the Indies, women had to stake out their place in the colonial project of hygienic modernity, and the evident influence of Dutch maternalism was tempered by developments in other Muslim-majority areas and colonized territories in Asia. Conscious mothers, informed by science but rooted in their traditions and beliefs, would bring about the emancipation of women and a postcolonial nation.

In the 1920s, literate (and mostly upper-class) indigenous women had started to find scientific validation of their traditional modes of mothering, and similarly began to write about the broader impact of their biological and social reproductive labor on the shaping of a *maju* nation. They reflected on the impact of birthing clinics and infant care on the advancement of colonized Filipina women;[117] they celebrated the mother of Shaukat Ali and the wives of Tagore and Sun Yat Sen as "the most important women in the world of *kemadjoean*" and across nationalist movements;[118] and argued that only with widespread birthing reforms would the Indies have a nationalist hero as China, India, and Turkey had.[119]

These reflections were not envisioned as the exclusive purview of elite women, as articles printed in the women's press circulated further than to the few who could acquire and read them (as discussed in Chapter 1). Soerti Tirtotenojo, Sapartinah, and Marsidah had focused on the dissemination of biomedicine and hygienic practices to improve the conditions of infants and mothers across the territory, working with women from different backgrounds. With few women trickling through Java's medical schools, their role was to transmit practical knowledge relevant to everyday tasks of caregiving by modelling behavior to those around them, as well as formally train others, including the *mantris* and *dukuns* who would then advance hygiene work with rural women in their homes.

The impact of the work pursued by female *mantris* would become evident to the Dutch colonial establishment only when Dr. Postmus, as director of the Institute for Nutrition in Batavia, began collaborating with Hydrick at Purwokerto in the late 1930s. He was interested in further pursuing his research on local diets and the impact of vitamin-enriched milk consumption on rural children; after a few weeks spent surveying local families, during which time he had been supported by one male assistant, Postmus requested that his second assistant be a "female mantri in order that he [Postmus] can compare the work of the two." He was soon convinced that female *mantris* could better connect with those in the family who were in charge of hygienic matters—i.e., women.[120] The incorporation of nutrition work at Purwokerto in 1938–1939 further supported Hydrick's intuition that female *mantris* would engender "still better results" than those obtained employing men.[121]

As under- and malnutrition were long-standing and ever-worsening problems in Java, food became a core concern of colonial health propaganda. And with infant feeding and cooking being seen as womanly matters *par excellence*, women were then directly identified as primary interlocutor. In the next chapter I show that indigenous women staked out their authority on matters of nutrition and piety as aspects of their gendered roles of social reproduction. Bringing into conversation nutrition science and hygiene with local practices and religious epistemologies, then, they filled the discursive gap left empty in the colonial project of hygienic modernity by the marginalization of women and Islamic frameworks in the Indies' racialized colonial society.

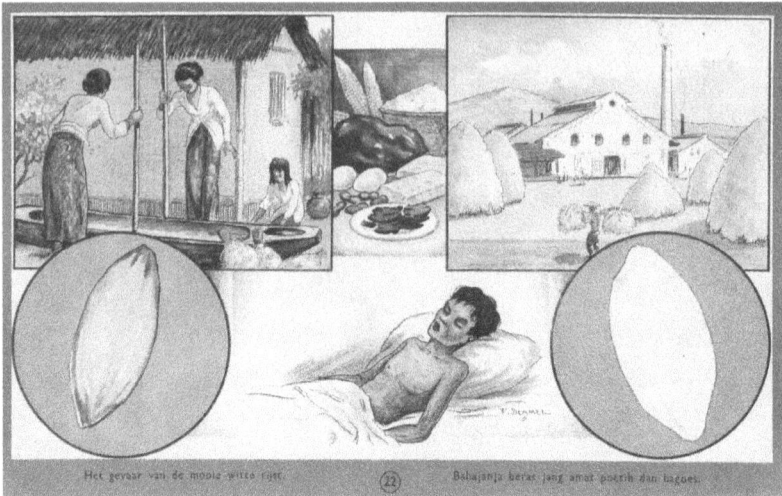

FIGURE 3.1 "The dangers of rice that is too polished." Source: P. Peverelli and F. van Bemmel. *Blyf Gezond! = Sehatlah Selaloe*, 1933, Plate #22, Leiden University Library

3 | FOOD

FOOD HAD BEEN A FAVORED Dutch topic in discussing the
Indies' backwardness in the 1800s. At the turn of the century, fears of food-
borne diseases compounded with social and political demands, resulting in
further separation and differentiation between the colonizers and their colonized subjects. Home, food, and children sat at the center of these conversations. As imperialist circles maintained that breastfeeding was the root
cause of "native" civilizational difference, Dutch women distanced themselves from their infants and kept their children away from local habits and
individuals. For this construction to be effective, indigenous women were
represented as inherently backward and unable to bridge the gap. But when
it came to advertising, this position was softened; as marketers sought out
new consumers, it was convenient to present some products as *potentially*
able to ferry indigenous women into modernity. On the other side of this
equation were indigenous women themselves, who countered, or ignored,
this framing by writing about local foodways, combining nutrition science
with Islam and customs.

This chapter advances a parallel analysis of indigenous women's writings and colonial advertisements. In doing so, food emerges as a site where
ideas of hygienic modernity and the labor of mothering encounter the an-
alytical realms of Islam, consumption, and the Great Depression. I frame
care work as multifaceted—inclusive of domestic, intellectual, and professionalized endeavors—to show that Muslim women in Java and Sumatra

leveraged their role as nourishers to establish their own authoritative voices and occupy a discursive space. They could characterize their appearances and choices as modern in the name of hygiene, nutrition, and Islam—even as these choices differed from those of their European counterparts.

Far from flatly reproducing colonial understandings or aspirations, literate women used the burgeoning vernacular press as a platform to rearticulate modern motherhood in a way that was inclusive of traditional practices and Islamic precepts, while also taking science into account. This dynamic was most visible in women's responses to the emerging threat of breastmilk substitutes.

Conversely, though, while marketers relied on some of these elements—the Muslim identity of women, along with a scientific notion that their products were proven hygienic and nutritious—they failed to acknowledge the "modernity" of the same Muslim women. In the mid-to-late 1930s, Muslim women were conceptually identified as agents of progress in consumer culture and advertisements (through their expanding gendered roles as hygienic caregivers, nourishing cooks, Islamically conscious modern mothers, and shoppers), yet their iconography remained steeped in racialized views that—literally—would picture them as "backward natives" until the 1940s.

FOOD AND COLONIAL HEALTH

The production, handling, and consumption of food had commanded much attention in the field of tropical medicine since the second half of the nineteenth century, as these matters influenced the colonial administration's ability to control, rule, and exploit colonized territories. Food-borne contagion and infectious diseases—such as typhoid, bacillary dysentery, and cholera—had caused the death of many soldiers through the decades, as did beriberi.[1] The hot, humid weather, combined with the presence of flies and near-absent sanitary infrastructures (at least any recognizable to the Dutch), had exacerbated the impact of outbreaks caused by contaminated water and foodstuffs. Similarly, nutrition had been a source of long-standing concern for the Dutch administration, first because of the colonials' own need to adapt to a "tropical diet," then because of the widespread incidence of beriberi, and eventually because of significant levels of under- and malnutrition among the Indies population.[2] It was no accident that Christiaan

Eijkman (1858–1930) had pursued his groundbreaking research on beriberi in Batavia, leading to his discovery of vitamins in the 1880s.

Publications offering advice to Dutch men embarking on the long journey to the Indies focused on their physical wellbeing. Van der Burg's 1884 manual for physicians practicing in the Indies gave much space to food, approaching it through the double lens of cleanliness and nutrition.[3] Milk and meat, coveted staple goods of the European diet, received most of the attention: Van der Burg was clear that in the Indies butchers operated in "bad hygienic conditions," and cow milk was "very difficult" to procure.[4]

Dairy farms were few and far between, and more importantly their operation required supervision: "Even if the native is honest, one will have to deal with the usual messiness and lack of care for cleanliness. . . . Without strict supervision, the bottles are not clean." The comment on "honesty" related to the issue of tempering; milk adulteration was reportedly ubiquitous, especially at the distribution stage, once the milk had left the supervised farm. Ditchwater, coconut milk, oil, and more rarely sugar water, were all substances used to dilute the milk and sell more bottles.[5]

Marketers of canned milk knew they had a captive and desperate audience in the overseas European population. It was in the 1880s to 1890s that advertisements for multiple brands first appeared in the Dutch-language press of Deli (Sumatra) as well as of Semarang and Surabaya (on Java) alongside other imported luxury goods such as wines, cigars, champagne,[6] and margarine (I return to this last product later in the chapter). In the 1895 revised edition of his manual, Van der Burg still argued that it was not easy to find "good" milk because of the failure to prevent both human adulteration and climate-induced spoilage in the milking, storing, and transportation processes.[7]

Van der Burg was caught between the need to warn his European readers against the risks of "unhygienic" animal products and the belief that animal-derived fats were nonetheless important.[8] Van der Burg deemed it "incorrect that people needed less meat in hot climates," meat being "needed for nourishment" and for avoiding an overall negative impact on one's health.[9] Hence, he argued that a "fully Dutch diet" was "undesirable," as too heavily reliant on bread and cheese. The manual instructed physicians to encourage a gradual transition to the "native table," establishing a "golden middle way" between local and European diets.[10] The "European table," then, was to be modified with the insertion of "native foods," shaping what Van der Burg now referred to as the *rijsttafel*: a meal comprising rice, cooked vegetables, and fish or meat.[11]

Food was key to the imperialist project. Van der Burg had clearly stated that "good nutrition [was] important for the provision of life,"[12] and from a colonial perspective, care of food was similarly decisive in avoiding "the serious danger of a breakdown of [European] authority in the Archipelago."[13] Far more ubiquitous and harder to control than mosquitoes and rats, the "Oriental latrine fly"—or Chrysomya Megacephala, a.k.a. the blowfly—was responsible for transmitting the food-borne diseases that most commonly decimated soldiers, at higher rates than malaria and more frequently than the plague (see Figure 3.2).

Dairy farms and slaughterhouses, alongside kitchens and markets, were identified as places commonly infested by flies, like manure and trash piles, thus spurring the sanitary reforms and infrastructures already introduced in Chapter 1.[14] Early twentieth-century interventions in matters concerning food laid bare the fact that although these projects were presented under the umbrella of the Ethical Policy, the primary motivation behind their establishment was the colonists' fears of their own contamination by the environment and "native" interferences. Excessive heat, local diseases, and undesired human contact were deemed dangerous to the health of the Europeans, whose bodies they considered weakened by the tropical climate.

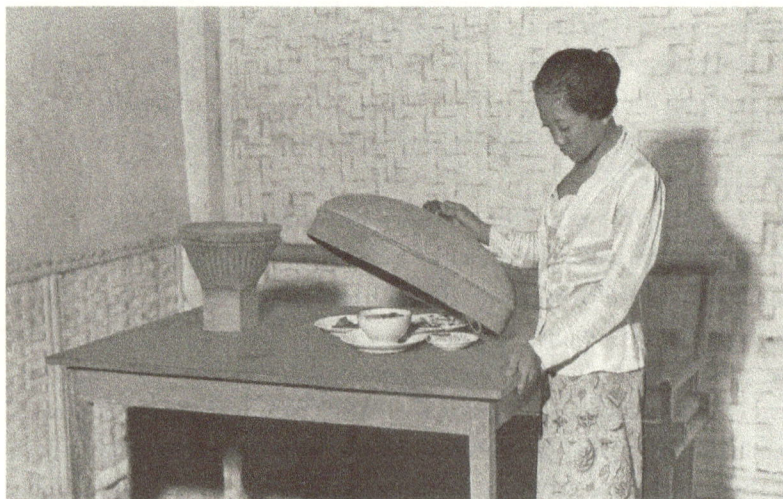

FIGURE 3.2   "Covers of bamboo protect the food from flies." Source: Rockefeller Archive Center, 655 Java circa 1905–1980, Photographs, Series 100–1000

By the early 1910s, Solo, Bandung, and Medan had opened new municipal abattoirs, while Surabaya, Batavia, Semarang, and Medan had issued
regulations for the production and sale of milk. In 1917, when the Dutch-Su-
rinamese professor Paul Christiaan Flu published his didactic text *Tropenhygiëne*, much importance was given to slaughter, from blood and water
drainage to the mindful handling of the animals (with important reverberations on Islamic sensitivities).[15] While milk was only tangentially addressed then, the later 1920 revised edition expanded greatly on the topic,[16]
as the industry still struggled to find ways to guarantee enough supply.
Safeguarding of hygienic processes remained a challenge in the tropical
setting, despite known advances in other countries.[17]

Rules on hygienic production were only as good as the systems put
in place for their control and enforcement, such as inspection. To moni-
tor compliance, the chemical laboratories of Weltevreden (in Batavia) and
Medan (in Sumatra) ran analyses of hundreds of samples of various consumer products—from Chinese medicines to health tonics and alcoholic
beverages. Milk and its by-products and substitutes (fresh, powdered, and
canned milk; butter and margarine) featured most prominently.

Flu was appointed director of the Weltevreden Medical Laboratory in
1917, and, shortly after, the laboratory expanded its activities to include a
dedicated chemical department. Its primary task was the monitoring and
research of food, especially milk. As anticipated in the previous chapter,
several women were employed there, regularly pursuing the testing of milk
samples collected "under supervision" in order "to guarantee its being un-
adulterated."[18] The laboratory compiled a *codex alimentarius* for milk to
determine its standards of hygiene and nutrition; and its (largely female)
staff developed a method to detect small amounts of common impurities,
such as exogenous sugars, coconut milk, and salicylic acid (a plant-based
preservative that extends the shelf life of milk, but also happens to be toxic
for humans).[19]

Research on milk was so important that the only significant change in
Flu's 1920 revised edition of *Tropenhygiëne* was the expanded discussion of
that product with an added chapter on food. There (differently from Van
der Burg's manual) the attention focused on strategies to ensure and mon-
itor hygiene and safety. The publication now included a section dedicated
to milk production, and another one on hygiene in markets. This version
was translated into Malay as *Kesehatan didalam Kampoeng* ("Health in the

Kampung") in 1922 for the instruction of health inspectors and indigenous doctors.[20] While the government pursued efforts to specifically supervise milk production,[21] the broader industry of hygiene propaganda came to focus on flies—often referred to with the monicker "queen of dunghills" (Dutch: *koningin der mesthoopen*).[22]

Beginning in the 1920s, food hygiene and nutrition concerns proceeded on separate yet related paths. The laboratory continued to pursue its nutrition work on vitamins—stemming from Eijkman's research on beriberi, the original goal for the whole institution—by creating vitamin B tablets (primarily for Mecca-bound pilgrims), developing menus for convicts and soldiers, and researching the nutritional value of local fruits, vegetables, and grains. In the early 1930s, research publications increased,[23] and in 1934 an Institute for Nutrition (Instituut voor Volksvoeding) was established in Batavia. This marked the recognition of nutrition as an element of public health policy, and government expectations for the growth of its public relevance. A sign of this transition can be seen, for example, in the DVG's bilingual magazine for children *Gezondheid Brigades* ("Health Brigades"). Launched in 1929, by 1933 its masthead pictured a (European) boy holding a shield and sword against a fly. Its contents, in Malay and Dutch, reflected much of the hygiene and nutrition research conducted by the colonial establishment.[24] Similarly, flies were in the spotlight at the 1930 hygiene exhibition at Pasar Gambir;[25] and the following year, the same Batavia fair focused on nutrition. Illustrating how to make "good food with little money," it was seen as "very instructive for the native population."[26] The exhibition was "a hymn to vitamins . . . a vitamins' kingdom."[27] Nutrition was gaining attention in public health propaganda.[28]

Even while food was situated at the intersection of hygiene, nutrition, and imperialist concerns, it also came to be associated with "womanly" domestic matters, anchoring it to expectations of modern mothering. These were not exclusively official matters of policy, nor topics for—sometimes disengaged and perfunctory—hygiene propaganda booths. It was the women's press which initially brought scientific literature to the attention of literate women, and others in association with them. This was largely possible as this body of journals, in both Dutch and Malay, experienced an unprecedented expansion in the 1930s as a result of increasing numbers of indigenous girls gaining an education: matters related to milk safety and infant feeding could now be broadly popularized through accessible scientific articles, reports, and (at times fearmongering) advertisements.

While results from the laboratories regularly confirmed that most milk samples were of "sound" composition and quality, efforts to popularize the consumption of fresh milk were to no avail. It was expensive[29] and faced competition from marketers of substitutes, who were keen on amplifying the potential risks of fresh milk. The first issue of the Dutch-language women's magazine *Huisvrouw in Indië* ("The Housewife in the Indies," a publication distributed by the homonymous territory-wide association),[30] opened with a full-page advertisement placed by Nestlé. Reproducing a news clipping reporting that police had filed a report about a local milk distributor diluting milk with water from a ditch, the advertisement ran: "It could have been YOUR milk! Only buy reliable milk—use milk products from Nestlé."[31] The same issue of the magazine published another advertisement too, this one for a "European" Model Farm Menteng of Batavia, which felt compelled to announce that it processed its milk in "the most hygienic manner," "under the control of municipal and government veterinaries."[32] Starting in early 1932, the Surabaya bulletin of the abovementioned association came to regularly publish a "Milk Report," this one compiled by the municipal veterinarian, Dr. H. Fooy.[33] The women's vernacular press joined in this effort to follow milk safety in the second half of the decade, as seen in the case of the Indonesian periodical *Keoetamaan Isteri*, which is explored in the next section. Scientific propaganda was followed by an even stronger commercial messaging from the marketing industry, stressing the importance of nutrition and hygiene in the kitchen to women's responsibility in that task.

MOTHERS AND NUTRITION: INFANT FEEDING

The *Volksalmanak Melajoe 1929* had featured a ten-page article titled "On Health." It was primarily dedicated to scientific principles of nutrition, including references to medical treatises, and it aimed at amplifying the efforts of the health office in promoting better hygiene among the Indies population. An appended table listed the nutritional values of over forty foods available in the Indies—from sago and bananas to milk and chocolate.[34] As in the 1920 edition of the Almanac, discussed in Chapter 1, here once again the women's section showcased an entry on eating.

The shorter article "Principles of Eating" oversimplified the science, as it had done a decade earlier. It used some new medical terminology—like "saliva" and "gallbladder"—but the message was basic: female readers were told to chew well and not eat too much because "this is [what is] beneficial to our body." Indexing an epistemological tension between promoting biomedicine and not discounting traditional practices, it offered advice that countered local habits—such as suggesting eating plain food and mild condiments because "excessively spicy foods are not good for the stomach"—while encouraging behavior in opposition with the hygienic mandate.[35]

Despite these contradictory messages, the premises of imperialist mothering and the colonial capitalist need for healthy productive laborers would eventually engender a medicalized approach to feeding. As introduced above, the knowledge produced by the laboratories did not stay within their walls. The dietary guidelines developed for colonial institutions, and assessments of the health claims of commercial products available to the broader public, were all disseminated through the specialized and popular press alike.

Likely spurred on by the desire to impact the colonial project, this popularization of science also engendered the rearticulation of biomedical knowledge in conversation with extant indigenous practices and traditions, including Islam. As Soekarmi (quoted in the introduction) would point out in 1931,[36] these "new" scientific discoveries were just a different articulation of knowledge commonly held by indigenous women in the Indies. Christiaan Eijkman's "discovery" that the consumption of unpolished rice prevented beriberi was nothing more than what women in the villages had been doing all along—the only difference was that he had explained it through the modern, western, medicalized framework of "vitamins" (see opening Figure 3.1). Similarly, physicians called on mothers to breastfeed infants because of the hygienic and nutritional deficiencies of substitutes, but Muslim women in Java and Sumatra reminded their audiences that the Qur'an had already prescribed that.

In this section I explore how scientific knowledge about nutrition reached indigenous women (thanks to their ascribed role as nourishers), and how they acquired, made sense of, and rearticulated such knowledge. Fully visible as agents of progress through their responsibilities of feeding healthy food to the children and families they cared for, in the 1930s indigenous women emerged as active subjects in the arena of modern nutrition.

In Chapter 2, I showed how international conversations on modern birthing advanced a nationalist agenda. Similarly, here women were not passive enablers of hygienic maternalism. Literate women appeared in the press as authors and producers of knowledge, merging multiple epistemologies according to their own priorities, and articulating an indigenous, gender-specific, Muslim point of view.

———

As birthing had been a space where women were to be educated in the science of hygiene, so infant feeding came to occupy a liminal space between biological reproduction (perceived as vital to the sustaining of empire) and "mere" domestic care. Two of the booklets introduced in Chapter 1—"Caring for Nursing Infants" (1919)[37] and "A Guide to Teaching School Children How to Care for Infants" (1922)[38]—thus addressed the issue of infant feeding directly.

"Caring for Nursing Infants" placed emphasis on a mother's milk as the healthiest option, and argued that a key step in reducing infants' chances of death was to not "stop breastfeeding the baby without a reason, and then give the baby artificial food."[39] The booklet accepted only mother's milk as a "natural" source of nourishment. "Lesser-quality or counterfeit milk, contaminated milk,"[40] and anything else that was not breastmilk was identified as a common source of illness for infants, leading to the condemnation that "bottle-feeding, whether with cow milk or canned milk, is a very dangerous calamity." Inadequate nutrition was secondary to the threat of bacteria, which in the heat of the tropics reproduced quickly, causing high risks for the contamination of cow milk.[41] The harm of bottle-feeding, then, pertained primarily to the handling and preparation of the bottles themselves, and could only be avoided with extreme care regarding hygiene and cleanliness, using boiled clear water and keeping the environment dirt-free.[42]

Similarly, the 1922 "Guide" identified mother's milk taken directly from the breast as the best course of action to ensure the good health of infants. But as the book was explicitly aimed at young girls caring for infants while their mothers were away at work,[43] this emphasis reinforced the shaming of indigenous lower-class women who needed to seek employment outside of the home.[44] Both booklets echoed European trends blaming the ignorance and negligence of working-class mothers for their infants' malnutrition and death.[45] This included highlighting inadequate milk substitutes such as sweetened skimmed condensed milk—likely the only product most mothers would be able to afford, especially if forced to work while caring for an infant.

Breastfeeding had been the norm across the Indies for centuries. And as observed by Europeans, and attested in textual sources, mothers in Java, Sumatra, and other islands tended to breastfeed on demand for many months if not years. It was only with the expanded footprint of colonialism in the early twentieth century—its transformation of the economic system, the airing of racialized civilizationist views, and the physical presence of newly arrived European women—that the practice had started to be questioned in the first place.

In his 1830 *History of Java*, Thomas Stamford Raffles had stated that "women of all classes suckle their children."[46] A Javanese text composed in 1907, illustrating various rituals and life-cycle events, noted that infants should be breastfed for over a year, with boys weaned at sixteen months of age and girls at eighteen months.[47] Notably, Van der Burg had argued the same thing in his 1895 manual for Europeans in the Indies, as he instructed that weaning should not start any sooner than ten months, and breastfeeding should be kept up for sixteen to eighteen months.[48] Several physicians had also emphasized how breastfeeding, when conducted in a hygienic and structured manner, was better than any alternative available to the Indonesian lower classes. And the 1919 Malay version of "Caring for Nursing Infants" explicitly sanctioned breastfeeding as a local practice that complied with science. As "mother's milk is the best food for infants . . . by custom" (*kepada 'adat*), it presented the practice as part of women's cultural heritage.[49] We will see that indigenous women continued to maintain this position through the 1930s.

Yet, some European commentators focused on what they saw as breastfeeding's corollary practices, and their potentially negative consequences. The absence of a feeding schedule, bed-sharing, and keeping infants and toddlers in the *slendang* (a shawl used as a baby sling), were all taken as causes of what colonials perceived as the common indolent nature of indigenous men.[50]

The Dutch physician Kohlbrugge was representative of this thinking. At the beginning of the century he had argued that "the constant giving of the breast" translated into the "natives'" inability to control impulses.[51]

Observers continued to note that women across the archipelago carried their babies in the sling, and were prone to answer any calls from their babies with the breast. The conclusion drawn was that native infants were overfed and overly dependent.[52] In open criticism of indigenous practices, Dutch mothers in the Indies were advised to feed their infants on a schedule and to keep them either in a baby carriage or a playpen.[53] A similar approach was retained even in postcolonial scholarship: in 1961, Hildred Geertz argued that swaddling, carrying, and extensive feeding encouraged passivity in Java's infants, a view reiterated in the late 1970s by James Peacock.[54]

European practices—physical separation of mothers and babies, self-reliance, and self-soothing—had established a model of "modern" mothering that allowed middle- and upper-class mothers to be freed from the burden of infant care.[55] In parallel, this model of care claimed to foster (male) individualism, which was a desired transformation believed to lead to the eventual expansion of economic enterprises. Dutch women in the Indies embraced the rejection of breastfeeding, then, as both a desire to emulate the motherland, and the need to distinguish themselves from the local population. As motherhood had become part of the imperialist project, though, Dutch colonizers faced one more challenge. Whereas upper-class mothers in the Netherlands had been able to distance themselves from their infants by relying on wet-nurses, in the Indies the Dutch feared that personal characteristics could be transmitted through breastfeeding. Mothers were instructed to not let their babies drink the milk of "native" women for fear of racial pollution.[56] Furthermore, Dutch children in the Indies were said to need protection from the "'extremely pernicious' moral influence of babus," the nursemaids who would have otherwise cared for them.[57] Food was understood as a recurrent potential vector of contagion,[58] and if in the everyday preparation of meals the challenge seemed to be resolved by avoiding the sharing of cutlery and plates and the maintenance of a European diet (at least symbolically),[59] the feeding of infants revealed itself to be much more complex.

Non-human milk enabled Dutch women to model their behavior on the new mode of motherhood widespread in the middle-class metropole. At the same time, this maintained the cultural, racial, moral, and political superiority—and purity—of their offspring as demanded by the empire. Cow milk posed its own challenges—discussed earlier in this chapter—but other substitutes came to the rescue, first among them condensed and powdered milk.

Canned milk had been developed to feed soldiers and cure the debilitated during various wars in North America and Europe, but later came to be marketed in industrialized England as a cheap and long-lasting infant food for the rapidly swelling number of working-class mothers who could not afford to stay home and breastfeed. Its shortcomings soon became apparent to physicians, including in the Netherlands and its colonies. The Indies' Dutch-language press had publicized scientific discoveries conducted in Europe proving "the great value of breastfeeding" beginning in the early 1900s.[60] By the mid-1910s and 1920s, the colonial press and various popular fairs' exhibitions regularly showcased work pursued in the Netherlands through *consultatie-bureaux* and *moeder-cursussen* (courses for mothers). This work had successfully reduced infant mortality rates by promoting breastfeeding in the metropole.

European women in colonized territories, however, operated with a different set of priorities. The Dutch-language press had previously presented multiple viewpoints on infant feeding, but by the early 1930s bottle-feeding had been asserted as the "modern" option. This approach inevitably affected indigenous women, as colonial consumption and behavior were often seen by the emerging upper middle classes as necessary and "constitutive aspects of modern lifestyle."[61] In the mid-1920s there had been scores of Dutch-language advertisements marketing Ovomaltine and Quaker Oats as foods that helped breastfeeding mothers produce more milk, but in 1931–1932 the only advertisements addressing breastfeeding were milk substitutes: formula brands Glaxo and Lactogen.[62] Similarly, two doctors took turns presenting their divergent opinions in the Dutch colonial press: one stipulated that "breastfeeding is best," the other presented the advantages of all possible alternatives.[63] The popular magazine *Marriage and Household*, in its third issue of 1932, included an article on bottle-feeding,[64] and the 1934 Exhibition for Housewives showcased and distributed instructions for bottle-feeding.[65] During the same period, Malay periodicals were similarly flooded with advertisements for condensed milk, and Nestlé had just opened a showroom in Batavia.[66]

Despite the powerful marketing, bottle-feeding was met with substantial opposition from indigenous Muslim women. In their formulation, as it appeared in the vernacular press, breastfeeding was not a mere reflection of traditional (i.e., possibly backward) customs, nor was it simply protection from the "dirt" and "bugs" of unhygienic bottles. Instead, they focused on breastmilk's nutritional advantages and the Qur'anic mandate to pursue it.

A late-1926 issue of the Sumatran women's magazine *Asjraq* printed an article on infant care warning readers that canned milk and Nestlé's *kindermelk* (infant formula) should be used only sparingly because it could lead to beriberi.[67] In 1928, the Dutch-educated editor of the women's page of *Bintang Hindia*, Anna Sjarif, did echo the Dutch criticism of answering every baby's cry with the breast ("what often happens is that [the infant] is given too much food"). But she was also clear that it was not right when young women who could speak French, German, and English, could play the piano and tennis, and who were well-read in literature, "had no idea how to care for a child" and how to nurse.[68] In 1929, the first issue of *Isteri* similarly included an article on infant care. There, it warned that cow milk—although better than powdered milk substitutes—would "lose its vitamins" when boiled for too long, and should thus be supplemented with "food that contains vitamins," such as mashed and cooked bananas (specifically mentioning the "ambon" and "raja" varieties), or well-cooked porridge with a handful of spinach leaves, fish broth, or broth from chicken skin.[69]

Women's writings from Java and Sumatra intersected with, and complemented, colonial Ethicist approaches to the caring of infants. In 1931, a long article appeared in *Isteri*, dedicated to "Mother and Child." The author (who signed herself as *Iboe*, lit. "mother") argued that breastmilk was "God's bounty, [as] mother now contains the food needed to satisfy the hunger and thirst of her child, giving it strength for life." Indeed, "if possible, the infant should not be given any other food besides mother's milk, because other milk, no matter how good it might be, cannot match the mother's own." Whereas the author suggested that a mother should consult a doctor for supplementation should she not be able to feed the child "due to illness or insufficient quantities," there was no display of kindness for the mother "who does not like to nurse her baby even if she has enough milk, woe is the mother who has such thoughts!" Drinking the milk of one's own mother was a "right given by God."[70] Similar advice circulated in Sumatra. In an article published in *Soeara Iboe*, the local women's magazine in Sibolga-Tapanuli, on the west coast of the island, the (anonymous) author divided her attention between the imperative of cleanliness—meaning regular soapy baths and changes of clothing—and that of feeding infants the healthiest diet, namely mother's milk.

Religion was used to lend support to an argument based on nutrition, asserting that newborns and infants ought to nurse from their mothers.[71] But the approach advocated now was not "traditional" breastfeeding as observed by Thomas Stamford Raffles, for example. As explained by Iboe, infants should feed for only about fifteen to twenty minutes, seven times a day at regular intervals, and with a night-time break between midnight and 6.00 am, during which the baby was supposed to sleep through, on its own mat, separate from its mother. Before and after each feeding, the child's mouth and the mother's nipples would be cleaned with boiled water to avoid any disease,[72] and in order to be sure that the "baby is drinking well and enough," mothers were to weigh their children before and after every feeding.[73] These women owned watches and used scales; they had separate beds and possibly separate rooms for their children. Obviously, they had access to clean water and would have at least had the option to feed milk substitutes to their children in a safe and accurate manner, if they had so desired. They followed western "modern" rearing and feeding scheduling practices most diligently, to the full extent of their capabilities. But they deliberately chose breastfeeding over bottle-feeding.

For Ethicist doctors, breastfeeding was just a local practice, an advantageous expedient for working mothers who could not afford expensive patented infant formula or clean water. But colonized women made a more nuanced argument. Milk substitutes were lesser than breastfeeding because of their harmful potential. The superiority of breastfeeding was asserted on the grounds of scientific discoveries and medical opinions as well as traditional practices and Qur'anic mandates, and was demonstrably superior to its substitutes.

Appropriating the essence of "modernity" as "healthy" and "hygienic," and interweaving it with religion, these women's perceptions of healthfulness could be separated from colonial paradigms of modernity. They rearticulated colonial knowledge through their own worldview, reclaimed practices that the colonial establishment saw as backward, and promoted them as modern. This counter-imperial undertaking stood against the marketing campaign of the industrial behemoth Nestlé. In 1926 its subsidiary Lactogen had launched its first advertisement for infant formula that featured an indigenous woman. The caption as it appeared in *D'Orient*, a

Dutch-language illustrated magazine often propping up colonial Ethicist policies and points of view, was unequivocal in its civilizationist stance: "Who said the native is backward?"[74] (Figure 3.3).

The woman in the image appears to be seated on a chair, rather than the floor; the can of Lactogen is placed on a table next to her. She is well put together: her hair is pulled up, she is adorned with jewelry, and dressed

FIGURE 3.3 Advertisement for Lactogen milk powder. Source: *D'Orient*, 1926, n.p., Leiden University Library

in a *kain-kebaya* outfit. She is clearly a "native": European and Eurasian women wore *kain-kebayas* at home, but they were never represented wearing them in the press. Similarly, her body was shaded, to indicate dark skin, as was that of the baby. Thus, the pictured woman was not imagined as a *babu* (servant) in the service of a European family—in which case the infant would have been drawn as unequivocally white skinned. She is represented as an urbanite holding some socio-economic status: her sitting on a chair and donning earrings contrasts her with images of women squatting on the floor (Figure 3.4) or their families sitting on a mat (Figure 3.5) as depicted, for example, in the Maggi advertisements below. Her implicit class status explains how, beginning in January 1927, this very same Lactogen advertisement came to be printed on the cover of the vernacular magazine *Pandji Poestaka*, notably, without the caption.[75] Two years later, yet another publication employed the same image: the 1929 *Volksalmanak Melajoe* had printed a four-page long commercial story introducing Lactogen as the best food for a fussy baby, and included the same image, also without the caption.[76]

I have not found any other reproduction of the original, complete advertisement as it had appeared in *D'Orient* in 1926. It is unclear who the marketers envisioned as their intended audience, and how they thought this framing would encourage readers to purchase the product. I am inclined to see it as playing into the racialized civilizationist discourse prevalent in the Indies at the time. In what could be seen as a tongue-in-cheek message, they may have believed the copy presented their product as so exceptional and modern that it could even elevate a "backward native." The following year the same magazine printed the special issue celebrating the EHTINI hygiene exhibition discussed in Chapter 1 and I see strong discursive parallels between Kelling's article printed then in *D'Orient*, the overall Ethical Policy, and this caption.[77]

The caption rendered explicit the subtext embedded in the image: indigenous women were subordinate colonial subjects (they wore *kain-kebayas*, not European dresses) who could—potentially—find opportunities for advancement (civilization) through the adoption of Euro-American modern behavior and products, such as bottle-feeding. With this choice, advertisers may have intended to provoke a laugh, or foster a sense of entitlement to the status of modernity. It certainly perpetuated racialized views of colonial society that marked "native" women as only *en route* toward civilization. The Lactogen advertisement, possibly the first one in the Indies to depict an indigenous woman, leaned heavily on popular understandings

FIGURE 3.4 Advertisement for Maggi Cubes. Source: *Pemimpin*, November 1938, n.p., Leiden University Library

of colonial hierarchies. Implicit in the image, they were rendered explicit to a Dutch-speaking public through the caption. This advertisement represented a distillation of decades of racialized civilizationism, as well as public health propaganda, and the changing global economy.

Oentoek mendapat
poela tenaga.

Satoe potong Maggi-bouillon di taroeh didalam mangkok dan toeangkan air panas dan toean lantas dapat kaldoe jang menjegarkan jang memperbaik penjakit2 dan membikin badan koeat dan sehat.

 MAGGIS
BOUILLON BLOKJES

FIGURE 3.5 Advertisement for Maggi Cubes. Source: *Pemimpin*, February 1940, n.p., Leiden University Library

MODERN CONSUMPTION: HYGIENE, ISLAM, AND GENDER

In the rest of the chapter I explore the interweaving of gender, consumption, modernity, and Islamic cultural behavior following the colonial perception, imagination, and representation of indigenous Muslim women vis-à-vis "modernity" as reflected in the published conduits of consumerism, still keeping mothering and infant feeding central.

As economic demand in the imperial metropole shrank with the 1930s crisis, the expanding colonies emerged as a destination for consumer products, prompting a reassessment of capitalist markets and distribution strategies. This vision was encouraged by the emergence of a new "middle class" in Java and Sumatra, a transformation that had been in progress for at least a decade.[78] This growing consumer culture inserted itself into the long-established logic of imperialism that placed motherhood and child-rearing at the center of colonial discourse. As discussed in previous chapters, the colonial state had needed both a "healthy" colonized population able to support productivity—thus leading to sanitary reforms and the medicalization of childbirth among the local population—and a European colonial population representative of the Dutch metropole.

The financial crisis in the imperial metropole instigated further change in the colony: colonized women were increasingly seen as consumers with purchasing power. The Great Depression was also pushing more American and European women into the workforce, conferring upon them a new role in "economic production" in addition to their sustained labor in social reproduction. This turned them into consumers with spending capacity on the one hand, and less time to invest in food preparation on the other: the ultimate audience for marketers. In Java and Sumatra, most women had always engaged in economic production, and from the perspective of marketing, this new approach to gendered consumption further narrowed differences.

The marketing industry, then, caught up with the reorientation toward indigenous women already underway in health propaganda, even though visual strategies were not representative of indigenous women's identities. From the late 1920s most advertisements in the Indies press—in Dutch and vernacular languages alike—promoted food products on the grounds of their "healthfulness," "nutritiousness," and "hygiene." These ranged from

Milk Maid condensed milk and Glaxo baby formula to Quaker Oats, Molenaar baby flour, and Maravilla Oats; from Del Monte fruit preserves and Sunvita raisins to Cocomalt drink, Droste cocoa, and Blue Band margarine. Advertisements for household appliances followed the same pattern: products both imported from the Global North and produced locally claimed they were nutritious, clean, and healthy. This was especially so for the kitchen, where gas stoves, hot-water boilers, and refrigerators were changing women's lives. Gas—"for light, energy and warmth"—was first announced ahead of the 1927 EHTINI exhibition as a hygienic and economic solution.[79]

The electric refrigerator, the ultimate modern kitchen appliance which arrived in the Indies shortly after its appearance on the American and European markets, marked the peak of this phenomenon. The first refrigerator made its appearance in 1928, "to bring comfort and hygiene in your home."[80] The 1932 advertisement from General Electric stated: "The modern housewife, in the modern Indies' kitchen, with the modern electric fridge."[81] Inevitably, this modern housewife in the Indies not only read Dutch but was also racialized as European.

The refrigerator was able to conjure colonial images of both health and quintessential modernity—from technological advances to women's enjoyment of life. The fridge was necessary to maintain "a healthy body" through a "healthy diet";[82] it was described as "clean, healthy, modern"[83] and necessary to "preserve vitamins."[84] Competitor manufacturer Westinghouse adapted the ancient adage "a healthy mind in a healthy body" for its audience of upper-class (European) mothers in the Indies, claiming that the refrigerator could be used to preserve milk at its freshest "thus preventing feeding disorders that could seriously hinder a child's development"; health was similarly improved by keeping vegetables fresh.[85] By 1936 Frigidaire claimed health and hygiene as the identifying markers of its flagship appliance.[86]

The primary audience was women—European women, in particular. Consumption was both gendered and racialized. Even as emerging indigenous middle-class consumers became important to the uplift of the overall colonial capitalist economy, their representation in advertising was limited. And when the Frigidaire and Westinghouse refrigerators, for example, came to be commonly advertised in the vernacular press in the mid-to-late 1930s,[87] images of indigenous women remained absent.

However, other products—ones that could project modernity while remaining affordable to a large sector of the population—did target the indigenous consumer base by picturing indigenous women in the advertisements, some even branding their products *halal*.

———

Through their mothering role providing nourishment, by the second half of the 1930s indigenous women consolidated their modern societal role as guardians and promoters of health, and as gatekeepers of religious piety. As I show here, this multifaceted role was recognized by marketers and came to be reflected in advertisements that now targeted indigenous women as primary audiences: relying on the dual endorsements of the colonial medical laboratory and religious authorities, marketers promoted their products as Islamically permissible in addition to being "hygienic" and "healthy."

Two products in particular stand out as marketers interwove modern mothering, religion, and consumption: the Maggi Cube and Blue Band margarine. Both were already products with a long-standing presence in the Indies, having been marketed consistently to Europeans as their primary consumers since at least the 1890s. But in the 1930s they started to court indigenous women, stressing their products' conformity to Islamic principles of permissibility. With this adaptation of the message came a gradual change in visual representations of the expected audience, too, although this transformation would be much slower.

The pivot to Islamic branding was the outcome of two separate dynamics. On the one hand was the crunch of the Great Depression, which pushed producers to consider a broader consumer base.[88] On the other was the increasing visibility of Sumatran and Javanese people's Islamic identity, whether in the context of the Islamic turn in anticolonial politics in the 1930s, or the strengthening of religious reformist movements in education and society. Instead of analyzing the political tensions that surfaced from this transformation, here I look at how non-indigenous economic actors sought to gain from the Javanese and Sumatrans' relationship to piety—whether actual, performed, or merely perceived.

Maggi products had been omnipresent in the Indies for decades, often expected in the pantry of any Indies household. But their advertisements visualized a Dutch audience. Maggi Cubes were used for weaning infants,[89] as a nutritional supplement in low-salt diets,[90] as a health-booster,[91] for picnics,[92] or just as an appetizer: "The earth . . . is spinning . . . times are changing. It is increasingly recognized that the tasty, easily digestible, yet highly nutritious soup prepared from Maggi's Cubes is an appropriate and welcome starter," claimed one of the many advertisements in the Dutch press of the Indies.[93] To Dutch readers, the bouillon was an enabler of a modern healthy diet, but it was also "cheap," an important feature amid the economic depression.[94] In 1934, *De Indische Courant* opined that Maggi's presence at the Surabaya Fair (*Jaarmarkt*) was odd, precisely because it was ubiquitous:

> Maggi products are so highly appreciated that it really makes little sense to recommend them in particular. This would be tantamount to carrying water to the sea. The well-known Maggi bottle—and at the stand there are a few hundred, in all sizes, on display—can be found on almost every table.[95]

The advertisement for the Maggi Cube printed on the front cover of *Pandji Poestaka* in March 1932 showed only slightly modified copy, which however marked a conceptually major shift. The text now asserted that in the cubes there was "not even a little pork meat or pork fat."[96] Similar advertisements continued to appear in this magazine for close to a decade,[97] with a spike in 1938 (as in Figure 3.4).

The fasting and feasting season of 1938 was exceptionally prolific in terms of the presence of *halal* products in the press, but it started even earlier that year. In February, a Maggi advertising campaign combined affirmations of the Cube's health-granting qualities with clarifications about the fact that: "In Maggi Bouillon Cubes there is **no** *haram* meat."[98] And from November (coinciding with the beginning of Ramadan) through July of the following year, every printing of the Maggi advertisement in *Pemimpin* (the magazine for Java's civil servants) specified that the cube contained "no pork."[99] Meanwhile, in May 1939 Maggi had a stand at Solo's Grebeg Maulud *pasar malam*, i.e., the week-long night fair held on the occasion of the Prophet's birthday. There, the newly crowned ruler Pakubuwana XI and his wife "made a visit to the stand of the well-known Maggi products . . . The royal party showed great interest in these articles, which was reflected in their tasting of the world-famous Maggi broth."[100] And in October, at that year's Surabaya *Jaar-markt*, the Maggi stand was tended by "four Javanese ladies [who] were engaged in this [expansive] campaign, and they will convince the public that these [cubes] are delicious by [having them] tast[e] the bouillon."[101]

Notably, Maggi was not the only company to claim its product to be *halal*. A slew of margarine brands would soon follow. In 1938, Van den Bergh—the foremost importer and producer of margarine in the Indies—announced that its Blue Band margarine was "*halal* for Muslims" on the authority of the Chemical Laboratory of the Industry Branch of the Dutch East Indies' Economic Affairs Department.[102] (This was the same laboratory that had been testing milk and other commercial products.) As with powdered and condensed milk, margarine had been a food staple for Dutch colonizers since the 1880s, as local dairy production failed in the tropical climate. Made to be as close as possible to the "real thing" in taste, texture, and nutritional profile, and already known as an affordable butter substitute for the urbanized and poor working classes of the European continent, margarine had become a popular product among the colonial elites, gaining a rapidly growing share of the cooking-fat market.

Maggi and Blue Band had been consumed across communities, but in the 1930s, advertisements for both products flooded the Indies press, now specifically speaking to the Indies' indigenous population. Not only did they place advertisements in Malay-language magazines; to further expand their consumer base they engaged with them as Muslims. Aware that even less-pious Muslims tended to avoid pork,[103] and possibly attuned to the increased visibility of Islamic reformist ideas, Dutch entrepreneurs and marketers saw the key to their expansion in branding their goods as *halal*, alongside health and nutrition.

In the increasingly medicalized, science-based domestic environment, religious claims needed to be mediated by the laboratory. This was not just a matter of substance but also a visual projection of authority. As some magazines had printed copies of the certification, the first Blue Band advertisement announcing its *halal* designation displayed a microscope, symbolizing the product's purity in both chemical and Islamic terms.[104]

All margarine brands insisted on displaying their product's vitaminic and hygienic profiles. In late 1933, Palmboter was advertised as nutritious.[105]

In 1934, Blue Band's primary claim was cleanliness: "Be on the safe side! Blue Band is a Dutch product, prepared in the most hygienic way from the very best raw materials."[106] In 1936, when a Blue Band factory opened in Batavia, it was described as: "A jewel of technology and hygiene . . . Blue Band is no longer an ordinary margarine—it is a natural product with a high caloric value and practically 100% digestibility—a product that can completely replace cow butter and only costs half."[107] Like the Maggi Cube, its affordability was just as key as healthfulness. Even though margarine's harmful health consequences would be first suggested only in the 1950s,[108] the claim that it was "nutritious" had already been challenged in the Indies, as in the Netherlands.[109] The development of extracted, supplemental vitamins came to the rescue: companies could further amplify their products' healthfulness. Shortly after Archa margarine had stated that it contained vitamin A in late 1938,[110] Blue Band similarly launched a new campaign announcing that its margarine was "rich in vitamins A and D, which until now were only expected in fresh butter."[111]

The announcement in February 1938 that Blue Band was *halal* seemed to raise no commentary for months, until an article in a provincial newspaper in Palembang (Sumatra) challenged the colonial laboratory's authority. At the beginning of August, T.M. Oesman—a physician also involved in producing *halal* health tonics—wrote on the pages of *Pertja Selatan* questioning whether any margarine could really be without pork, and brought to the readers' attention a recent case from Singapore.[112] Later that month, *Pedoman Isteri* (*Pemimpin*'s companion magazine for the wives of civil servants) printed an official statement from the Batavia civil court's Imam affirming the suitability of Blue Band for Muslims as it did not contain *haram* ingredients, all employees were Muslim Malays, and the facilities were "very clean."[113]

Nothing more on the topic would appear in the press until October. As the fasting month of Ramadan approached, the firm Van den Bergh disseminated its advertisement as broadly as possible. First was *Pedoman Isteri*, which printed a new advertisement that brought together nutrition, purity, and *halal*-ness: "Blue Band margarine now contains vitamins A and D like in fresh butter"; the bottom banner, which in previous iterations had stated that the product was "fragrant and healthy," now underlined its being "pure and not *haram*," using the Malay *soetji*, discussed in Chapter 1 (see Figure 3.6).[114] Then came *Doenia Kita*, whose November

FIGURE 3.6   Advertisement for Blue Band. Source: *Pedoman Isteri*, October 1938, p. 114, Monash University Library

issue included this same advertisement, but here supported by a reproduction of the official certificate signed by Dr. Koolhaas (head of the chemical laboratory), and by an article authored by Haji Agus Salim, the well-respected Islamist politician and leader of the Sarekat Islam Party.[115]

That same month, *Pandji Poestaka* printed a similar certification for Planta (another Van den Bergh margarine product),[116] as well as advertisements describing the product as "holy and healthy," "permissible to Muslims,"[117] and "without pork" or other *haram* ingredients.[118] In December, Sumatra's Islamic reformist magazine *Pandji Islam* followed suit, reproducing the analysis reports for both Blue Band and Planta,[119] as well as the already mentioned article by Agus Salim.

When T.M. Oesman questioned Blue Band's claim, he opened the doors to indigenous challenges; the authority of the colonial laboratory was now under scrutiny. Further questions had reportedly been voiced by "the residents of Kepahiang" (a city in Bengkulu residency, on the west coast of Sumatra).[120] In response, Agus Salim had been allowed to visit the Blue Band factory in Batavia in late September, to verify the firm's claim and offer his legal opinion (*fatwa*) on the matter. As articulated in his popular article, for Salim, such a "matter concerning Islamic law" required "an answer based on knowledge, which can only be obtained with investigation." During the visit, Van den Bergh had "answered all [his] questions, and showed [him] everything," dispelling concerns that this factory might have used animal fats. Salim was thus able to answer the question posed to the magazine:

> With certainty [. . .] in the butter (margarine) and oils . . . made by the van den Berg [*sic*] factory in Angke (Batavia) there is no pork fat mixed in, or any other thing that is forbidden in Islam, neither in its basic ingredients, nor the chemicals or additives used in its preparation.[121]

Throughout the process, the product was "very well cared for and its hygiene and purity are guarded, too." The same article was printed in *Doenia Kita* (in November), *Pedoman Masjarakat*, and *Pandji Islam* (both in December).[122]

The trajectory of these advertisements and related articles underscores two important points: first, that Islam was an important discursive element beyond circles primarily identified as pious; and second, that women were preferred interlocutors in matters relating to pious consumption. To the first point, it ought to be recalled that the earliest advertisements with *halal* claims (Maggi, Blue Band, and Planta) had been printed in magazines envisioning a general middle-class audience: *Pandji Poestaka* was printed by the government printing house Balai Poestaka, and *Pemimpin* was the civil servants' magazine. Neither publication was affiliated with religious groups. Similarly, the first and (to my knowledge) only direct challenge to these *halal* claims was printed in a non-religious newspaper, Sumatra's *Pertja Selatan*. To the second point: none of these platforms were gendered, suggesting that initially marketers had sought to cast a net as wide as possible. However, when the validity of such *halal* claims had been questioned, the attention shifted to women's magazines. Reassurances were first broadcast in *Pedoman Isteri* and *Doenia Kita,* and it was only at a second stage that the conversation surfaced in outlets for the general public (specifically, *Pandji Islam* and *Pedoman Masjarakat*).

Whereas neither *Pedoman Isteri* nor *Doenia Kita* had an explicit religious leaning, both *Pandji Islam* and *Pedoman Masjarakat* did. This shows how, even though initially women might have not been assumed to be the primary audience for religious-based marketing, they emerged as the most important constituency to be reassured of the product's compliance. Furthermore, whereas the matter of Islamic permissibility was considered compelling to indigenous women in general (suggesting a confluence of concerns about food quality and religious piety), the only men engaged in the conversation were those who sought out specifically religious perspectives.

REPRESENTING MUSLIM MODERNITY

With the transition to the Malay-language press, the audience for products like margarine and bouillon was just as clearly gendered as it had been in the Dutch-language press. But the glamor of bobbed hair and dinner parties that exuded from Dutch-language advertisements (see Figure 3.7) was completely absent here. The process of iconographic adaptation that would eventually include indigenous women and visually convey a message of modernity similar to their European counterparts, would be much more gradual.

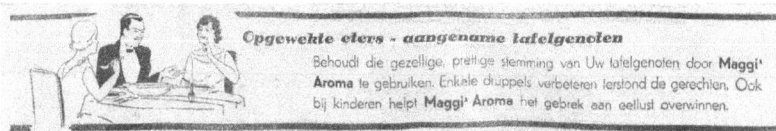

FIGURE 3.7   Advertisement for Maggi Cubes. Source: *Bataviaasch Nieuwsblad*, December 21, 1938, p. 4, National Library of the Netherlands

I contend that this slow pace was a by-product of the marketers' choice to engage with indigenous female consumers as Muslims, a marker the colonial establishment continued to equate with backwardness. Indigenous women were thus depicted differently from European women, not just in their physical features, but more saliently in their embodiment of modernity, as anticipated in the 1926 Lactogen advertisement's analysis. In the Dutch-language periodical *D'Orient*, the Javanese woman was presented as "performing modernity" in virtue of her use of a bottle, and *despite* her ascribed native backwardness: this was made explicit by the caption. This was in stark contrast with representations of European women associated with the same product. For example, a 1933 issue of *De Mode-Revue*—a monthly fashion magazine "for the tropics"—featured another Lactogen advertisement. This one displayed a toddler with a teddy bear: "Mothers! Feed your baby yourself. If you can't, buy Lactogen."[123] While the mother was not shown in the advertisement—possibly reflecting the Dutch preference for separating mothers and infants—on the same page we see the drawing of a female model posing in a fashionable dress, accompanied by two children. This European mother was drawn with an elongated figure and sported bobbed permed hair. This was not the only instance where figurations of European women complied with dominant European gender roles, at the same time projecting an image of stylish womanhood (see Figure 3.8).[124]

FIGURE 3.8 *De Mode-Revue*, no. 3, April 1933, pp. 26–27, Leiden University Library

In vernacular periodicals, both Maggi and Blue Band downplayed the more flamboyantly western elements of "modernity." When they began to visually include the Cube's local consumer base in the late 1930s, Maggi advertisements showed women in other modes: wearing everyday garb, working explicitly as servants, cooking, or welcoming their husbands into modest homes.[125] By contrast, advertisements in the Dutch press had

FIGURE 3.9   *Keoetamaan Isteri*, no. 11, December 1938, p. 26, Leiden University Library

depicted European-looking figures and deployed many of the most recognizable symbols of modernity—from boats[126] and airplanes[127] to bobbed haircuts[128] and medical charts.[129]

Indigenous women were never, it seems, represented as canonically modern in the 1930s, even though we see some hints of this in advertisements for products considered accessible to the emerging middle class. In the mid-1930s indigenous women began to be visually represented as consumers, showing some minimal markers of "modernization." In 1935, the marketers of factory-produced Verkade cookies had switched from an image that simply showed an Indonesian mother with her children[130] to one that depicted her sharing the tin box of cookies with her family at a picnic (Figure 3.10).[131] Indigenous women were depicted in a variety of contexts: showing off a new Kodak camera to a servant,[132] embroidering at the table under a Philips light bulb,[133] and going on a road trip with her husband (Figure 3.11).[134]

**SAJA MINTA – SAJA MINTA
BISKOEWIT ENAK – BISKOEWIT ENAK**

FIGURE 3.10   Advertisement for Verkade biscuits. Source: *Pandji Poestaka*, no. 97, year 13, December 6, 1935, p. 1903, Leiden University Library

FIGURE 3.11   Advertisement for Balsem tjap Matjan. Source: *Pemimpin*, no. 4, October 1936, cover, Leiden University Library

While the context of these advertisements showed women in a surrounding environment undergoing "modernization" (as a process), the attire these women displayed—as an indicator of their own condition—was consistently reflective of "traditional" clothing. I have come across no advertisements depicting a Javanese or Sumatran woman matching, in any approximate way, the canonical characterization of the Modern Girl as Weinbaum et al. identify her.[135] The absence of *the* Modern Girl, even as a "heuristic device" to understand the common imagination of the time, is in itself an indication of how colonial society gendered and racialized the possibility of modernity through hygiene propaganda efforts and in popular representations of modern consumption. Islam was a core element in the construction of this imagined "backward" indigenous Muslim woman.

However, things were beginning to change. I see the first indication of this in the drawings accompanying the fashion section of the Malay-language women's magazine *Keoetamaan Isteri*. Echoing the models of *De Mode-Revue* of five years prior (Figure 3.8), these indigenous women wore fitted *kebayas* with foulards, heeled sandals, and pochette bags—but included headscarves too (Figure 3.9).

An embodied modernity began to emerge more explicitly at the turn of the 1940s, but it was still partial and redacted. Palmboom, a competitor of Blue Band previously known as Palmboter, displayed an indigenous model wearing a *kebaya*. She was shown half-bust, an elongated arm extended out to greet the brand's mascot; with a serene smile, closed eyes, and painted lips (Figure 3.12), she closely resembled her European peers, who populated other Palmboom advertisements in the same vernacular magazine.

The advertisements for Quaker Oats clearly show the transition. In earlier years, the company printed advertisements that either showed its iconic metal container, or a European doctor; but in the late 1930s to early 1940s these became more elaborate. Quaker Oats would not only come to feature indigenous women, but it began to represent them as "modern women" who managed a household or enjoyed a leisurely lifestyle—while remaining concerned with health matters.

In May 1939, *Pandji Poestaka* illustrated an Indonesian mother in a short series of visual scenes: at the bedside of her ill son, taking him to a doctor, feeding him Quaker Oats for breakfast, and eventually watching him play soccer with his friends (now with the father alongside her).[136] Two years later, in 1941, the trope of the woman consumer *qua* mother was sidelined, now favoring a young woman in search of a husband and aware of her own projected beauty (and health). This indigenous woman in *kain-kebaya* saw herself in the mirror as sickly, and after seeking counsel from a friend (not a doctor) she shifted to a daily breakfast of Quaker Oats. The result

FIGURE 3.12   Advertisement for Palmboom. Source: *Pandji Poestaka*, no. 15, February 21, 1940, n.p., Leiden University Library

was not only regained health, but marriage too: in the last frame, we see her driving off in her traditional wedding dress.[137] The young woman was represented as entangled with a localized mode of being even while gesturing to the modern. She wore traditional clothing and yearned for companionship in a framework that required marriage; the mirror, conversely, revealed a

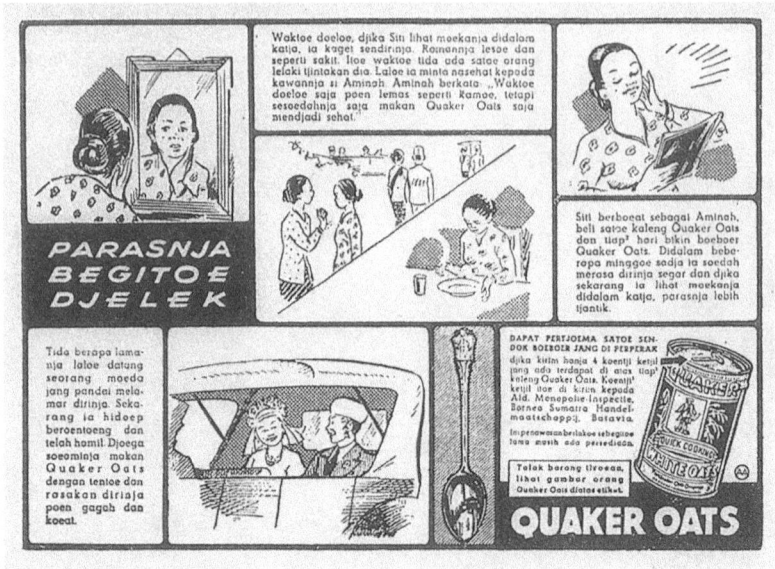

FIGURE 3.13   Advertisement for Quaker Oats. Source: *Isteri Indonesia*, March 1941, p. 19, Leiden University Library

desire to project physical beauty, and attract a partner. In the end, whereas she was married in her "ethnic costume," she drove off in a chauffeured car (Figure 3.13).

In 1941, a Balai Poestaka booklet of "affordable but good" recipes had on its inside cover a new Blue Band advertisement (Figure 3.14). This one depicted an elegant woman in *kain-kebaya* carrying a tray of food; the caption recited,

> Blue Band is a pure food, it is good and strengthens the body. Blue Band is made in Batavia, using as an ingredient oil from Indies plants; therefore, this food is *halal* for people who embrace Islam. Blue Band contains lots of vitamin A and D which make our bodies healthy and strong. Use Blue Band for cooking and frying, as well as for bread.

The product was first characterized as *soetji* ("pure"), then delicious, and finally healthy. While it was said to support a European diet that privileged bread, the model in fact carried rice and side dishes. The drawing shows a slender woman in a form-fitting *kain-kebaya*, her foot lifted in mid-step,

BLUE BAND makanan jang soetji, énak dan mengoeatkan badan.

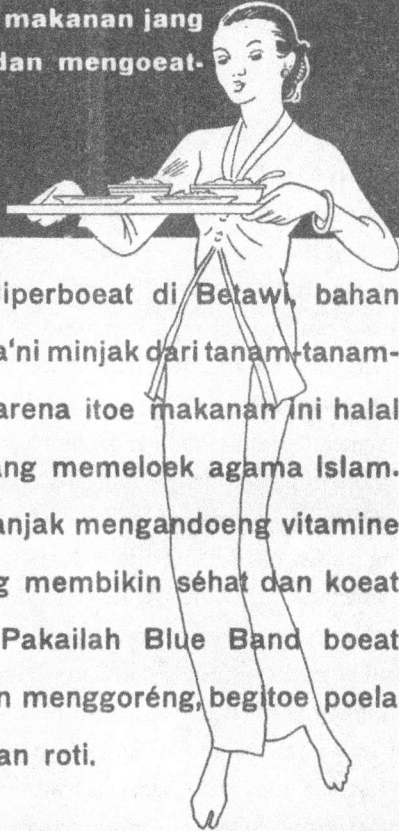

Blue Band diperboeat di Betawi, bahan jang diboeat ja'ni minjak dari tanam-tanaman Hindia; karena itoe makanan ini halal bagi orang jang memeloek agama Islam. Blue Band banjak mengandoeng vitamine A dan D jang membikin séhat dan koeat badan kita. Pakailah Blue Band boeat memasak dan menggoréng, begitoe poela boeat pemakan roti.

BLUE BAND
DIPERBOEAT HANJA DARI MINJAK TANAM-TANAMAN

VAN DEN BERG'S FABRIEKEN (N. I.) N. V.
BATAVIA-C.

FIGURE 3.14 Advertisement for Blue Band. Source: Instituut voor Voedsvoeding, *Makanan Jang Moerah Tetapi Baik*, Batavia: Balai Poestaka, 1941, n.p., Cornell University Library

swaying sensually as she carries the tray. And whereas she is depicted in an elongated form, with a narrow waist and defined lips, she is nonetheless wearing "traditional clothing," performs a domestic task, and is implied to be Muslim, as the copy mentions Blue Band being *halal*.[138]

In this analysis of advertisements, I recognize that agency cannot be determined, one reason being that it is difficult to identify the creators of the images. Instead, I have approached these representations as shared idealizations and projections of acceptable desire. Consequently, the transformation I trace through the decades indicates that the range of possibilities available to indigenous women was expanding, within the sustained limitations imposed by Indies society. The drawings in *Keoetamaan Isteri*'s fashion section suggest that the representations of indigenous Muslim women were changing, too (not merely reflecting the tools of outright marketing.) Strikingly, *Keoetamaan Isteri*'s images are from the early 1930s, whereas the advertisements begin to show indigenous women as approximating the idealized "modern woman" only years later.

It was only in the 1950s that Blue Band placed Indonesian women poolside, playing tennis, and hosting dinner parties. But these women remained in *kain-kebaya* and hair buns, while their husbands wore western suits. Such were the expectations for Indonesia's citizens, in advertisements as well as in public imagery. As noted by Jean Gelman Taylor, in reproductions of the iconic photograph representing the first raising of the Indonesian flag on August 17, 1945, women wearing western outfits were usually "cropped out," therefore excluded from national historiography. One of the women in the photograph is dressed in "Javanese costume," another has her head covered; neither was too westernized.[139]

Yet images of Islamic piety would similarly disappear from public display. Only the vegetable oil Delfia, a subsidiary of the Dutch Calvé, would be marketed as "non haram" or *halal*, endorsed by the *penghulu* of Jakarta and Gambir in 1950.[140] Two months earlier, a cooking column on a women's magazine introduced Chinese food, with the expressed caveat that "clearly, we are going to have food that does not use meat forbidden by Prophet Muhammad. Right?"[141] Again, in August 1951, when more recipes were shared from the famous Chinese American book *Easy Chinese Dishes for Today*, the columnist had stated that "of course you are not going to use lard or pork meat, as it should be done in Chinese cooking. Chicken meat and fat can be used as substitutes for pork and lard" instead.[142] A 1957 column on Chinese food made no mention of avoiding pork. Delfia's statement of *halal*-ness would remain the only explicit engagement with Islam in marketing and food conversations, until it too ceased in 1958,[143] when Dutch citizens were expelled from Indonesia and their companies were nationalized.

————

The diffusion of knowledge about nutrition in the 1930s aligned science with household "domestic matters," providing an avenue for women to enter the world of biomedically defined health through their ascribed roles as mothers and wives. The popular press had discursively reshaped the paradigms of infant care and feeding into what Rima Apple has dubbed modern or "scientific motherhood,"[144] and hygienic propaganda and marketers both perpetuated racialized views of colonial society that marked "natives" as constantly *en route* toward civilization. This held true in visual representations, too.

However, the indigenous voices we heard in this chapter reconceptualized modern mothering and conspicuous consumption in conversation with traditional and religious practices. These women rejected a projected "modernity" that countered traditional and religious practices, as in the case of bottle-feeding; they embraced *halal* consumer products, such as Blue Band margarine and the Maggi Cube; and they visually presented themselves through a gendered modernity that rearticulated colonial iconographic models in a deliberately new type of image (as seen first in *Keoetamaan Isteri*).

Public health propaganda had unfolded by treading a fine line between two ideas: first, implying that the Indies' subject population was not yet modern, and, second, that the population could nevertheless achieve modernity (at least in theory) through the implementation of daily activities. Yet, as detailed so far, in their own circles, indigenous women advanced the idea that in their own actions, words, and representations, they were already modern. While these conversations appeared to be primarily grounded in the home-domestic sphere, they also had political implications, both at the time and in subsequent developments. The Japanese occupation and National Revolution would change public perceptions of women's roles, at least temporarily. As the Indies were pulled into World War II, gendered responsibilities would become recognized as public concerns—the "domestic" arena would be recognized as political.

FIGURE 4.1   "First-aid training for women." Source: *Djawa Baroe*, September 1, 1943, p. 18, Cornell University Library

4 | WAR

THE IMPERIAL PERIPHERIES BEGAN TO notice the reverberations of World War II even before the Netherlands surrendered its neutrality in 1940. In this new environment, Z.—a woman writing in the magazine *Keoetamaan Isteri*—noted that the economy was the first to suffer, and thus "one's livelihood, and then one's household needs, such as eating and drinking, clothing, and daily affairs"[1] were affected by war before politics would be, too. In such circumstances the line between men's and women's affairs began to fade. Domestic responsibilities gave women participatory rights in politics, as war amplified the fact that life in the household could not be separated from broader social and political developments.

Food shortages began in 1939, and the situation was soon to worsen.[2] In December of that year, women were officially mobilized through the "Central Committee for Women's Work in Time of Mobilization" to take over jobs left vacant by men. Women with diplomas took up teaching jobs to keep schools and offices open. Others, in turn, were encouraged to support those now employed by pursuing domestic duties on their behalf, caring for their children and homes. Many were expected to enroll in first-aid courses and be ready to contribute to the war effort. The announcement, made by Raden Ajoe Abdoerrachman—a leading figure in the women's organization Isteri Indonesia—concluded with an exhortation to all Indonesian women: "We must be ready. If asked to help, we women will join in maintaining the safety of our homeland and its inhabitants."[3]

In this chapter I bring to the fore how, in the 1940s, Indonesian women were left to manage the "home front," as the Japanese, Dutch, and nationalist regimes conscripted Indonesian men into the war effort. Indonesian women became the heart of the labor force, and their ordinary tasks of cooking, cleaning, and caring—for which they remained responsible—also took on fundamental political relevance. As vividly shown by Margaret Steedly in her study of the anti-colonial struggle in Karoland, North Sumatra, politics happened in the physical space of the home: "Cooking, shopping, and doing the laundry [turned] into political acts" as the outcome of military engagements would depend on them. She saw a "domestication of political space," as well as a "politicization of domestic space" in Karoland.[4] But this reality applied more widely: Raden Ajoe's speech indicated that such dynamics were already at play even before Japanese troops landed in Sumatra and Java.

Another question woven into this chapter is how—and under what circumstances—was Islam made visible, or not. The announcement transmitted by Raden Ajoe identified women's organizations as the primary avenue for the colonial government's effort to garner civilian support. While these had been religion-neutral spaces of associationism—a strategy seen by women themselves as necessary to keep an expansive and inclusive membership—piety surfaced in many articles. At the end of 1941, for example, the magazine *Isteri Indonesia* (affiliated to the homonymous organization) called on its readers who still resided in the areas affected by warfare to "pray and work, *ora et labora*; this needs to be our motto now. Pray, to ask God for protection; and work, so that our thoughts are not overwhelmed by worry and fear to the point that our mind and health can be damaged."[5] The author, whom we only know as S. Dnl., was telling her peers that in this time of war, they needed to hold on to their faith. But rather than lose themselves in this devotion, they ought to use it as a source of strength to actively engage with the circumstances.

By the late 1930s, Muslim associations in Java and Sumatra had a far-reaching presence and broad sway over their members. Their importance would remain relevant through a series of wartime governments. The Japanese authority built on the bottom-up network of the associations, and continued to foster federative structures initiated under the Dutch, until it merged them all in a centralized organization, Masyumi; it appointed leaders, and set up newsletters in order to mobilize what was the single largest sector of the civilian population. Toward the end of the Occupation, the authority also made provisions for an armed wing of the organization, Hizbullah. During the Indonesian revolution, multiple militias formed on the basis of religious affiliation, and splinter political groups rallied for the formation of Islamic polities.[6] While these phenomena spanned the archipelago, Islamic affiliation was especially visible in Java and Sumatra, where in the 1940s Islam was a core marker of many Indonesians' identity, mobilization, discursive vocabulary, and representative imagery. Women in headscarves (*kudung*) had been regularly featured in women's Islamic magazines, but by the 1940s the *kudung* was a "consumer commodity," as Sally White has suggested.[7] In this time of impending war, a 1941 advertisement for women's fashion in the reformist *Soeara 'Aisijah* listed styles suitable for "mobilization" alongside other "modern" styles of Islamic clothing.[8] The opening picture reproduced here (Figure 4.1), taken in 1945, shows Muslim women joining in a first-aid training course—all participants made explicit their religious identity, as did the vast majority of women we see depicted in the sources of the time.

In this chapter I focus on the lives of Indonesians, and women in particular, throughout a decade that spans three different regimes: the Japanese period (Occupation, 1942–1945), Indonesia's struggle to assert independence (Revolution, 1945–1949), and its international recognition of sovereignty (Sovereignty, declared in December 1949); I conclude the chapter with a section that looks into the 1950s, foreshadowing developments expounded on in Chapter 5. Despite such political heterogeneity, I see this period as a coherent unit of time dominated by precarity, food insecurity, and the threat or experience of violence. As I center the context of sustained crisis, I strive to offer a perspective on the opportunities created by such circumstances without obfuscating the tragedy, foremost being the abuse of women's bodies under conditions of systematic sexual violence during the Japanese occupation.[9]

In the social, political, and economic environment engendered by the war, care work and hygiene were primary fields for the employment of female labor, bringing to the surface the first layer of Indonesia's "domestic nationalism," as domestic work was recognized as fundamental to the goal of independence. Indonesian women had engaged in home-based hygienic care work as a gendered duty for decades now, but their impact had been obfuscated by the Dutch. However, the war rendered women's daily labor of social reproduction visible; its relevance to social, economic, and political developments was no longer relegated to remain behind the scenes. In the 1940s, care work came to define a "domestic arena" wider than a conventional reading of the term, now encompassing in a single discursive domain home and nation at once.

Additionally, many among them were being trained to step into the roles vacated by militarized men, creating a window of opportunity for Indonesian women to transition in larger numbers, and with less-pronounced class boundaries than before, into the professional world. The role of women in healthcare increased dramatically with such new opportunities for education, mobility, employment, and authority.[10]

Beginning with the Japanese invasion and encouraged by the context of Occupation and war, this trend would have lasting repercussions in the postwar era. In the early years of independence many Indonesian women leveraged the wartime role of "health" in military victory, imperialism, and nation-building to cross the boundary from the domestic and social (volunteering) fields into the professional public arena. Others, writing about household duties as a space for social and political change, primed their readers to see themselves as drivers and enablers of national development in a variety of fields and roles.

CRISIS AND OPPORTUNITY: THE JAPANESE OCCUPATION

In this section I address the tragedies that unfolded during the Japanese occupation—not least those which befell women—and attempt to disentangle them from some moments of possibility that emerged during this time of war. As I focus on the "tangible impacts" of Japanese rule, I echo Kelly Hammond, whose work centers Sino-Muslims in Japanese-occupied China, and attempt not to minimize the violence and destruction that affected Indonesians.[11] Rather, I simultaneously probe the opportunities created for women by war[12]—as has been done by scholars of Europe and America—in order to identify the historical trajectory that enabled women to enter the fields of politics and healthcare in the postwar era.

I approach this situation from the viewpoint of changed patterns of labor. As recently argued by Katharine McGregor, Japan's vision of Southeast Asia as a space for resource extraction included Indonesians as forced laborers, often referred to as *romusha*.[13] From the second half of 1942 onward, progress on Japan's most ambitious infrastructural project in the region—the Thailand-Burma railway—languished, and increasing numbers of laborers were sent from across Japanese-controlled territories to work on clearing the land and laying the tracks. By October 1943, the Japanese regime further intensified its appropriation of manpower, along with food and supplies.

Because of Java's vast, and often unemployed, population, large numbers of men from the island were drafted as *romusha* laborers. In all, according to Shigeru Satō, over ten million Javanese men were mobilized in the Japanese war effort.[14] In theory voluntary service, joining in the ranks of the *romusha* was the outcome of coercion. Most of these laborers never returned to their villages, and often their families did not receive the promised compensation.[15] As concluded by Ethan Mark,

> from the point of view of the peasantry and the working class, the Japanese occupation, welcomed at its inception, evolved into a system of extreme exploitation and oppression that undermined every semblance of legitimacy to the claims and urgings of Japanese Greater Asianism.[16]

What had started as an originally appealing discourse of liberation was voided by the daily tragedy of Occupation.

One consequence of drafting Javanese men as *romusha* was that the majority of those left behind to work were women. Indonesian women had already worked outside the home before the war, but usually within their villages or neighborhoods, and in under- or unskilled positions—as plantation workers, in rice fields, and all sectors of the informal economy. Amid the dire economic circumstances of the Occupation, however, more young women sought work further afield, and their labor was in demand for skilled jobs too. They enlisted in the military, were sent to the front lines as soldiers and nurses, entered new fields, moved to new places, and were mobilized in every sphere of the war effort—from factories and battle lines,[17] rice fields and kitchens, to laboratories and hospitals.[18]

Many were also coerced, tricked, and lured into physically exploitative roles, primarily as what the Japanese called *ianfu*, usually translated as "comfort women" but better articulated as women subjected to unfree labor under conditions of systematic sexual violence. Throughout the Occupation, Dutch, Eurasian, and Indonesian women were forced into prostitution for the benefit of Japanese soldiers and officers. This was often the outcome of abduction, and sometimes also the result of women's responses to fake advertisements offering employment in restaurants and factories, as nurses and domestic servants, or even training opportunities as midwives and nurses.[19] The outcome was, however, often different, as these women found themselves in military brothels.[20] Recent estimates indicate there might have been between 200 and 400 thousand Indonesian women who were forced into military prostitution.[21]

The promise of being trained or employed as nurses or midwives was credible. Education and work in healthcare was not a far-fetched fantasy, as Indonesians were being trained in those fields.[22] Under Dutch rule few Indonesians—and even fewer women—had access to the medical profession; out of necessity, though, the Japanese tried to expand the indigenous presence in the field, and more broadly make healthcare accessible to ordinary people. We see this featured prominently in the pages of a bilingual Japanese-era periodical.

Because of the scarcity of surviving sources, the brief timeframe of the Occupation, and the heavy control the Japanese exerted over the press, it is hard to parse out what was just propaganda and what was truly attempted. The primary publication still available today is *Djawa Baroe*, a bilingual Japanese-Indonesian newsletter printed and distributed in Java. With more illustrations than text, many scholars have considered it pure political propaganda. In the words of Anton Lucas, its contents must have "seemed totally bizarre" to Indonesians in the context of economic crisis, food shortages, and physical abuse.[23] However, Lucas also acknowledges that during the Occupation "some Indonesians ... gained new skills and experiences. . . . Women had new roles to play as well as the traditional old ones."[24] It is that latter experience that I explore here, combining *Djawa Baroe* with oral histories of the Occupation collected in a 1980s publication curated by the National Archives of Indonesia.[25]

Since its early days, the Japanese occupation government had taken some steps toward improving healthcare infrastructure and medical education in Java. *Djawa Baroe* announced how Indonesian doctors were placed in leading positions in the reopened medical schools, how more training facilities for nurses and *mantris* were established, and pharmaceuticals began to be produced in Java. The Japanese focused on recruiting and training more medical professionals, and women were prominent among them as most of the men, regardless of education levels, had been diverted to the direct war effort as soldiers and *romusha*.

A postwar official history of Jakarta (formerly Batavia) noted that in 1943 the city had doubled the number of medical centers available to the people.[26] Yet, as pointed out by Hans Pols, "Despite their impressive medical ideals, the Japanese accomplished little in Indonesia. . . . Indies' physicians could not help but notice that the health of Indonesians was rapidly declining."[27] Similarly, the 1952 publication *History of Jakarta* commented that: "The state of medicine during the 3 ½ years of occupation was very deplorable for the common people. The death figures in these years of occupation show an increasing trend. . . . The reasons are easy to find, namely the lack of food and Japan's lack of attention to people's health, while the supply of medicines was [also] very disappointing. . . . There is a shortage of food, [and] there is less attention to cleanliness."[28]

Before looking at the healthcare sector in more detail, it is worth sketching out the broader economic circumstances that so exacerbated the health crisis in Java. During the Japanese occupation, disease thrived as war, malnutrition, poor infrastructure, and shortages of supplies accumulated, while the economy collapsed. The Japanese had been attracted to the archipelago because of its raw materials (from rubber and oil to tin), but the breakdown in inter-regional transportation caused by war itself and the failure of logistical infrastructure made its extraction and use challenging. Bringing in food supplies from other regions was equally difficult. As assessed by Anne Booth, the Japanese had to resort to "regional self-sufficiency" and discouraged trade.[29]

Java, like other Southeast Asian islands and the mainland, suffered losses barely short of catastrophic, in both food and non-food production. Rice output declined, and what little was available the Japanese taxed heavily, trying to procure it for their own imperial and military purposes; it was the same with rubber and quinine. Oil extraction decreased due to Dutch disruptive actions, and the situation was further exacerbated by the unavailability of both spare parts and imported raw materials. The lack of cotton meant that clothing was scarce, too. Conversely, the impossibility of exports caused enterprises producing consumer goods—such as coffee and sugar—to shut down, furthering unemployment. Within the first year of Occupation, inflation soared, shortages were the norm, and the black market widened extant inequalities even further.[30]

It was against this background that Japanese efforts to advance infrastructural changes in healthcare failed. As the Dutch before them, the Japanese turned to health and hygiene propaganda and women's care work to ameliorate the challenges posed by inadequate sanitary conditions and nutrition. And again, like the Dutch, the Japanese never acknowledged their own role in creating those circumstances, but rather embraced a civilizationist discourse disparaging of local practices and beliefs. One article on yaws prevention exhorted, "if you sweat, take a bath!"[31] While implying the audience's ignorance of this basic fact, the article neglected to mention that the real problem was the short supply of soap, making bathing a difficult endeavor.

Similarly, the practices encouraged to keep malarian mosquitoes at bay promoted since early 1943 were almost impossible to execute.[32] On the occasion of the first gathering of the newly established Java Medical Service Association (Djawa Izi Hookoo Kai) in 1944, malaria and dirt were identified as primary topics for the forthcoming "People's Health Day," as the cleanliness of bodies, homes, and the environment was called upon as part and parcel of a strong and healthy society.[33] Hygiene improvement targeted drinking water, vegetable gardens, and food, as well as the home (WC, clothes, yards, etc.), farming (fishing, cattle, etc.), mosques, and the need to "change traditional habits that go against principles of health and cleanliness."[34]

The rhetoric of civilizational difference and the primacy of scientific knowledge—based on the assumption that Indonesians needed to be educated in matters of hygiene—appears to have seamlessly continued from Dutch times into the Japanese era. In an article printed in the popular *Pandji Poestaka* magazine in 1944, the director of the Japanese public health services, Dr. T. Sato, complained about the Javanese people's lack of physical and spiritual health, and stressed the importance of knowledge- and practice-based prevention (as opposed to medicalized cures) to improve people's conditions. The explicit goal was the success of Greater East Asia. In the absence of strong infrastructure or basic supplies, the only viable strategy was to reform the behavior of the population.[35]

In August 1943 the Japanese had reopened the Pasteur Laboratory in Bandung,[36] which conducted research on vaccines; a few months later they opened a new pharmaceutical laboratory: "During the Dutch period—*Djawa Baroe* claimed—all the ingredients to make medicines were usually imported into Holland, and processed there. Then, those medicines would be sold at high prices to the Indonesian people. . . . But the government now has established a laboratory to make many efficacious medicines," which were putatively going to be sold at affordable prices.[37]

Much propaganda was interwoven in these short articles. The new pharmaceutical laboratory, for example, primarily catered to Japanese soldiers, and oral accounts attest to the lack of medicines across Java and Sumatra. Hajjah Aminah Roezin, married to a doctor who practiced at Koja Hospital in Jakarta during the war, would recall how

> in the hospital itself, the medicines that were available were only basic, and many had run out. I found out from my husband that there were only medicines for malaria and diarrhea, and many were made in the hospital; bandages were also very limited, and syringes were rarely used.[38]

Similarly, Dr. Ali Akbar, a physician stationed in West Sumatra, recalled that

> everywhere was the same, there were no medicines whatsoever, or were set aside by Japan for their war effort. . . . I myself made many of the medicines for skin diseases that were prevalent there, including ointments made by mixing the ingredients [listed] in the book's instructions together with certain types of leaves that are easily available in the villages. It turns out that the medicine I made really helped, many people were relieved from [the discomfort of] skin diseases.[39]

Dr. Akbar was not the only one resorting to homemade remedies. In fact, that became a main strategy of the Japanese authority itself. In mid-1944, the military administration had formed a committee for the study and research of herbal medicine under the guidance of the Health Office. Underscoring once again how the Dutch had preferred to keep Indonesians dependent on expensive imported pharmaceuticals, the Japanese instead claimed that their "health officials have been paying attention to herbal medicines [*jamu*] for a long time and have carried out examinations of them, and have investigated how to make some of them into 'medicinal drinks.'"[40] A series of articles in *Djawa Baroe*, then, provided scientific and medical information about "medicinal herbs found throughout the island of Java . . . quite a few of which are simply unknown to people, treated as grass on the side of a nameless road."[41]

The importance of conducting scientific research on herbal remedies had been a point of order for decades. As discussed by Hans Pols, physicians and botanists had been collecting information about *jamu* since the mid-1800s, but never from actual healers (*dukuns*), many of whom had been indigenous women. Researchers, instead, relied on traders, pharmacists (mostly Chinese), and Indo-European women who had compiled manuals of domestic medicine based on their own interactions with indigenous acquaintances and servants.[42] When the Association of Indonesian Physicians gathered its congress in 1940, two doctors "call[ed] for the integration of indigenous herbal medicine [*jamu*] in medical practice."[43] This strategy would have had a double outcome: on the one hand, it would have framed medicine as "nationalist," rooted in indigenous practices. On the other, Indonesian physicians might have been able to leverage the authority common people conferred on traditional healers, while providing their patients "with remedies they knew actually worked" because of their established scientific testing.[44] This logic revealed the deep stigmatization of indigenous women's practices. Not only was their trust of *dukuns* over physicians usually presented as a trope of women's backwardness (even though here it was turned into a potential asset), but the indigenist and nationalist argument for traditional medicine also did rely on the expertise and mediation of Indo-European women and European scientists, perpetuating the displacement of indigenous women's epistemological authority in matters of health.

Throughout the Japanese era, indigenous women would gradually be reinserted into the broader effort for health improvement, even as they

remained far from reclaiming any position of authority. Before reopening
the Pasteur Laboratory, the Japanese had already revamped other Dutch-
era medical infrastructures. First among them were the school for health
inspectors (*mantri kesehatan*) in Banyumas,[45] and the Jakarta medical
school (which now combined staff from Surabaya and Jakarta, and came
to enroll 500 students[46]). Next were first-aid courses. These efforts, while
perhaps minimal, left a mark nonetheless.

Women featured prominently in the images accompanying the narratives. Young women were portrayed among their male peers as medical
students and pharmaceutical factory workers,[47] while women were alone in
filling the ranks of emergency first-aid trainees and nurses (see Figures 4.1
and 4.2). The Japanese Health Office had opened first-aid courses for
women in August 1943, arguing that "Indonesian women wish to be able
to contribute" and "they had realized that first aid had become common
knowledge for housewives."[48] Presented as housewives who understood the
importance of basic emergency-management skills, the role of Indonesian
women was to expand as circumstances worsened. A year later, the Ministry of Education determined that female students graduating from five-year
primary schools would be granted access to nursing schools where they
would learn about childcare and surgery assistance, for example, alongside
how to act in the case of air raids.[49] In the words of *Djawa Baroe*, "many
of them have become 'angels in white'" supporting soldiers on battlefields
across Java.[50] By February 1945, the Red Cross had provided training for
the first group of Indonesian nurse candidates, also made up of primary
school graduates. With the original goal to "spread knowledge about health
among the Indonesian people and to educate nurses in Java," these women
were now expected to "carry the Red Cross flag on the front line in this
holy war."[51] Being awarded their certification from the army, Indonesian
Red Cross nurses—like their peers around the world—were embedded in
the military effort.

Djawa Baroe emphasized the presence of women in the medical establishment, with female nurses becoming iconic: they showed up in the imagery
of model villages,[52] on the magazine's cover (Figure 4.2),[53] and in advertisements for all sorts of medical supplies, from pharmaceuticals to stretchers
(Figures 4.3 and 4.4).[54] If in earlier issues from 1943 women were only depicted in advertisements for soaps, vitamins, and fertility medicines—thus

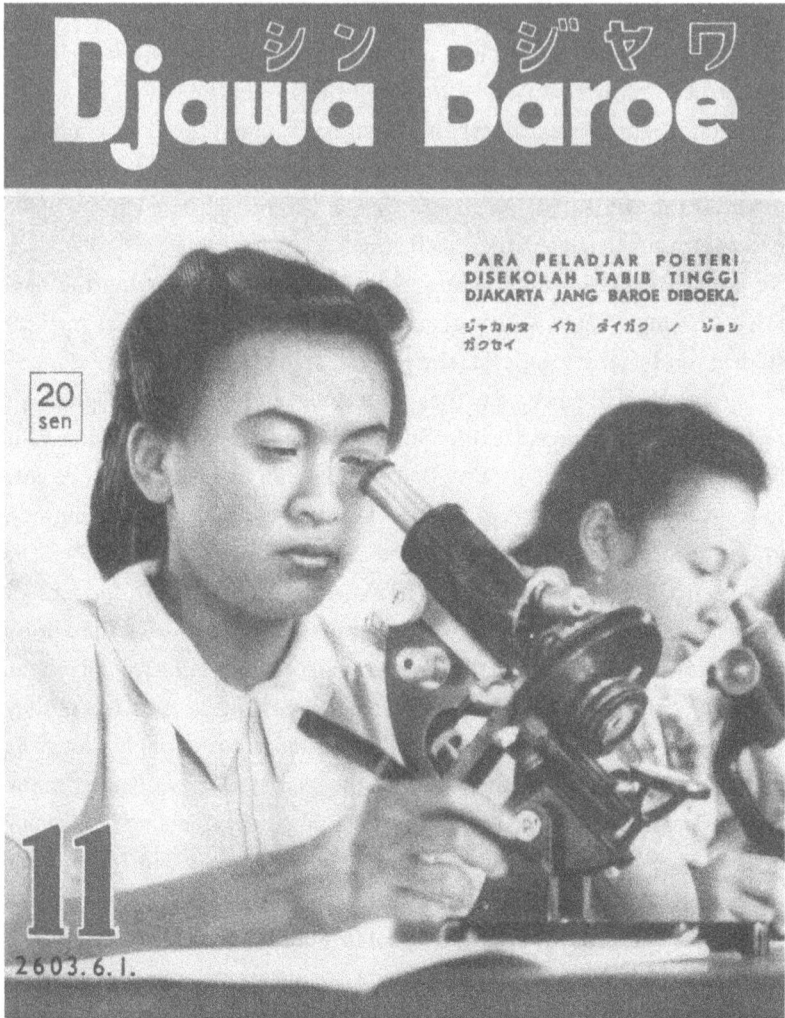

FIGURE 4.2   "Female students at Jakarta's Advanced School for Medicine, which just opened." Source: *Djawa Baroe*, June 1, 1943, cover page, Cornell University Library

performing roles of biological reproduction and home-centered domestic care—by 1945 they were represented as healthcare professionals working in situations relevant to their expertise.

The oral accounts available complement the picture depicted by *Djawa Baroe*. They illustrate the hardship of the era but also confirm the increased responsibilities put on women as providers of healthcare—whether at home,

FIGURE 4.3 Advertisement for Odopharm. Source: *Djawa Baroe*, August 1, 1945, n.p., Cornell University Library

FIGURE 4.4 Advertisement for Moethalib. Source: *Djawa Baroe*, August 1, 1945, n.p., Cornell University Library

in clinics, or on the battlefield. *Nyonya* Baheram Iskandar, a midwife, re-called her daily activities of care:

> At that time, the Tanjung Priok area [of Jakarta] was still forest. We have lived here for a long time, in this house. No one was our neighbor yet, it was still sparsely populated. I often went on duty here and there,

up to Cilincing [a neighborhood east of Tanjung Priok], helping people who were about to give birth, sometimes with other women, such as *Ibu* Aminah, *Ibu* Entin. I am a midwife, you know. Oh . . . the people here really listened to me. I said this . . . they would do it. I said that . . . they would do it, yeah, all kinds of things. During the Japanese era it was difficult. I was not just a midwife, but I helped with all kinds of things, especially those related to illnesses. I brought some medicines along, if I happened to have any, but it was very difficult, [I might find] as little as just a few quinine tablets and diarrhea medicine which were provided by Doctor Roezin, *Nyonya* Aminah's husband, [only] once or twice. Meanwhile, from the village head and the sub-district head Endong Natawinangun, we didn't get anything. With my skills and knowledge, at the time I did not only help people who were about to give birth, but also often helped those who suffered from hunger, dysentery, and malaria. There were a lot of people who got dysentery and malaria in the Cilincing area, maybe because it was dirty and the area is swampy. But what I do know, is that dirt and insufficient food will invite all kinds of disease.[55]

Ny. Baheram Iskandar's recollection exposes many of the challenges faced by ordinary Indonesians, and the role played by women in managing such difficulties. We hear about the lack of medicines and the failure of institutions to provide help, but also the initiative of private individuals—like Ny. Iskandar and her friends—who stretched their networks and expertise to bring as much relief to others as possible. And, with much gravitas, we hear that regardless of medication, many ailments could be prevented— or at least limited, considering the extreme circumstances—by "ordinary" care work.

Such reflections were not unique, and the Japanese, too, were well aware of the importance of hygiene and nutrition in mitigating the negative impact of warfare. Cognizant of having exhausted the available resources, and with no strong infrastructure in place, the Japanese, then, turned women's care work into an element of empire-building. The key to victory, or at this point mere survival, shifted towards cooking and cleanliness, especially in the kitchen.[56]

As in the Dutch era, knowledge was disseminated in multiple ways. Periodicals published instructive materials, and (some) girls were enrolled in

Japanese-styled home economics schools where they learned to cook, along with other skills such as sewing, cleaning, and household upkeep.[57] Additionally, the Japanese had established the Fujinkai. This was a women's organization which, as with all similar organizations set up by the Japanese, cast a wide net to mobilize as large a share of its expected membership as possible. With a broad vision of the goals of this gender-based organization, Fujinkai brought together women of all social strata, from the wives of civil servants (who were required, or at least expected, to join) to illiterate women from the villages; although within the group social class operated as a sharp wedge, especially in the rural areas.

At the most basic level, Fujinkai branches taught literacy and mobilized women to support the war effort through manual labor, caring for wounded soldiers, entertaining them, receiving military training, and running public kitchens.[58] Fujinkai regularly offered discussions on matters of hygiene and nutrition for those who did not attend school because of age, location, or socio-economic status; or because the schools had actually shut down. Women instructed their peers on how to cultivate cotton and how to "cook healthy food," and the organization offered health services, too.

Healthcare was a core responsibility for women during the Japanese occupation, and that reality was embedded in Fujinkai's activities. According to one Indonesian voice, "at a minimum, the Japanese wanted this organization to become a kind of health promoter in the cities' kampungs, especially through outreach, providing medical assistance."[59] As its members walked around the kampungs, they carried some medications for malaria and diarrhea, provided by the sub-district or doctors, and encouraged those who appeared to be "really sick" to go to the hospital.[60] At the Fujinkai congress, held in Java in mid-1944, the contribution of women to the war effort was defined as stretching from nutrition and health to participation in air-raid training,[61] not unlike Red Cross nurses.

An article published in *Djawa Baroe* in early 1943 argued that every woman could contribute to "building this new society." This might well have been Japanese wartime propaganda, but it had been authored by Maria Ulfah Santoso; the first Indonesian woman to graduate in law (travelling to the Netherlands to achieve that goal), she would also become the first woman cabinet minister in independent Indonesia. During the Dutch era she had been vocal on matters of marriage law and women's legal rights, and under the Japanese regime she was employed in the ministry of legal affairs, thus standing by default as a leading member of Fujinkai. But she also regularly wrote to advocate for women's rights, and their role in the independence movement.

I read her article as a call for women to recognize, acknowledge, and engage with the fact that in a mobilized society every action counted, whether one joined from an office, school, business enterprise, or the household. For those who were limited to the "surroundings of the home," they had to "pursue their duties at their best, keeping the home in order, and preparing food" that was "cheap and healthy." Maria Ulfah saw these domestic efforts as equally important as those pursued in public spaces, both being crucial to the establishment of a postcolonial society: a "new society" that would be free of foreign control and characterized by gender parity was a double goal to be achieved through a variety of channels—from legal reforms to cooking.[62]

In addition to the Fujinkai network, the Japanese regime relied on publications to spread instructional materials. *Djawa Baroe* printed articles illustrating how to maximize the potential of available ingredients, and how to protect foods from germs.[63] Embracing a well-established civilizationist discourse, *Djawa Baroe* often underlined how Javanese cooking techniques were flawed, and kitchens in Java "were known to be dirty." Women had to take extreme care to avoid diseases and thus clean themselves and their kitchens before starting to prepare a meal.[64]

Another recurrent piece of advice was to follow Japanese cooking techniques. Frying vegetables in oil with spices (*bumbu*, the usual way of cooking in Java) was said to make nutrients disappear, while the Japanese practice of eating fresh vegetables was considered better.[65] The benefits of a raw diet of fruit and vegetables had already been discussed at the 1944 gathering of Indonesian physicians, when Dr. Aulia offered a speech on the topic.[66] This was an excerpt from his booklet *Makanan jang Sehat* ("Healthy Food"), first published in 1937, later serialized in *Isteri Indonesia* in 1941, and eventually reprinted under Japanese auspices in 1943.[67] Japanese habits were promoted as superior in how rice was cooked,[68] as well as in the consumption of the Japanese sweet potato (*ubi*). This root was presented as a symbol of Japan bestowing progress upon Java. Deemed far more nutritious than rice or any other carbohydrate usually consumed on the island, *Djawa Baroe* explained how to cultivate it and how to cook it "like the Japanese peasants."[69] The actual advantages, in the current conditions, were that yam could be easily cultivated in one's backyard and had a short growth time (around four to five months), making it far preferable to rice and its laborious cultivation process.[70]

As reminisced in the oral accounts collected by the Indonesian national archives in the 1980s, staple foods were scarce. Rice was rationed, and of subpar quality. When *Nyonya* Barkas's younger brother found himself stepping over heaps of unbagged premium polished rice—"white rice, number one, rice from Cianjur"— at the harbor in Tanjung Priok, he wondered where it was being shipped to, as at home they could only eat "rice with stones."[71] Vegetables, too, were rare: "Not even carrots were available at that time; they had disappeared from the markets. Sometimes also potatoes disappeared from the market back then, taken . . . for Japanese soldiers."[72] Ny. Hafni Zahra Abu Hanifa, married to a doctor, recalled how they lacked sugar and rice, and they "resorted to growing vegetables in the yard, so that there would be eggplants, string beans, and tomatoes."[73] She remembered their transfer from Jakarta to Sukabumi, in rural West Java:

> As soon as we arrived, the next day, we immediately ordered chilies for cooking. For side dishes, sometimes we got papaya, we made . . . what is it called . . . we grated it, and the skin [. . .] we made it into a stew. That was our situation in Sukabumi, it's unimaginable, just the slightest difference from our situation in Jakarta.[74]

Djawa Baroe had opened 1945 reminding Indonesian readers that eating was not just about filling one's stomach; it answered the call of a nation's development, as health was the basis of progress.[75] Aware that a weak and dying population was not going to be able to support the military effort, the Japanese authority broadcast the idea that hygienic and nutritious food was a key component of good health for each individual, and therefore would lead to military success.

Sukarno, who would be appointed by the Japanese to lead Indonesia to independence, had already expressed, in 1943, the idea that a strong nation required healthy subjects: "The task of doctors is not only to cure the ill, but also to guard and guide, so that the Indonesian people become very healthy and strong."[76] The statement exuded Japanese propaganda—which stressed physical strength as a pillar of national assertion[77]—while at the same time it hinted at the aspirations Sukarno had for an independent Indonesia.

The Japanese had accepted that preventive care was an unachievable goal for the (very few) doctors scattered across the archipelago, and had thus resolved to directly mobilize women's daily domestic labor as a front against disease (even as women also stepped into training and waged employment as men were sent to the warfront). Notably, though, Sukarno focused on physicians alone in his vision of a healthy nation. Sukarno's apparent omission of women's everyday contributions to health could be pegged to the context of his remarks—he was speaking to an audience of doctors. But it also reflected his broader paternalistic vision of the proper role of women in nation-building.

Sarinah was Sukarno's book-length elaboration of women's "duties" (or "responsibilities," Ind. *kewajiban*) in Indonesia's struggle for independence. Published in 1947, it had a longer history as it built on ideas first expressed at the nationalist party (Partai Nasional Indonesia, PNI) congress of 1929, and its publication had been announced as early as 1940, before the war altered that schedule.[78] Whereas the prewar manuscript is not available, ideas expressed in 1929 are found in the 1947 edition of the book, where Sukarno lamented that Indonesian women had "no concerns other than the kitchen." They were, he explained, in the first of three stages of the emancipation movement, still lacking social and political awareness.[79] Sukarno exhorted Indonesia's women to join in the National Revolution:

> Indonesian women, your duty is clear! Now you must join in the effort to save the Republic, without reservations, and then when the Republic is safe, you must join, without reservations, in the effort to establish the National State.[80]

But Indonesian women, he said, remained in the first stage of emancipation, just as in the 1920s. Sukarno's demand, then, was that the leaders of the women's movement should unite across organizations, class, and ideologies "to instill awareness, awake, and invigorate" all other women.[81] They should do so despite different perspectives on education, health and midwifery, on involvement in para-military groups, or on gender equality of rights.[82]

Women's socio-political awareness was "an absolute requirement" for building society,[83] and in Sukarno's view, Indonesia's women had not become aware. Middle-class women were either concerned with capitalist consumerism, or so absorbed in feminist ideas of gender equality and professional achievement that they refused to have a family. Lower-class women, in contrast, worked around the clock on factories' floors and at home, leaving no time for socio-political activism. While proclaiming his belief in Islam and nationalism,[84] Sukarno postulated that only a socialist state could "bring happiness to women,"[85] "synthesizing" women's natural desires (*kodrat alam wanita*) for homemaking and motherhood,[86] with their own need for financial independence, and the revolutionary needs of the nation.[87] The socialist collectivity would attend to domestic chores, and women could work outside the home while still having a family, thus solving the contradictions of Euro-American feminism (which prioritized work at the expense of family), the exploitation of the proletariat,[88] and Indonesia's Islamic conservatism (*kekolotan*) that kept women "like a pearl in a box."[89]

As the socialist state would take care of women's daily duties of social reproduction—providing daycare, mess halls, and laundries—Indonesian women could attain political awareness for the benefit of the emerging nation-state. Sukarno rejected any form of "domestic nationalism" that the state could not control: women were neither encouraged to pursue activism, nor to see the political—and socio-economic—value of their mothering beyond biological reproduction. They in fact were dispossessed of those roles, as children needed to be socialized and molded by state institutions into desired future citizens. The contribution of Indonesian women was exclusively shaped in terms of direct economic productivity and biological reproduction.

ORDINARY TASKS IN EXTRAORDINARY TIMES: REVOLUTION (1945–1949)

In the aftermath of Japan's surrender on August 15, 1945, Navy Admiral Maeda—stationed to Indonesia since the early days of Japan's occupation—made real the 1944 promise of independence given by Japan's then Prime Minister. Sukarno and Mohammad Hatta announced Indonesia's independence on August 17, 1945, and shortly after established a Jakarta-based government as president and vice-president, respectively. Sukarno had envisioned the fledgling nation-state as a unitary republic corresponding to the Dutch East Indies' widest geographical footprint, embroiling the Indonesian republic in years, and in some areas even decades, of conflict (both political and armed, internal and international).[90]

Immediately following the proclamation, armed conflict involved the newly constituted Indonesian People's Army, multiple Indonesian militias (representative of communist, Islamic, and various regional groups), and Allied forces, represented by British, Dutch, and Australian troops. It soon became clear that the Dutch expected to "return" to the Indies as the ruling authority—and archival documents show that the Dutch government had been planning for that since at least 1943.[91] While the international community timidly expressed caution and reservations on the matter, in July 1947—and again in December 1948—the Dutch launched direct offensives in Java and Sumatra. The Dutch called them "police actions," thus labelling them as an internal affair, but Indonesians would refer to them as "military aggressions."

In the long string of internationally brokered agreements, and their recurrent failures, the Dutch continued to launch military attacks on areas controlled by Sukarno's Republican government. Between 1947 and 1949, Dutch bombing campaigns and land incursions forced mass evacuations and displacement, while prominent political leaders and members of the cabinet were arrested. One—intended—consequence of the Dutch operations was to intensify shortages of food and medical supplies. By early 1948 the Republic controlled non-contiguous territories in Java. Its capital relocated to Yogyakarta, and masses of refugees crossed the "van Mook line" to reach Republican-controlled areas. Worse still, the Dutch established "export-import controls" that effectively constituted a blockade.[92] Consequently, the Dutch

> refused to permit the entry of medicines into Republican territory. As far back as July of [1948], the United Nations Committee of Good Offices, in its sharp comment on Dutch policy in Indonesia, reported to the Security Council that the Dutch blockade was preventing rehabilitation in the Republic of Indonesia.[93]

––––––

Ravaged by years of human and natural resource extraction and exploitation, as well as armed conflict, in the 1940s the archipelago faced sustained difficulties in tending to rice crops, labor shortages, and disruptions to distribution of food and medical supplies.[94] In the second half of the decade, the newly established Revolution-era government began to set up services, and various international organizations became involved in the improvement of conditions, but the fundamentals of care remained in the purview of ordinary women's domestic work.

The Republican government attempted policy interventions even while engaged in revolutionary, armed conflict. The February 1946 "Economy Conference" established as priorities the supply of clothing, plantation management for commodity export, and—most importantly—the domestic production and distribution of food.[95] Ignatius J. Kasimo—junior minister of welfare and previously minister for people's food supply (Menteri Persediaan Makanan Rakyat, 1946)—devised a three-year plan (1948–1950, often referred to as the "Kasimo Plan") aimed at increasing the production of subsistence crops as well as the relocation of people out of densely populated areas,[96] but much of this would remain ink on paper until the 1950s.

A 1946 account to the British Broadcasting Corporation noted that clinics operated by the Netherlands Red Cross across Java were swamped by hundreds of patients each day. Near Bandung (West Java), for example, over a third of the outpatients had been admitted for undernourishment. Of all the admitted patients, none was "well nourished" and the nutrition level of two-thirds of them was labeled "bad."[97] Around the same time, the Dutch Red Cross's Nutrition Research Team had just completed a survey to provide advice to the authorities and medical personnel on how to "combat the after-effects of [wartime] starvation," as well as conduct research and provide guidance on systematic nutritional deficiencies.[98] But as Java and Sumatra, and other islands, were still mired in armed conflict, the idea of structured policy-driven improvement was largely aspirational.

Throughout the years of Revolution, in Java and Sumatra public kitchens and women's networks of solidarity provided basic access to food, as other scholars have shown. The testimonies collected by Margaret Steedly from women in Karoland, Sumatra, are similar to Saskia Wieringa's analysis of Java, with both showing that girls and women came to be deeply involved in the revolutionary struggle as nurses, messengers, cooks, and fighters.[99] Steedly's informants reminisced how "During Independence Time women were really the most important. . . . They did the cooking, they did whatever had to be done."[100] And the relevance of those tasks to the revolutionary struggle was widely recognized at the time, at least on the ground. Based on his words in *Sarinah*, though, Sukarno seemed to remain detached from daily reality, more interested in making political and ideological statements.

In women's experiences of the struggle, "ordinary, daily acts [were] transformed by the startling circumstances of warfare."[101] Finding and preparing food, whether for families or soldiers, was a pressing and complex challenge, one among many of such now-extraordinary tasks, and a recurrent theme in the stories Steedly collected.[102] Throughout the period, "young educated women found a public voice,"[103] and by mid-1947, "home front and front lines were hopelessly entangled,"[104] blurring and dissipating the distance between them. For some women—especially young unmarried ones—this was empowering, opening up possibilities; for others—primarily those already married and with children—the expectation of contributing to the struggle was exploitative.[105]

In the words of a 1952 nationalist history issued by the Indonesian government, when Dutch troops attacked and occupied Jakarta in early 1946, women were "tested" in their efforts to procure and prepare food while holding onto the spirit of freedom with "firmness and tenacity," and they did "not let [that spirit] fade because of some cheese, did not let it die because of the distribution of foreign goods by the opposing party."[106] The anonymous bureaucrat-narrator shrugged off the betrayal of the few "women who [were] seduced by sweet offers and join[ed] those [opposing] groups," and focused on the many others who stood strong in their nationalist aspirations: "those women are the pioneers of the Proclamation."[107] Their efforts were not just for their own (and their family's) survival. Rather, in the eyes of the fledgling nation, they were for the broader community. As urban and rural starvation were regular fare,[108] mobile kitchens would remain a staple until the end of the decade, with the Indonesian Red Cross and independent women's organizations operating as many of them as possible, and as widely as they could.[109] In the 1950s, women's roles had entered the visual imaginary of Indonesian artists too, as we see in Raden Mas Sajid's inclusion of Red Cross nurses in the *wayang kulit* shadow puppet theater repertoire (Figure 4.5).

In 1952, then, women who had been involved with public kitchens could be depicted in laudatory terms, as they had spared no efforts to feed

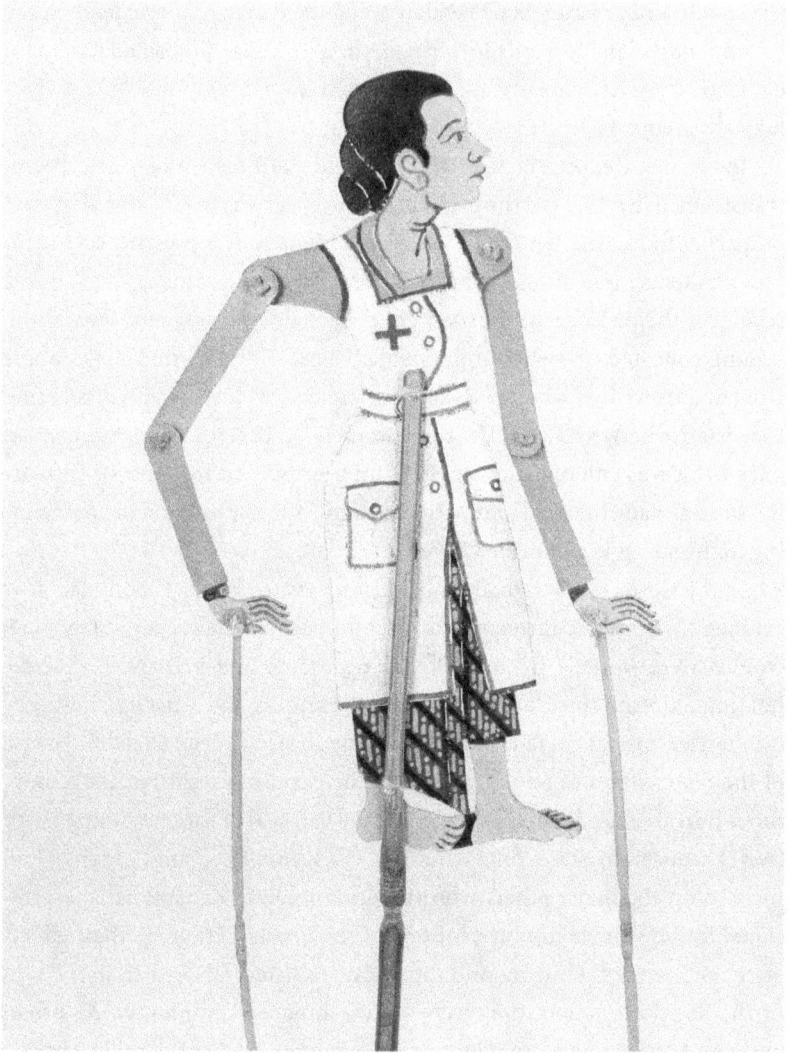

FIGURE 4.5 Raden Mas Sajid, Red Cross nurse, circa 1955. Source: Collectie Wereldmuseum Rotterdam, WM-57188 Creative Commons

nationalist soldiers on the front line, and other members of the anti-colonial resistance:

> The spirit of the Proclamation gave birth to national women's organizations. . . . As a fighting group [*badan perdjuangan*], WANI [Wanita Negara Indonesia, Women of the Indonesian Nation-State] endeavored

to support the struggle for independence. . . . Among other things they established public kitchens and distributed foodstuff to the families of fighters and residents in need. In the further development of the fight for Jakarta, the WANI Public Kitchen, under the leadership of Nn. Erna Djajadiningrat, played a role of no little significance.[110]

This official publication did mirror many women's experiences of their actions at the time. But official discourse would change during the 1970s to 1980s. Then, as Karo women reminisced about their wartime role with Margaret Steedly, nostalgia for the spirit of the time would be palpable, with women disheartened by the then-predominant perspective:

> But [in the 1980s] it's as if women had no part in the struggle, isn't it? . . . Then we were the best, at the beginning of independence we were the best. But now there's no more meaning in being a woman.[111]

OUT OF WAR

Amid mounting international pressure on the Netherlands, including the US threat of withdrawing Marshall Plan aid, in mid-1949 the Dutch relented and agreed to transfer sovereignty to the Indonesian republic. The landmark Roem–van Roijen agreement was signed in May 1949, making provisions for a roundtable conference that met later that year in The Hague to stipulate the details of the transfer. Post-Revolution Indonesia first took shape as the "Republic of the United States of Indonesia," thus acknowledging regionalist desires in a federal structure. Now, Sukarno's Republic was just one of sixteen federated states within RUSI, with its capital located in Yogyakarta. But since this federation was seen as a "foreign" structure—the Dutch and Americans had advocated for (or imposed) it—Sukarno quickly moved to dismantle it. On the fifth anniversary of the proclamation of independence, in August 1950, Sukarno announced the establishment of the unitary Republic of Indonesia, with its capital in Jakarta, and himself as president.

Marking the end of a decade of struggle, media and consumption infrastructure regrouped, now, for the first time, in a non-occupied, non-colonial context. With a government strapped for resources, health and hygiene propaganda were common themes in the popular press, and especially in resurgent women's magazines. In this section I bring to the fore the combination of gendered care work, nation-building, and religious piety to show that, in this period of transition, women consciously wove those strands together, explicitly writing about this in the dedicated press, while other ungendered publications often sidelined their role.

The importance of small, home-based actions was evident in late 1949. On the pages of the now bilingual magazine of the Association of Housewives, renamed *De Huisvrouw in Indonesië* to mark the transition to independence, a Jakarta City Council member, Mohammad Sjatrie, stressed the significance of everyday nutrition.[112] Sjatrie wrote about topics familiar from previous decades, now made even more explicit by the intervening years of women's wartime service: cleanliness was the basis of health, and health the foundation of a strong nation. And women's daily activities with their families and in their communities were vital, in part because broader efforts in hygiene education were needed.

> Don't we often see and read placards and various medicines' advertisements proclaiming "[with] a healthy youth, the Nation becomes strong"? . . .
>
> These words can be understood to mean that, to eradicate any disease, first of all we need to guard the cleanliness of our bodies, households, yards and villages too. . . . To prevent disease, to spare our society from being affected by a great catastrophe, it is better if we make every effort to advise and enlighten our society on the benefits of maintaining cleanliness, especially if such information is given to Women.
>
> Because of the emphasis on "cleanliness" of the household and children, this [effort] lies in the hands of Women in particular. The same is true of information in matters of food and guarding against the dangers brought by flies.[113]

A translated article in a Red Cross newsletter, also printed in 1949, similarly centered the domestic role of women in the sanitary drive—but this is the only article I found in the ungendered press that specifically acknowledged women's labor. Following a long complaint about unhygienic behavior in public places—from markets to trams and restaurants—the article identified the kitchen as the focal point of hygienic concerns. Hence, even though "every person must understand their social responsibility," women had an additional responsibility in ensuring the overall hygiene and health of the household through their management of the kitchen.[114]

Between 1949 and the early 1950s, women also contributed to this perspective, often authoring articles on related subjects, such as the importance of health, hygiene, and good nutrition; the responsibility of women in pursuing those goals; and their relevance to nation-building.[115]

One of the first women's magazines to be published in the postwar period was *Wanita*, printed by Balai Pustaka, which had remained a government publishing platform, now under Indonesian control. Described by some scholars as "Sukarnoist" and promoting a "nation- and community-building project"[116] centered on the household, *Wanita* nonetheless pushed against discursive efforts to inscribe women solely to the narrow space of the household in name of their "nature." While *Wanita* fit a conventional vision of domestic womanhood, it also made explicit its entanglements with politics and nation-building. The magazine saw itself as a space for learning "important and useful" things for the management and improvement of a woman's world, namely the household, its surrounding environment, the yard, and crops.[117] These were not merely domestic matters, but outward-facing goals too. In its very first editorial from August 1949, the board made this perspective explicit, although perhaps timidly so:

> All Indonesian women have the same interests in matters of the household. Building an independent and sovereign nation cannot but include the struggle for women, bringing [and] nurturing the spirit of independence and sovereignty in the household.[118]

Beginning in 1950, the editorial board pushed the boundary further, underscoring how the building of society and the nation depended on women's multifaceted responsibilities. In January, the editorial column opened with a celebration of Indonesian citizens' independence, noting the transition of their collective struggle "from fighting to building." Similarly, it noted the continued role of women in advancing "the realization of [this society's] ideals. . . . Indeed, women can't be left behind in all that happens outside of their home. The field of work is very broad." This was meant both professionally—"There are among us [some] who with their skills will go forward, shoulder to shoulder with the men"—and beyond: "If her family at home does not demand all of her effort, *madjulah ia*, let her advance, contributing her thoughts to [women's] organizations."[119]

It was women's ideas that, brought to the organizations, would shape their activities for "decades" ahead. Despite all the past efforts, women had not yet "moved forward" enough in "the advancement of the living standards of the common people; the advancement of education; the improvement of health; the monitoring of the standards of daily life."[120] And these were the issues that demanded their attention, for the benefit of the nation.

Hence, as Indonesia entered the phase of national development,

> the duty of women is obvious, as it was in the previous phase of struggle: [we ought] to be the "back-bone" [English in original, and glossed as *tulang-punggung*] behind the screen [*kelir*] in a society that is busily working to realize its ideals.[121]

This sentence appears in the first substantial paragraph of the 1950 editorial, and should thus be connected to the previously mentioned three-partite articulation of women's labor: at home, in women's organizations, and in professional areas alongside men. The double metaphor asserts a fundamental role in stimulating such developments. First is the image of women as the core pillar of society, the steadfast "back-bone," or *tulang-punggung*, that sustains the entire national body.

Next is the image of the screen. Notably, this is not the "curtain" (*tabir*) meant to segregate men and women in Islamic reformist settings and which Sukarno had loudly criticized in the late 1930s, and again in *Sarinah*. The one here is the *kelir*, the screen behind which the *dhalang* (puppeteer) sits to choreograph the shadow puppet performance, maneuvering the *wayang kulit* figures. Being behind this screen does not denote marginalization, but rather authority and skill—the *dhalang* embodies Islamic, mystical, and creative authority; traditionally a man, he holds power and is the only one with full knowledge of the play. It was on these very grounds that Sukarno himself was often referred to as Indonesia's *dhalang*: he could manipulate, control, and influence others, and would—as he did—create his own narratives.[122] But in *Wanita*, it is ordinary women who play the role of *dhalang*.

With this article, *Wanita*'s editors placed themselves and their peers at the very center of Indonesia's developmental narrative, continuing along a path that had taken decades to take shape, but was only now clearly visible. They still felt the need to "comply with the will of the times and the people," but the editors had staked out their authority as the architects of this new phase in Indonesian history.[123]

A similar connection between the home, good health, and nation-building can be seen in advertisements, popular books, and government policies of 1950, the same year of the *Wanita* editorial. As noted by Sjatrie, a resurgent consumerism was mining the political preoccupations and social trends of the new era. When Unilever re-launched Blue Band margarine, the April copy appearing in both *Karya* and *Wanita* read: "Pemuda Sehat, Rakjat Kuat," or "A healthy youth, a strong people" (Figure 4.6). It thus evoked the populist appeal to the *rakyat* (the masses) and the double meaning of *pemuda*—as both the youth in general, and those who had led the Revolution[124]—in order to connect its brand to the now-commonly accepted importance of nutrition for nation-building. While some illustrations pictured a young child wearing an iconic *peci* hat (like the one Sukarno would wear), many others portrayed a mother preparing food for her children, husband, or friends, underscoring the multiple valences of cooking.[125]

FIGURE 4.6 Advertisement for Blue Band. Source: *Karya*, no. 7, July 1950, p. 12, Leiden University Library

A year later, in 1951, the Dutch company making Friesche Vlag ("Frisian Flag") condensed milk—locally renamed Bendera ("Flag") in an attempt to soften its Dutch identity—was marketed as "Strength to Build." "To build you need a strong body. For a strong body, you need pure milk." In the foreground we see a young child playing with building blocks, while his shadow is that of a man building a brick wall (see Figure 4.7).[126] Under the ever-present rhetoric of "development" (Ind. *pembangunan*), building a wall was akin to building the nation; and whereas the responsibility of equipping the new generation of strong-bodied citizens was here placed on home-based food consumption, the women in charge of purchasing groceries and feeding citizens were not pictured.

A similar dynamic is apparent in the branding of a Jakarta publishing house, Djambatan, and policies issued by the Ministry of Health, as both remained ambivalent to women's roles. Whereas Djambatan had adopted the motto "Rakyat Sehat, Negara Kuat" ("Healthy People, Strong Nation") for its "Indonesia Sehat" ("Healthy Indonesia") outreach book series (the new embodiment of the DVG health books), its volume on birthing and newborn care had omitted the slogan.[127] Similarly, in his 1952 *Membangun Kesehatan Rakjat* ("Building People's Health"), Minister Johannes Leimena asserted that "Rakyat Sehat, Negara Kuat" was "not just a slogan": good health was necessary for farmers and workers to be productive, for children to learn, and for soldiers to defend the country. He had pulled together decades of public health propaganda, demonstrating its relevance to the economy, the wellbeing of future generations, and its military purposes. And as had many of his predecessors, Leimena left women out of the picture: their work was vital, but their role was invisible.[128] Whereas these official publications had omitted any explicit reference to the pivotal role played by women, policies on the ground in the 1950s would lean heavily and explicitly on women's labor.

In the women's press, however, women themselves brought nation building into conversations about care work. In 1951, two articles centered women's domestic and professional labor: one, printed in *Suara Perwari* ("Voice of Perwari," the periodical of Indonesia's foremost feminist organization), had included the photos of newborns attended by nurses at a clinic, and captioned it as: "Anak2 sehat, negara kuat!" ("Healthy Children, Strong Nation!").[129] Another one, in *Wanita*, had presented learning how to cook "beneficial food" as contributing to "shaping a strong state."[130]

FIGURE 4.7   Advertisement for Bendera condensed milk. Source: *Suara Perwari*, no. 8, May 1951, n.p., Cornell University Library

These reflections appeared alongside many other articles that called upon women's duty and responsibility (*kewajiban*) to keep their families healthy, through hygienic practices and wholesome foods.[131] Scholars of the women's movement have argued that these concerns, framings, and publications simply reflected upper-class elite worldviews of "housewifery."[132] In fact, I suggest that these (and many other) articles addressing matters of child-rearing, health, hygiene, and nutrition went far beyond the shaping of "good wives," and instead signaled women's awareness of their role in nation-building as a social, economic, and political endeavor. This was an argument made by the editorial board of *Wanita* in mid-1950: when a reader criticized the magazine for limiting itself to superfluous household matters, *Wanita* responded by making explicit the political importance of domestic work.[133]

That note echoed the editorial printed earlier that year, and the sentiment was shared in other circles, too, as religious platforms hosted women's thinking on the connection between social reproduction and national progress. The Islamic reformist magazine *Suara 'Aisjijah* provides a good example. In April 1952, the article "Women and National Development" expressed a view similar to that of *Wanita*, yet in a different framework, quoting an "Arab saying" which asserted that: "Women are the pillars of the nation." Further, it stated that when *maju* women are in the public realm as teachers, community organizers, government officials, office workers, or clerks, such work should be instilled with the skills of mothering. These "skills" were a force and framework that could ensure that the nation's development, and its people, would not stray. Women were guardians of piety, and the author concluded: "Our women can offer their services to fulfill the needs of the state, so that they can bring the state and people towards the divine pleasure of the Lord."[134]

A year later, a Siti Isnadijah Aly of Semarang suggested that Khadija, Aisyah, and Asma, important female figures close to the Prophet Muhammad, were exemplars of respected and influential Muslim women known for fulfilling duties and expectations in the realms of economy, faith, and domestic care. They combined their *kodrat* and advanced the needs of their society, each in her own way. Khadija had been a dutiful mother and wife and an economics expert who financially supported the early community of Muslims. Aisyah, a dedicated wife and "mother of the community" (*Ibu masjarakat*), had "committed her intelligence and skills to the state." An *ahli hukum* (legal expert) and "driver of Islamic politics," she had fulfilled the call of society with her expertise. Sitti Asma, daughter of Caliph Abu Bakr, had been a mother and educator of three martyrs who sacrificed their lives on the battlefield.

However, Siti Isnadijah Aly continued, contemporary Indonesian women's "progress" was far from these ideals, not being "in accordance with the desires of a state as articulated in the basic laws of the One Almighty." She argued that among Indonesian women there were some who had taken their freedom too far, poured themselves into work and neglected their families. Others, modeling their emancipation on the western experience and embracing licentious lifestyles, in this "age of development" were in fact undermining the achievements of national independence which God had granted. Lastly, a third group simply ignored society to only dedicate themselves to the kitchen—also a mistake, in Siti Isnadijah Aly's formulation.

This article in *Suara 'Aisjijah* was similar to Sukarno's *Sarinah*, both maintaining that major obstacles to Indonesia's development could be found in the two polarized behaviors exhibited by women: the "excessive westernization" of careerism or self-indulgence; and domestic withdrawal from society. To both authors, either behavior was seen as equally neglecting of women's social and political duties.

For Siti Isnadijah Aly, though, differently from Sukarno, the fundamental conceptual problem of the time was the neglect of the connection between women's labor of reproduction (both biological and social) and the improvement of society (economic, military, political, and civic). The solution, then, was not in detaching (or alienating, we might say) women from their religiously mandated, politically fundamental household labor, as Sukarno had suggested with his ideal socialist state. Rather, for Indonesia to achieve development there needed to be stronger Islamic values and therefore increased awareness—among men and women alike—about the intrinsic, even spiritual, value of women's domestic work, and, crucially, its idealistic connection to nationwide betterment. The models ought to be Khadija, Aisyah and Asma, who had stood as pillars of the early Islamic community, precisely because their activities of care work had been in the service of, and led to the benefit of, society in the areas most in need of development. She concluded her article with the following exhortation: "Let's together fulfill and guard *kemerdekaan* with *kesedaran* [awareness], and adorn it with faith and fear of God."[135]

These Indonesian women writers called on their peers to put their gendered roles to work in service for the new nation-state. Sukarno, and even some recent scholars, have pointed at these activities as "social" and reflective of women's "nature," in antithesis to the (masculine) field of politics. However, Indonesian women themselves saw mothering not just as a moral imperative, an aspect of their "nature," a social necessity, or to satisfy patriarchal views of "womanhood"—rather, they saw mothering as a profession and part of a political agenda, in the hope that their work would impact the nation as much as it would impact other women.[136]

———

The promise of sovereignty opened an era of possible transitions and deep contradictions. The end of international armed conflict was in sight, but what would soon come to be known as "anti-nationalist rebellions" were just starting. Islam had been an organizational basis for Japanese-era mobilization, and it remained a framework for many writers and "rebel" groups advocating for an alternative vision of an independent Indonesia. In the postwar period, however, Sukarno would push Islam out of public discourse as much as possible. And while Indonesia was taking shape as an independent nation-state vowing to strive for self-reliance in its "forward movement" (kemajuan), it had to rely on international support and foreign aid to achieve that status and prosperity.

The prominent role of women in the public sphere would nonetheless remain firmly in place, at times even expanding, despite the fact that postwar Indonesia was a "masculine enterprise," to borrow from Elleke Boehmer.[137] Sukarnoist visions of a "new society" saw women as confined to biological and economic production, leaving the political value of gendered care work hidden; yet, the conditions of war had enabled Indonesian women to put themselves on the front lines, making apparent a layer of "domestic nationalism" that had been there, but barely acknowledged in public media or policy, for decades.

As the priorities of nutrition and health remained pressing for the fledgling nation, some ministerial offices actively recruited women as participants in enacting their policies, lending a new dimension to this analysis. As explored in the next chapter, the Ministry of Health took the official position that "the issue of nutrition is a National matter,"[138] and domestic matters of the home—with women as key actors—were pursued as policy explicitly leading to national improvement. Women were trained and employed as healthcare professionals and outreach workers, and many more caregivers embraced change in their own homes. Women were tasked with achieving the greater prosperity of the nation through quotidian activities of care work, making Indonesia, in Sukarno's own words, "stand on its own feet." The emancipatory possibilities of their wartime gendered experience, akin to Europe's 1910s "wartime cultures of care,"[139] might have been rooted in the values of domesticity and the rhetoric of motherhood, but were nonetheless deployed to political ends.

Keluarga Pontjodarmo jang terdiri dari ajah, ibu dan dua orang anak lelaki dan perempuan, bernama Sadhono dan Sri.

FIGURE 5.1 "The Pontjodarmo family, consisting of father, mother, and two children, a boy and a girl, named Sadhono and Sri." Source: Suwardjo. *Menudju ke Kemakmuran Desa*, 195?, p. 4, Cornell University Library

5 | PROSPERITY

THE 1950S PUBLICATION "TOWARDS VILLAGE Prosperity," authored by Suwardjo, the head of the Office for People's Agriculture (Djawatan Pertanian Rakjat, an office within the Ministry of Agriculture), presented a model family leading Indonesia toward agriculture-based prosperity.[1] *Pak* Pontjodarmo's family lived in a rural village somewhere in Java. The couple and two children, depicted in the image above, inhabited a small but well-fitted home: each room had large enough windows to let in good sunlight and facilitate airflow; the floor was paved, "dry and clean"; they had a latrine and sewer; and alongside larger crops, the surplus of which they sold, they grew vegetables and medicinal plants for their own use too. Both children attended school, while the parents took care of the land; when in difficulty, they reached out to the government-sponsored Village Education Center (Balai Pendidikan Masjarakat Desa, BPMD) for advice, and shared their knowledge with neighbors and friends. *Ibu* Pontjodarmo worked the land and produced items to sell at the market; also, she had recently learned how to read and write, and regularly participated—and led—discussion sessions with the other women of the village on matters of nutrition (see Figure 5.1).[2]

We can find a counterpart to *Pak* Pontjodarmo's prosperous family in *Pak* Mertani, who appeared in 1958 on the pages of the outreach newsletter "Agriculture," issued by the Ministry of Agriculture. He was the epitome of a "poor peasant." The article presented the challenges of poverty in mid-century rural Java,[3] and the need for the government to improve life for the millions of *Pak* Mertanis: "The first goal is to provide employment and livelihood, so that our people have enough food, clothes, housing and health insurance. // Besides fighting to eradicate poverty, we aspire to improve the education and culture of our people too."[4]

His life "has consistently been below the minimum standard of decent living,"[5] asserted the author, but his condition was redeemable:

> In this age of independence [*kemerdekaan*] and progress [*kemadjuan*], we the Indonesian people [*bangsa*], are trying to achieve development in all fields. . . . We must provide practical guidance and education to *Pa[k]* Mertani and must also think further about efforts to improve his life.[6]

Ultimately, *Pak* Mertani was "ignorant,"[7] and what he needed most was guidance:

> [a] village man who knows nothing, has never owned shoes, has not yet used a toothbrush, and rarely bathes with soap . . . *Pa[k]* Mertani is satisfied with a full belly, even though he is far from fulfilling the requirements of the "4 for health, 5 for perfection" [nutritional guidelines]. . . . His [unsuitable] home is inhabited by husband and wife and four children, and obviously it does not follow health regulations.[8]

———

The merely oblique presence of an *Ibu* Mertani, versus the clear character of *Ibu* Pontjodarmo, is not coincidental. Neither is the fact that nutrition is given space as a matter of conversation and learning for *Ibu* Pontjodarmo, and one that is ignored by the Mertanis. For the first time, in the 1950s, women's labor of social reproduction was overtly pictured as crucial to Indonesia's projection of national stability and flourishing, and they were thus now targeted for basic literacy and broader education efforts.[9]

Indonesia's *kesejahteraan* ("prosperity, wellbeing") came to be articulated by political freedom (*merdeka*) and translated into active policy as socio-economic stability. Ideologically, as the fledgling nation-state struggled to assert itself vis-à-vis internal challenges and international pressures, the Surkanoist political establishment leaned heavily on non-confessional, if not outright secular, discourses. In the 1950s, then, Islam was mostly absent from the government-shaped public arena, even though, as I discuss further in the Epilogue, religious and Islamic ideals did find their way into writings about infant care and maternal health, including family planning, at this time.

At the highest levels of government, the prosperity of nation and people was to be achieved via increased agricultural output and good nutrition; biomedical maternal and child health (MCH) and public health in general; and improved education and literacy. In 1951, Minister of Health Johannes Leimena asserted that the "physical, mental and social wellbeing" of Indonesian citizens was necessary to enable people to work at their fullest, bringing "happiness and joy." Further, "This effort is part of a larger effort, namely state development."[10] A few years later, speaking to an international audience, he would assert "the importance of the health of the people for the upbuilding of the country."[11]

In his programmatic speeches, Leimena did not point at the role of women, but key policies developed by the Ministry throughout the 1950s explicitly called on them, and openly acknowledged their role. The increased awareness of this dynamic was most evident in the fields of nutrition and MCH. While this mirrored earlier attempts at pursuing policies that would foster professionalized expertise and health literacy, it is only in the 1950s that some women rose to higher positions of leadership, bringing a nationwide impact.

In 1950 Dr. Poorwo Soedarmo, director of the Institute for People's Nutrition (the colonial-era Instituut voor Volksvoeding, which was now the Lembaga Makanan Rakjat, or LMR for short), reportedly stated that the improvement of nutrition was "a national matter."[12] The LMR aimed to achieve this goal by transforming Indonesians into a *nutrition-minded* population—an English term frequently appearing in policy papers and reports. Since the driving force behind this initiative was seen in professionalized experts and informed consumers, particularly in rural areas, women were directly targeted for their involvement.[13]

This exploration, focused on nutrition improvement and MCH, brings to the fore two dynamics which operated on parallel tracks, but analytically connect with each other to further nuance our understanding of Indonesia's "domestic nationalism." On the one hand, I show that in the early years of postwar nation-building, the breakdown of the putative boundary between private "womanly matters" (home-domestic) and politics (national-public) appeared most clearly to policymakers and ordinary women themselves. Women were executors of new modes of food production, preparation, and consumption; they continued to further distribute knowledge to their peers in the press and through outreach activities; and they expanded their footprint, as professionalized experts and government advisors. Indonesia's quest for prosperity followed a pattern of national development that brought to the fore an explicit reliance on gendered activities of care work, whether pursued in the private space of the home or a public institution.

On the other hand, as I place these efforts in the context of the Cold War and the emerging landscape of international assistance for "underdeveloped" countries—a new take on the civilizing mission of earlier decades—it also becomes clear that Indonesia's apparent nation-building ambitions belied the country's interest in and partial reliance on global powers. As the leader of a postcolonial and non-aligned nation, Sukarno advocated for self-reliance and voiced reluctance to accept foreign aid—a position later articulated as Indonesia's desire to "stand on its own feet," or berdikari.[14] But behind the scenes much of his government's policy efforts relied on the support of the United States and international agencies. As shown by Sunil Amrith, the "ambivalent positions" of the non-aligned movement allowed for America's direct influence, and similarly allowed UN agencies to "carve a space, between American hegemony and the aspirations of Asian nation-builders."[15] The activities of the LMR, for example, had been revived in collaboration with the Food and Agriculture Organization (FAO); the soon-to-be head of the MCH Welfare Department had spent time abroad with World Health Organization (WHO) sponsorship; many ministerial officers had received support from the Rockefeller Foundation; and even as Sukarno publicly rejected American assistance, the US Foreign Service sent agriculture and health experts across Indonesia starting in 1951.

This was not a purely "ambivalent" strategy on Indonesia's part. As articulated by Soewardjo in 1955, Indonesia was not planning on blankly adopting exogenous models, but, in accepting aid, rather intended to engage in a process of adaptation, choosing its own pathways to implement the international support. One of such departures was to amplify the role of Indonesian women and their activities of care work; it is worth keeping in mind that this was taking place decades ahead of the global pivot toward the role of women in development.[16] Another divergence was an explicit rejection of the American model of capital-intensive mechanized agriculture.

With such balancing acts, the expanded "domestic arena" that had contained home and nation explicitly since the 1940s (and implicitly since the 1920s) would come to embrace the additional domain of geopolitical liminality. In the 1950s, "domestic nationalism" thus blurred the apparent dichotomy between national and international spheres as foreign aid was directed toward initiatives for national development rooted in nutrition and infant care, activities still conventionally conducted by women in the space of the home.

IMPROVING NUTRITION FOR NATIONAL STRENGTH

As discussed in Chapter 2, the colonial-era Instituut voor Volksvoeding had been established in 1934 as an offshoot of the Chemical Laboratory, with the primary goal of continuing research on vitamins, and then expanding to the nutritional values of local foodstuffs, and ensuring the safety of commercialized products; it will be recalled that in the 1930s the laboratory supported certain marketing claims about Islamic compliance too. But its postwar re-embodiment had set different priorities and strategies. Reopened in 1949, the LMR explicitly reformulated its goal "to assist in 'building a strong and healthy nation by improving people's nutrition and promoting family health and living conditions.'"[17] Their primary audience was women.

The work of the LMR was the topic of a mid-1950 article in the already introduced newsletter of the Association of Housewives in Indonesia (*De Huisvrouw in Indonesië*).[18] The anonymous author—who can be inferred to be an Indonesian woman with good knowledge of Dutch—presented the intentions of, and steps taken by, the new government to promote wellbeing through good nutrition; but she nonetheless criticized some of its outreach strategies, which she saw as ineffective in building connections with "village women." In this section I follow the insightful analysis of this anonymous author to explore the complex dynamics tying together nation-building, women's labor, and the politics of international aid.

Food and Politics

Throughout the 1950s, output growth had stagnated, as food production increases had not kept up with the population—which had been expanding at over two percent per year. Per capita availability of basic staples lagged behind prewar levels,[19] and malnutrition was widespread across Java and the archipelago.[20] Eighty-five percent of the population lived in the rural areas and engaged in agricultural labor,[21] with most farmers cultivating less than one acre of land. Hence, ninety percent of the available farmland was worked for subsistence rather than profit-making commercial purposes. Sukarno's developmental model, then, charted a labor-intensive subsistence agriculture, and most policies were directed to the nutrition and overall wellbeing of the farmers.[22] As argued by Soewardjo, Indonesian farmers needed to be lifted from "hunger and difficulty" through education. In the Pancasila framework, dominant at the time, this was aimed at the emergence of a vigorous rural society through mutual help.[23] People's conditions were microcosms of the national condition. Director Soedarmo's quote, "The issue of nutrition is a National matter," was then further glossed to clarify that "improving food means improving the prosperity of the population."

Readers of the women's press had been primed since the 1930s to be attuned to matters of nutrition as a pillar of good health alongside hygiene, and to see a broader relevance for "housewifery." And the Dutch government had seen health as fundamental to the maintenance of colonial order. But in 1950, our anonymous author writing in *De Huisvrouw in Indonesië* made it clear that with the advent of the nation-state, both the government and the people it administered—now citizens—were working toward a common goal. It was based on this connection that Blue Band and Bendera had launched their new advertisements (discussed in the previous chapter), and that *Wanita* had claimed that cooking healthy food contributed to "shaping a strong state."[24] The implications of nutrition had expanded much further than one's own home, becoming overtly political. Further, food not only linked home life to national prosperity, it also carried global importance, demonstrating a tension between national and international politics. The article in *De Huisvrouw in Indonesië* would conclude stating that "improving food is the first step to achieving world peace. Because peace will not be achieved unless most of the population no longer suffers from hunger."[25]

The Global North held a postwar concern for "hunger-eradication": in the new Cold War order, food security was seen as a bulwark against the spread of communism.[26] On the premise that hunger bred socio-economic discontent, in 1949 US President Truman had announced a development program for "underdeveloped countries." Not much different from the

Marshall Plan in spirit, the so-called Point Four Program aimed to distribute international assistance to support the "people who are barefooted, diseased and hungry."[27] Beginning in 1951, the Technical Cooperation Administration (TCA, transformed into the ICA in 1955), promoted public health, education, and advances in agriculture as necessary conditions for the assertion of peace and stability, and ultimately capitalism. Indonesia was one of its targets.

American physicians employed by the US Public Health Services, for example, were active in the TCA Mission to Indonesia since the earliest days of the initiative.[28] Sukarno's tightrope, however, would keep their visibility to a minimum. The US had made it known that they were "prepared" to support Indonesia with technical assistance under the Point Four Program as early as March 1950.[29] And Sukarno had initially appeared open to accepting it, "provided [the USA] did not make too big a beginning and 'too much noise about it.'"[30] For months Sukarno continued to state his "desire" for American "friendship and support," but asked for "no great publicity or US-flag-waving involved," expressing a preference for "more books but no agents," as quoted in Ambassador Cochran's note from March 1951.[31] No agreements were signed nor ratified for months,[32] and so Cochran shifted his focus. He suggested that the US could reduce its footprint in Indonesia, since several areas of governmental cooperation overlapped with those of UN agencies, and even with those of private organizations such as the Rockefeller Foundation. These areas were: agriculture, public health, and small industries.[33]

But the Western Bloc did not have monopoly over international aid. Indonesia was a leader in the Non-Aligned Movement, and as suggested by Bradley Simpson, it was "one of the few countries in the world where US and Soviet officials competed directly for influence."[34] In 1954 the Soviet Union, by then under Khrushchev, launched what *The New York Times* called "the Kremlin's Point IV Program,"[35] and hosted Indonesian medical officers at the USSR Medical Congress in Tashkent.[36] However, in matters of health the Western Bloc would prevail—largely because of its influence over the United Nations: whereas the USSR had withdrawn from the body in 1949, the US would use it to bring healthcare professionals and researchers to America and its allies for further training.

Amid the Cold War and Sukarno's desire to project a non-aligned stand, the United Nations' agencies emerged as far more visible than US aid, and

home-centered initiatives would be privileged because they were not perceived as engendering or indexing foreign political influence. In this context, then, the FAO, WHO, and UNICEF brought nutrition and maternal
and child health to the forefront, and a few Indonesian women would go to
the US with ICA funding to study home economics.[37]

The role of international agencies was evident to our anonymous writer,
and that involvement was discussed with no apparent criticism.

> The Institute for People's Nutrition in Jakarta has strong relations with
> other institutes abroad that also work on nutrition. // The FAO congress
> of the United Nations that was held in Southeast Asia in 1948 held very
> strong meaning for Indonesia.[38]

The FAO had established a line of communication with Indonesia even
before the transfer of sovereignty, laying the ground for a first visit and
immediate active cooperation as early as in 1950–1951. FAO nutrition expert
André G. Van Veen—whom we have seen in Chapter 2, previously employed at the colonial Institute for Nutrition (now the LMR) in the 1930s
and briefly again in 1948—had returned to Java in April 1951 at the invita-
tion of the Indonesian government to support the development of a nutrition policy.[39]

During this visit, Van Veen and Soedarmo charted a course of action
for the improvement of Indonesians' nutrition by addressing sustained
food shortages, the implications of malnourishment for overall health conditions and infections, concerns over infant malnutrition, and the lack of
knowledge about nutrition among the *rakyat*.[40] Showing the multipronged
approach to the challenge, this collaboration with the FAO led to the formation of the inter-ministerial National Commission for the Improvement
of Nutrition (Panitia Negara Perbaikan Makanan).[41] Housed in the LMR, it
brought together an enormous number of representatives, from the ministries of Interior, Health, Agriculture, Social Affairs, and Education, Teaching and Culture (PPK), among them.

Alongside many (male) technocrats were some women as well, who had
been active in earlier manifestations of that liminal space between gendered
care work and politics; they were few in numbers, but yielded strong influence on shaping policies. Both Soejatin Kartowijono and Erna Djajadiningrat, members of the Commission, had a past as teachers at girls' domestic

schools, Revolution-era activists, and leaders of women organizations; both had been in charge of public kitchens during the war, and were now upper-level officials at the PPK.[42]

Their perspectives and experiences shaped the work of the Commission, where the expansion of nutrition education emerged as its core strategy. Tasked with developing a holistic nutrition policy that would take into account all the various facets of the problem, from biomedical health and agricultural production to schooling and outreach programs,[43] in 1954 the Commission delineated a plan that relied on the formation of a new class of professionals and their employment as outreach workers and experts. Placed in hospitals, MCH clinics, and "home extensions" across the archipelago, these young women were expected to transform Indonesians into a "nutrition-minded" people.[44]

Forming Experts

As pointedly remarked by our anonymous author, "In Indonesia, there is still a shortage of food experts." This was the result of Dutch disinterest in fostering indigenous expertise (as already discussed), and the mass exodus of European scientists in the 1940s.[45] During the Japanese occupation and the years of Revolution, many Dutch professionals had either fled the Indies or died, leaving behind a vacuum of expertise. The few Indonesians that had staffed the laboratories were likely too few to maintain them, if still alive and professionally active.

The first response had been to welcome a new group of foreigners, now labeled "advisers"; preferably, they were not Dutch. During his 1952 trip to Indonesia, FAO Director N.E. Dodd recorded how "several [Indonesian officials] have explained to me that while they have high regards for Dutch technicians as individuals, they would be concerned because of their colonial background and would prefer to have technicians from some other country."[46] Some (like Van Veen) had evidently established good enough relations with their then-colonized colleagues to be welcomed back, but most "foreign experts" from now on would be North Americans.

Longer term, however, the solution needed to rest in the formation of local expertise. As indicated by the early conversations between Soedarmo and Van Veen, and further stressed in the work of the National Commission, Indonesia's plan to improve living standards was primarily to train Indonesians and pursue an education-based approach to the "nutrition problem." As outlined in the *De Huisvrouw in Indonesië* article,

> As a first step, it is urgent to establish secondary educational centers for girls to study cooking and knowledge about food, schools higher than the [junior high schools for domestic education] S.K.P. . . . // This year, it is hoped that the above-mentioned educational institution will open in Jakarta, where girls can be trained to become food experts. . . . In the future, this professional field will be open to many girls and women.[47]

The LMR established a School for Nutritionists (Sekolah Ahli Dieet) in 1950,[48] and shortly after a Vocational School for Nutrition Outreach (Sekolah Juru Penerangan Makanan).[49] The more advanced School for Nutritionists enrolled young women who had already graduated as teachers from the Schools for Teachers of Girls' Domestic Schools (Sekolah Guru Kepandaian Puteri, SGKP, senior high school level); its sister institution, the Vocational School for Nutrition Outreach, admitted instead graduates of the Girls' Domestic Schools (Sekolah Kepandaian Puteri, SKP, junior high school level).[50] These nutrition schools were somewhat reminiscent of John Lee Hydrick's *mantri* school at Purwokerto, but the hope was that these new institutes, requiring a lower level of education, could attract larger numbers of pupils.

These schools had a large pool of applicants. Data is scarce for these early years, but, for example, the SGKP in Yogyakarta had graduated on average thirty teachers at each of the three exam sessions held between January 1951 and September 1952, while that year alone in Jakarta the SGKP had enrolled close to 400 pupils, and the SKP had enrolled 340.[51] Yet, administrative and financial barriers prevented these schools from achieving their full potential[52]—often because of structural problems created by the government itself.[53]

There were at least two separate challenges: first, the lack of Indonesian expertise—which the schools were supposed to help solve—meant that in their earliest iterations the courses were taught by Dutch nationals.[54] A reliable pipeline would be achieved by 1953–1954, but the Minister of Health estimated that in 1954, after a few cohorts had finished their course of studies, there were only fourteen trained dietitians available. The plan had originally envisioned 160 dieticians available at the regencies' level, another 13 for the laboratories, and 10 stationed across the largest hospitals. The discrepancy was even more dramatic for assistant dieticians. Nevertheless, by 1957 the numbers of employed graduates had almost doubled, with twenty-five dieticians and sixty-eight junior outreach workers.[55]

The primary task of these schools was to train urban (lower) middle-class women seeking professional employment (as *ahli dieet*, or nutritionists, and *juru makan*, or outreach dieticians, see Figure 5.2); as stated in the article, "The employment of these girls will cover our entire archipelago." Under the broader umbrella of nutrition-education, their activities would vary.

FIGURE 5.2   The office of a nutritionist employed by the Ministry of Health. Source: Poorwo Soedarmo. *Dapur Indonesia Djaman Baru*, Djakarta: Djambatan, 1952, p. 51, Cornell University Library

The graduates of the higher-level School for Nutritionists would return to their positions as teachers in the Girls' Domestic Schools (SKP) with new specialist knowledge on nutrition. Graduates of the lower-level school would instead travel to the peri-urban kampungs for house visits, or to rural areas to offer lectures at the Village Education Centers (BPMDs)—like the one *Ibu* Pontjodarmo would have visited. Any of them would have been qualified to transmit their knowledge to the fast-growing numbers of literate women by writing in magazines such as *De Huisvrouw in Indonesië*, *Wanita*, *Karya*, *Suara 'Aisjijah*, *Suara Perwari*, and the many others that continued to pop up.

The second challenge faced by the schools for nutrition emerged from their geographic concentration in urban centers, which limited the potential for achieving broader results, both in terms of recruitment and impact. Mirroring strategies seen at play at Purwokerto, this challenge was obviated with short training sessions for local cadres in the rural areas. In Central Java, for example, where the FAO became involved through a regional "Nutrition Project" originally meant to be expanded nationally, the courses lasted about a week, and were run multiple times a year. In Semarang there were eight courses in 1955, another five in 1956, and nine in 1957.[56] This strategy was yielding positive outcomes, but financial support was not consistent, being only partially funded by the FAO. As noted by the FAO advisor Margaret McArthur, "In 1958 there was no budget for more courses, [and] by 1959 the Board had decided that sufficient cadres were already trained." Whereas the 1959 Indonesian document argued that "the 800 or so cadres scattered throughout Central Java [were] considered sufficient," the FAO complained: "It is much regretted that courses for various Services/Departments, although offered (by the Board), were not carried out because of difficulties within the respective Services/Department." McArthur offered the explanation that responsible units were not able to provide the funds necessary to cover students' expenses. Even when the 1961 budget had included all the expenses, "the Army took over the Training Center."[57] As made clear later in this chapter, and then in the Epilogue, such a development reflected the spirit of late 1950s Indonesia, which was experiencing another major transition: after the declaration of Martial Law in 1957, resources were reallocated, prioritizing the further militarization of the Indonesian state and society, and more generally women would be (once again) pushed to the sidelines of policy.

Outreach

The School for Nutritionists was meant as a site of knowledge transmission to the enrolled pupils, but, in addition, it served as a hub for propagation to a wider audience, as stated by our anonymous author: "They [these graduates] will also educate others and provide information to the broader population." That work would take a variety of forms.

In this section I look at multiple approaches to outreach pursued with the aim of shaping a "nutrition-minded" population. I first take the vantage point of two nutritionists. One was Soekamto, a nutritionist at the LMR who likely also had a masked persona, as I argue she wrote under a pseudonym in *Wanita*, the middle- and upper-class popular women's magazine. The other was the fictional Sukarsih, the main character in one of the LMR books; she represented an outreach worker in the peri-urban kampungs of Jakarta. Next, I explore nutrition outreach in the rural areas following the sharp criticism expressed on the pages of *De Huisvrouw in Indonesië*, and focusing on the differential efficacy of theoretical instruction and practical demonstrations.

Nj. Soelasmi Soekamto was one of the first women to graduate from the School for Nutritionists. Previously a teacher, Soekamto had been hired at the Institute for Nutrition as assistant to Soedarmo shortly after graduation, and strong in her skills, she was appointed to coordinate the efforts of the LMR with the office tasked with women's initiatives at the Ministry of Education. Van Veen also recommended her for an FAO fellowship,[58] and by December 1951 she was *en route* to Manila for a two-month study trip.[59] In 1953, Soekamto became head of the Vocational School for Nutrition Outreach, and joined the "Third Nutrition Conference" held by the FAO and WHO in Bandung. This was the first of several international gatherings she participated in throughout the decade,[60] until terminating her work for the LMR in 1957.[61]

Soekamto's impact was much broader, though, as—I suggest—she was extremely active in the women's press, educating the larger public under the pseudonym (or just abbreviated name, as was common practice in Indonesia) "S.K.T." S.K.T. had been regularly publishing on matters of nutrition in *Wanita*, reliably combining scientific knowledge—because "women ought to know about our bodies' needs"[62]—with practical suggestions for food preservation and meal planning. The focus was on ingredients readily available in Indonesia at the time, anchoring the theoretical message of "good nutrition" to the feasibility of feeding a family healthily and on a budget. Soekamto's influence on *Wanita* was acknowledged by her becoming a member of the magazine's editorial board in the first half of 1951,[63] just as *Wanita*'s influence was recognized by the monthly newsletter of the Organization for Scientific Research in Indonesia as the publication with the most articles on nutrition.[64]

We can get a glimpse of another possible life for a graduate of the LMR schools through Sukarsih, the main character of "The Indonesian Kitchen of the New Era." Published in 1952, this booklet was framed as "a book to fill the spare time of mothers" (or "women" in general), and as a reviewer noted, "the price (Rp. 4,50 in stores) should not be a big obstacle for readers in our nation;"[65] one might infer an imagined middle- and upper-class readership of women who had "spare time." "The Indonesian Kitchen of the New Era," then, instructed its readers on how to cook healthy and affordable meals "to achieve happiness inside and outside the home!"[66]

Yet, it was also a popular instructive booklet, and a manual to be used by outreach workers. Each chapter is modeled on the *sandiwara* theatrical vignette[67]—a narrative "method still today appreciated by many of our people," the reviewer reminded his readers.[68] The sketches presented scenes pertinent to a variety of settings: the young child who doesn't like to eat, the *becak* (pedicab) driver, the athletic adolescent, and the newly pregnant woman. In her conversations with the various people she encountered, the fictional character Sukarsih explained conversationally—"as simply as possible"[69]—the meaning of "calories" and the sources and functions of the different nutrients contained in various foods. She offered detailed instructions on how to cook rice and vegetables to maximize their nutritional value, suggested menus, and provided shopping lists appropriate to the energy expenditure and wallets of her "patients."

As graduates of the LMR schools, both the real Soelasmi Soekamto and the fictional Sukarsih, in their roles as professionalized experts, enjoyed mobility far beyond their own neighborhoods and had an independent source of income, all while conforming to societal expectations of gendered responsibilities, and fulfilling a national duty. They were government employees, worked for "the prosperity of the people," and in a field determined to be "a national matter" (Figure 5.3).

From the vantage point of the rural *rakyat*, however, the educational strategies embraced by the LMR seemed less effective, at least according

FIGURE 5.3   A nutritionist visiting a kampung. Source: Poorwo Soedarmo. *Dapur Indonesia Djaman Baru*, Djakarta: Djambatan, 1952, p. 11, Cornell University Library

to our source. The anonymous author I introduced earlier, who had written for *De Huisvrouw in Indonesië* in early 1950, had pointedly remarked that "information [about appropriate and beneficial food combinations] is mostly conveyed with illustrations and demonstrations at *pasar malam*,"— the night fairs the colonial-era public health propaganda office had often patronized. She continued:

> However, it would be better if such information were directly given to the people. *Initiatief particulier* [non-governmental initiatives] could provide a lot of help in this matter. We have heard that [the women's organization] Perwari has proposed to train some of their [members], so that they can [in turn] offer cooking demonstrations in the villages.

> These women would receive lessons [. . .] through the Institute [for Peo-
> ple's Nutrition]. What is primarily given attention to in these educa-
> tional events, is the preparation of food. In this way we can directly get
> close to the women in the villages.[70]

Our anonymous author thus suggested that the LMR could be more effective in propagating nutrition education if it adopted the hands-on strategies
of women's organizations, rather than methods promoting passive, indirect
modes of knowledge transmission, such as booths at fairs. The model was
Perwari, a group, the author claimed, which had devised a way to establish
a direct connection with rural women by going to the villages and showing
them how to prepare food. However, this was not a new strategy: it will be
recalled that demonstration units had already been the hallmark of Hydrick's rural hygiene work in the 1930s, and especially so in his work with
women—in addition to the Rockefeller Foundation's original approach that
privileged doing over telling, it had been Hydrick's concern with educating
rural women (and traditional birth attendants) that had supported the expansion of home visits vis-à-vis lectures.

Out of political necessity and a nationalist desire for self-assertion, in
the context of post-colonialism and the Cold War, Indonesia exhibited
skepticism toward the potential impact of colonial-era strategies and new
international assistance programs. At the same time, politicians, policymakers, and commentators all sought points of strength in indigenous
practices and national values. While superficially complementary, these
two dynamics render manifest an intrinsic tension in Indonesia's postwar
trajectory toward "modernization."

Extensions

The criticism we read in *De Huisvrouw in Indonesië* article was not an iso-
lated case. In the opening to this chapter, I introduced the Office for People's Agriculture and its Village Education Centers, the rural units the
Pontjodarmo family was said to rely on for their enrichment and education
in matters of farming, finance, literacy, nutrition, etc. The establishment of
BPMDs had been spearheaded during the Revolution but only came to full
realization beginning in 1950 through the work of Ignatius Kasimo, Teko
Sumodiwirjo, and Soewardjo.

All three had been involved in rural reconstruction projects since the colonial era, and in several ways these postwar institutions mirrored the Dutch agricultural extensions. However, as recently argued by Sebastiaan Broere, plans for the BPMDs were formulated in an anti-colonial framework, and the Centers themselves were shaped as crucial spaces for decolonization: the postwar Centers promoted mass education instead of "personal contact" between expert and farmer, and socialized the idea of community self-help (which they called "auto-activity") as a driver of national self-reliance instead of individual accomplishment. The BPMDs, then, "identified peasant participation as crucial to rural reconstruction, [and] value[d] local knowledge and peasant skills," in order to reject foreign assistance.[71]

However, the BPMDs, being rural extension services, became the site of sustained negotiations between two powers: foreign models of development—especially American—and Indonesians' visions of localized strategies for prosperity. This struggle becomes easier to see when pursuing an analysis of extension services that interweaves its multiple temporal, spatial, and thematic layers, moving from its origins in Progressive-era America to Cold War Asia, from political discourse to gender roles and, of course, involving economic development.

The Kasimo Plan had omitted any mention of international assistance. This had been a deliberate political statement, because the BPMDs' activities were instead being spearheaded and supported through international aid. As stated in Van Veen's 1951 report to the FAO, the rural extensions (namely, the BPMDs themselves) should be diffusion centers of FAO-directed nutrition propaganda.[72] By 1954, the same idea was featured prominently in the report of the National Commission for the Improvement of Nutrition, in which the rural "home extension" was deemed the main venue for rural activities aimed at turning Indonesians into a "nutrition-minded" people. Both terms were referred to in English. In 1953, the Office for People's Agriculture had been translated as "Extension Service" in a booklet illustrating the work of the BPMDs. Authored by Soewardjo and published by the Indonesian Ministry of Agriculture, it was in both Indonesian and English, and acknowledged the support of the TCA Agricultural Extension Specialist Fayette Parvin.

Despite Indonesian leaders' best efforts, it had not been possible to opt out of the increasingly eager international network of aid that saw extension services as a Cold War anti-communist strategy. In the 1950s, then, the US Foreign Service (and, by proxy, international aid agencies) deployed public health officers, agronomists and home economists throughout the "underdeveloped world" to promote a blueprint of the "American Dream" on the global stage. Concerned by the perception of skyrocketing population growth in Asia, the lion's share of international aid went into agricultural mechanization (i.e., the Green Revolution) as the preferred avenue for food security.[73] This approach was grounded in social scientific research, and it enshrined a new flavor of civilizationism not dissimilar from that of the colonial era. This developmentalist postulate promoted the American values of individualism and productivity in an ultimate bid to connect modernization and mechanization to capitalism and democracy.[74]

But this now-globalized American model of development differed much from Indonesia's. The latter's vision of mass advancement had been conceived within the political ideology of the Pancasila and connected to Sukarno's vision of a centralized economy grounded in subsistence farming. The BPMDs supported the rural peasantry logistically through strong social welfare, and psychologically by advancing principles of mutual help.[75]

So-called American values were not part of Sukarno's political agenda, which was already influenced by socialism, and had started to inch toward authoritarianism.[76] But public health was emerging as a "less politically sensitive" field, as noted by Sunil Amrith.[77] A few months after Sukarno hosted the "Asia-Africa Conference" in Bandung, which would lay the foundation for the Non-Aligned Movement, Soewardjo was in Bhopal, India participating at the "Workshop on Extension Program and Plan of Work" convened by the FAO, UNESCO, and ICA in 1955.

Indonesia was thus firmly situated in the global circuit of aid, but navigated this space on its own terms, often challenging suggested strategies. When Soewardjo presented his paper at Bhopal, he championed the strength of rural development in Indonesia, emphasizing the crucial role played by farm women with their initiative and labor. Conversely, he criticized the international model because it had structurally relegated farm women to their homes. It was not accidental that Soewardjo's booklet introducing the BPMDs had depicted *Ibu* Pontjodarmo as active in agricultural production as well as domestic work.

American women had historically assumed shifting roles as economic producers. If during World War I and World War II, they were fully mobilized, by the 1950s, they were pushed back into the confines of the kitchen—now spaces of status assertion, consumerism, and the "Western way of life," rather than economic production.[78] These dynamics mirrored developments of the Progressive era. Ideas of housewifery and domesticity had begun to spread then, when Seaman Knapp, Liberty Hyde Bailey, and Ruby Smith had devised the system of extensions to disseminate basic literacy, principles of hygiene, and agricultural innovations to rural men and women. Emerging in early twentieth-century America, they employed a dual structure in which farm and home bureaus became gender-separate sites of education and expertise. The former expected a male-only audience interested in agricultural production; the latter engaged women on matters of home management and childcare: what would later become "home economics." This division reinforced the paradigm of "separate spheres," but also allowed rural women in the United States to gain knowledge and professionalization in "gendered expertise."[79]

The 1950s Indonesian system of "extensions," then, differed from the originating American model, as women were cardinal actors in the agricultural production of food as much as in its preservation and consumption choices. We see this difference clearly as we focus on the active life of *Ibu* Pontjodarmo and the omission of a well-formed character for *Ibu* Mertani. Soewardjo further articulated this point in Bhopal. He was clear that in Indonesia village agricultural courses were explicitly held

> for the adult farmers, both men and women, who wish to advance in their agricultural efforts. . . . Classes are given separately to the males and females, although both lectures are performed for the purpose of developing a progressive farming community, with its agricultural undertakings. The lectures deal with improved farm practices in the village and its environment.[80]

The involvement of women in farming was not only a facet of nationalist propaganda. It was visually evident in publications for farmers too, as seen in pictures printed in the magazine "Agriculture," for example, which explicitly showed Indonesian women working in the fields.[81] This was recorded by anthropologists. In her book *The Javanese Family*, research for which took place in the early 1950s, Hildred Geertz explained the "very strong" position of women in Java as a result of men's ineptitude with money and

their inability to care for themselves. She saw women in charge of all financial matters, with husbands regularly surrendering their income to their
wives. In agricultural settings, women were responsible for harvesting the
rice, including managing its sale, and handling the subsequent profit and
other expenditures. Besides farming, village women were employed in a variety of occupations too—from petty and wholesale trade to manufacturing
and teaching.[82]

Decades before international agencies would begin to talk explicitly
about women's role in rural development,[83] Soewardjo, then, explained
at Bhopal why and how Indonesia differed from the path to development
that the West had imagined for it. Indonesia was one of the few countries
that both rejected capital-intensive innovations, and explicitly integrated
women in rural extension work, addressing them as decision-makers in the
process of agricultural innovation.

> In conclusion it should be noted that the farm women [in Indonesia]
> play a big roll [sic] in agricultural progress. This has been known since
> earlier days but the service has not yet given it appropriate attention. It
> is a fact that women have the leadership in the homes, men are only the
> executors. Besides being the leaders in the homes, the farm-women take
> an active part in the growing of rice and the cultivation of fields and
> garden. It sometimes happens that men get advice from the service, for
> instance concerning the application of fertilizer, which will mean a new
> expenditure. This will sometimes prove to be a failure because it does
> not have the agreement of the wives. The women have to be convinced
> before the new step can be carried out. This is easily understood since
> the wives are responsible for the maintenance of the homes. Because of
> this fact and many others the People's Agricultural Service in the last 3
> years [since 1952] devotes more attention to the education of the farm-
> women and girls and includes women in the daily activities.
>
> . . . Village agricultural courses for women, schools for farm-women
> and rural women clubs are found at several places on Java and the other
> islands.[84]

Soewardjo's paper appears to have been internationally influential,
at least until women were sidelined once again. The conference organizers identified the need to draw women and young girls into agricultural

extension programs—a task taken on by deliberation at the "Technical Meeting on Home Economics for South and East Asia" convened a year later (1956) in Tokyo.[85] However change would prove elusive. When delegates gathered for the 1958 "Pan-Pacific and Southeast Asia Women's Conference," they were tasked to specifically discuss "the role of women in the development of rural societies," but in fact the proceedings do not show any effort to include women in productive farming activities. Rather, on that occasion the focus was placed on "fundamental education" (for which UNESCO praised Indonesia as the best in Asia), and on education in health and nutrition to encourage the consumption of rice alternatives.[86] In international circles, the vision of women as actors in agriculture was now discontinued in conversations on actual agricultural production.

In an international environment of developmentalism shaped by modernization theory, international aid agencies were simply not attuned to seeing economic cultural differences as positive contributions. In these early days, even Clifford Geertz's work would lend substance to the idea that Java's economic development had been hindered by local culture as well as by colonial economic strategies, since the prominence of the collectivity over the individual had prevented "primary accumulation in the agricultural sector."[87] In the 1950s the expectations of farmers served by rural extensions—and those of the government officers who administered them—appeared unusual to those who looked at Java and Sumatra through the lens of twentieth-century Euro-America. Even when one of the many American agricultural extension advisers stationed in Java and Sumatra was tasked to work specifically with women, it remains unclear whether her program entailed crafts and handwork or agricultural production.[88]

At the end of the decade, the US had begun to rethink the efficacy of extension services abroad. In 1960, Indonesia was one of only eight countries that still had an agricultural extension adviser in the foreign service.[89] For Howard Beers—professor of rural sociology at the University of Kentucky, and head of the Bogor mission from 1962 to 1966[90]—extension education was an "unorthodox" area of expertise.[91] The focus now was on the transition from basic sciences and agricultural extension education to fisheries, food technology and agricultural processing,[92] reflecting the desire to move away from working with small farmers and push for larger-scale projects.

The withdrawal of extension advisers, including from Indonesia, had been the result of yet another misled application of the one-strategy-fits-all approach. Work in Latin America had revealed that the American model had been "adopted" without "adaptation," and extension services should therefore be stopped as they did not bring the intended benefit.[93] Withdrawing advisers stationed in Indonesia, American developmentalists must have thought that they were remedying a similar mistake in the making. In fact, the way to "adapt" to Indonesia would have simply been to *expand* agricultural extension services there, and to bring in more workers that engaged with women. But that would not occur until at least the late 1970s and 1980s.

In the 1950s the LMR and other Indonesian government scientific institutions leaned on international aid to develop national policies and foster expertise. But as these Indonesian strategies sometimes took such assistance programs in their own directions, and intertwined them with local dynamics, the work of nutrition improvement was advanced by women, at all levels: policymaking, expert knowledge production, outreach, and implementation. As the Village Education Centers provided the physical space to turn Indonesians into a "nutrition-minded" people, so the knowledge being imparted primarily took form as nutrition guidelines.

Guidelines

As seen in previous chapters, knowledge about "vitamins" and the concept of a scientifically balanced diet had been in circulation since the early twentieth century, and boomed in the 1920s to 1930s with the diffusion of nontechnical nutrition science and its marketization. The Japanese propaganda machine in the early 1940s had actively introduced new ingredients and "best practices" for cooking balanced meals in times of scarcity. By 1950, then, the idea that one should eat healthily was widespread, but amid prolonged food shortages and what was perceived to be a sustained lack of pertinent knowledge, many Indonesians remained under- or malnourished.[94]

The article in *De Huisvrouw in Indonesië*, then, zeroed in on the LMR's civic responsibility to guide the *rakyat* in their daily food-consumption choices:

> The primary duty of the Institute is to provide information about appropriate and beneficial food combinations. . . . The Institute for People's Nutrition has the duty to provide information about the make-up of menus, and methods for cooking rice and sweet potatoes with side dishes.[95]

While Soekamto and her peers had been writing about the importance of certain food groups and nutrients, or suggesting ways to handle and cook food, the LMR itself offered an institutional structure to build balanced meal plans. As in the case of outreach strategies and policy development, this analysis of nutritional guidelines offers insights into how food was a liminal space between national and international ideas of progress and between the home and public realms.

In 1951, Institute Director Soedarmo launched a new slogan—"4 Sehat, 5 Sempurna," or "4 for health, 5 for perfection." This general structure for composing nutritious meals (still followed today) promoted a meal of four elements "for health"—namely, carbohydrates, vegetables, proteins, and fruit—with the addition of a fifth component "for perfection"—milk. Its first appearance was likely the introduction to "A Guide to Develop Menus." Penned in November 1951, this booklet contained detailed sample meal plans for Indonesians of all extractions.[96] However, it was only about a year later that the formula came to be popularized, first through "The Indonesian Kitchen of the New Era" (already discussed above), and then in various articles in *Wanita*,[97] *Keluarga*,[98] and *Suara 'Aisjijah*.[99] Soedarmo, home economists, and women writers all discussed this new formula as providing a clear path for women to offer their families, regardless of socio-economic status, a scientifically complete nutrition.

As the many articles in the women's press tended to showcase foods available locally and at affordable prices—the only animal proteins were eggs and chicken, for example—Soedarmo's guidelines similarly reflected, for the most part, the extant limitations of Indonesia's agricultural production and market availability of goods. While some "foreign" foods which had been regularly advertised during the colonial period and were now gradually reappearing (such as oats, cornflakes, peanut butter, *worst*, and margarine) were featured in the meal plans, the illustration of the four fundamental elements of a healthy diet prioritized local produce (e.g., *tempeh*, jackfruit, rice, and eggs). This reflected an awareness of what foods could be available in Indonesia's households and might look familiar.

It is particularly jarring, then, to see milk featured as the fifth, perfecting element: based on established practices and historical dietary preferences, this was the most "foreign" item mentioned. A 1953 booklet presenting basic facts on Indonesia, written for those in the field of development and technical assistance, had, for example, characterized "milk and other dairy products [as] nearly unknown" to Indonesians.[100] And yet, Soedarmo's guidelines granted it a key position. This is the strongest indication of the fact that Soedarmo's slogan was an adaptation of the US wartime "Basic Seven."[101]

In "A Guide to Develop Menus," milk is glossed as "a food easy to digest and very rich in nutrients."[102] In "The Indonesian Kitchen of the New Era," milk held a central position both visually on the cover—where a bottle labeled "MILK," in English, parades alongside other encouraged foods (see Figure 5.4)—and in the narrative text.

In one of the vignettes included there, the fictional character Sukarsih visits Noor, a young woman who has only recently realized she is pregnant. Sukarsih's first suggestion to Noor is that she start drinking milk. Sukarsih explains that Noor's diet ought to be tailored to her new condition, and that she needs more calories to be able to move a heavier body; more proteins, iron, and calcium to build the baby's body; and plenty of vitamins for general health. The ingredient that gets the most attention, then, is milk, as Sukarsih insists that its nutritional benefits for both mother and child, during pregnancy and breastfeeding alike, are well worth the extraordinary expense.[103] Her financial concerns are apparent, even though they lie behind a veil of possibly excessive bourgeois consumption: Noor settles on giving up her desire to own a baby carriage in favor of budgeting for several months of milk consumption.[104]

Milk was not only present in advertisements and in scientific publications. International business interests and aid agencies strongly pushed its consumption too, even though some scientists criticized the trend. While the WHO and UNICEF pushed a global campaign to fight infant malnutrition and protein deficiency by distributing powdered milk and incentivizing dairy production, Van Veen had been adamant since the earliest days that fresh cow milk and powdered milk should both be avoided in Indonesia, or at least not recommended. When plans were made by UN agencies to set up factories to produce powdered milk in India and Indonesia, Van Veen expressed strong concerns over dry-milk degradation in the hot tropical climate.[105] His preference would have been to promote the production and consumption of soymilk, locally known as *susu kedelai* or *saridele*,[106] and already experimented with by Hydrick in the 1930s as a food suitable for infants.[107]

Marjorie Scott—a Canadian FAO nutrition officer—advanced similar criticism of American business interests that had successfully pressured the

Dapur Indonesia djaman baru

PENERBIT DJAMBATAN

FIGURE 5.4 "Choose Us," Cover showing a milk bottle parading among other foods. Source: Poorwo Soedarmo. *Dapur Indonesia Djaman Baru*, Djakarta: Djambatan, 1952, cover, Cornell University Library

ICA mission to Thailand to distribute public nutrition messaging emphasizing the importance of dairy products for a "well rounded diet." Marjorie
Scott's comment was sharp: "It certainly looks as if the Americans will have
all the world drinking and liking milk."[108]

Nevertheless, later in the decade, the monthly magazine of Central
Java's Nutrition Improvement Commission (supported by the FAO) promoted local milk production and consumption—even featuring the milking of cows on the design cover.[109] In 1958, Soedarmo would advocate for
Indonesians to be transformed into a "milking and milk-drinking people,"
and the "Farmers' Almanac" called it a "drink for the *rakjat*." In the 2020s,
Indonesians still consume less than half the per capita milk consumption
of China, and 7% of America's. No transformation materialized, and milk
consumption remains a middle- and upper-class phenomenon.

Soedarmo's decision to bestow the characteristic of "perfection" upon
milk—a product unaffordable for the *rakyat* and unpalatable to many Indonesians—bears echoes of the colonial era. As in the 1920s, when Lactogen
had depicted indigenous women's adoption of expensive infant formula as
their one avenue to potentially achieve modernity, so the 1950s nutritional
guidelines had put perfection out of reach for most Indonesians, suggesting they settle for a lesser alternative. While the cover of "The Indonesian
Kitchen of the New Era" shows a glass bottle with the English writing
"MILK" on it (Figure 5.4), "A Guide to Develop Menus" shows it as a tin of
condensed milk, with a label stating *"susu"* (Ind. "milk").

MOTHERING AS NATION-BUILDING

To conclude, I circle back to mothering as biological labor, a stand-in for
care work, and a discursive framework for nation-building, occasionally
within an explicitly religious framework. In the first half of the twentieth
century, women's contributions to the social, political, economic, physical,
and religious development of Indonesia had been grounded in their "natural" gendered qualities of caregiving. Charged with masculine patriarchal
values, this discursive space could have led to a variety of possible futures.

Through this book I have shown that one outcome of this peculiar
trajectory was the emergence of women as fundamental drivers of progress, and key contributors to the establishment and consolidation of Indonesia as a modern, independent nation-state. Primarily because of the

loss of lives, and the precarities and challenges brought about by extended colonization and exploitation, and by warfare and occupation, women in Java and Sumatra were able to carve out a niche in the professional fields of health, education, and nutrition—in government, private, and religious institutions—crossing domestic and public life, urban and rural settings, class and literacy boundaries.

In the 1950s public discourse, nutrition was transformed from a tool of imperialist assertion and stability (looking back at the origins of the Dutch Institute for Nutrition as well as Japan's reliance on Indonesia as a wartime resource), into a priority for the advancement of the nation. In a parallel rearticulation in metaphor and fact, hygienic birthing—which in the colonial period had been the symbol of gendered modernity—was now a key element to nationalistic ambitions for a labor-intensive agricultural economy. While I return to this more extensively in the Epilogue, it is worth reflecting briefly on the fact that safe birthing was read differently from the political establishment vis-à-vis women. For the former, it meant numerous and strong future citizens; for the latter it translated into a healthier future-self.

In January 1952 the Ministry of Health established a maternal and child health (MCH) welfare unit under the leadership of Dr. Julie Sulianti Saroso. Its primary goal was to expand the government's education efforts beyond professional midwives, and thus include ordinary mothers, *dukun bayis* (of whom over 1,500 had been "educated" in modern techniques of home-birthing by late 1953), and a new cohort of home visitors.[110] The WHO and TCA were heavily invested in the development of Indonesia's medical resources, but writing in the pages of a women's magazine, Sulianti—similar to our anonymous author discussing the work of the LMR in *De Huisvrouw in Indonesië*—underscored that the establishment of this new unit had been driven by women's organizations. Women had shown commitment toward "building a healthy Indonesian nation" through their labor.[111]

When the government publication *Berita Hygiene* announced the same new MCH initiative, it presented the grim outlook of mortality rates as a political problem: a survey of two Jakarta neighborhoods had found that 25.5% of infants had died in their first year of life. The newsletter was clear in its current political purpose: "[Such numbers] hold us back as a people of an independent nation."[112] The implications were clear to Sulianti too. Her mandate was expressly nationalist: infant and maternal health was the "keystone . . . of a healthy Indonesian nation" and women were "the steady pillars" of any infrastructure aimed at improving people's health.[113]

This was in line with S.K.T.'s reflection on the work of nutritionists. Writing about the School for Nutritionists ahead of the March 1952 course,[114] she had argued that

> a big and important responsibility of an independent nation is to shape a strong state. The strength of a nation depends on the condition of its society. Only a healthy society can really work to strengthen its nation. Health is what we must preserve. One way to guard and preserve health is by preparing our daily food with care. And don't think that beneficial foods can only be obtained with a lot of money. And conversely, do not assume that if one has a lot of money, they will necessarily eat healthily. To choose, combine, and prepare our food carefully, with the money we have, is something which needs to permeate in our society, in short: the Indonesian People need to become *nutrition minded* [sic].[115]

The intricacies of nationalist priorities and international assistance, like those of local practices and "foreign" approaches, were similarly made clear by Sulianti when she wrote about MCH for Indonesia's anglophone community of women. In 1953 Sulianti further underlined how the international development approach of focusing on medical professionals would not take Indonesia where it needed to be in terms of MCH:

> But we must not only look at the conditions in countries that in this respect are far ahead of us, but we must try to solve the problem under present circumstances, and we must take into consideration the needs and habits of the population that lives here.[116]

Identifying in the education of mothers the key for improvement, Sulianti reported how the Ministry of Health was seeking young village women interested in becoming "assistants who, after a certain apprenticeship under supervision of trained instructors, can then work especially among the rural population." Female home visitors ought to be at least 18 years of age, and have completed the "Sekolah Rakyat" (between four and six years of primary school).[117] The course duration would add between a year and a year and a half to their studies. Sulianti's mother-centered health education drive stressed three key points: the reasons why better nutrition translated into better health; how to handle food to retain its nutritional potential; and which foods were locally available and had the best nutritional outlook.[118]

It was of utmost importance that these home visitors be "from the *desa*" (rural village) and that upon graduation they would "be appointed there," thus being able to transmit their knowledge to (other) village women as peers. Depending on their starting level of education and the kind of course they had attended, graduates of these courses received varying degrees of medical training and scientific instruction. At times it would be just enough to bridge the gap between ordinary *desa* women and midwives. But they were expected to understand local mores too, and be attuned to potential complications emerging from non-medical aspects of their interlocutors' lives. They were to be "the all-seeing eye (eyes on stalks) of the midwife, looking around on her behalf in the houses and reporting anything and everything abnormal." Alongside improved economic conditions, the key to lowering mortality rates for mothers and infants was identified in broad education efforts and the ability to detect "abnormalities."[119]

The peer-like position of these trained home visitors enabled them to establish "direct" connections, seen as crucial for effective knowledge transmission; this perspective was common to MCH and nutrition. As articulated in a 1980 government publication reflecting on the 1950s, the fostering of local expertise had been pursued to fulfill the awareness that "Nutrition improvement can only be carried out by Indonesian personnel who have sufficient knowledge about Indonesian society and the social conditions of the Indonesian nation." Students were trained in "practical lessons on how to get to know the community closely" and in *kesejahteraan* ("prosperity" or "wellbeing"). Graduates were thus expected to "be able to investigate nutritional problems, plan efforts to improve nutrition at the family level and in the wider community," and inform the work of other ministries as well as community groups.[120]

These new MCH initiatives were in alignment with the LMR's nutrition work and Leimena's nationalist vision of people's holistic health: Indonesia was going to achieve national prosperity and stability through reduced rates of maternal and child mortality. This strategy, harnessed to improved hygiene and nutrition, relied on women's indigenous ways of knowing and knowledge transmission, and focused on reaching as many women as possible.

All these women, across fields and levels of expertise, could see their domestic and community-oriented activities now turned into a remunerated profession. Their contribution to nation-building was closer to the realm of public service through social work as we understand it today, than to the volunteerism embedded in both colonial-era associationism and New Order visions of women's social involvement of later years. As we have seen in the fictional Sukarsih, the *ahli dieet* was a lower-middle-class woman who had gained an authoritative voice through education; she enjoyed freedom of movement, and she was a paid government employee—not a community member volunteering her time. Further emphasizing the public relevance of the job, S.K.T. exalted the role of nutritionists: "With the establishment of the Sekolah Ahli Dieet, the Ministry of Health is bringing into being another militia [*barisan*] to guide Indonesia's society towards that goal!"[121] Indonesia could emerge as a strong nation only if ordinary women were to learn about nutrition, infant care, and hygienic birthing. Further, S.K.T. underlined the importance of outreach—in village centers, through home visits, and in the women's press—for national development: "Knowledge, research, and understanding about healthy food is pointless if it can't all be pursued and realized by the people."[122]

With women and their "domestic" arena now officially part of the effort to establish the nation-state, it was only apt, then, that both the National Commission for the Improvement of Nutrition and MCH saw in primary positions of leadership women who had a strong public presence. Erna Djajadiningrat and Soejatin Kartowijono had a deep past of activism in the colonial era; during the war, they had been in charge of public kitchens, and held leading positions in the women's movement, within the Indonesian Women's Congress (KOWANI) and Perwari. Dr. Sulianti Saroso had practiced medicine at the Bethesda Hospital in Yogyakarta during the Japanese occupation; when the Dutch entered Yogyakarta in 1948, she joined the revolutionary effort on the northern coast of Java, running public kitchens and first-aid activities.[123]

These exceptional women—from privileged backgrounds, with opportunities to be publicly active in the struggle for independence, and now involved in national-level healthcare policy making—were among the most visible, and they led a much wider base of women employed in the healthcare profession. The numbers might have been small for a population of about 70 million, but women nonetheless outnumbered men in the field.

In 1950 there were 1,446 midwives and 3,500 nurses, all of them women; the mere 1,200 (almost all male) doctors paled in comparison, making the vast majority, and the public face of, Indonesia's healthcare personnel female.[124] This footprint was also expanded by the fact that midwives, nurses, and outreach health workers regularly travelled to the rural and peri-urban areas to visit patients, while physicians worked in hospitals (all located in major urban centers), or in their own offices. Further, as just seen, these professionals relied on assistants, who were also women, and whose training enabled them to support their peers in making informed choices for a healthier life.

The prominent role of ordinary women in nation-building was evident in the government's reliance on their everyday labor to advance sweeping policies. A survey of the *Berita Hygiene* newsletter, a publication targeting physicians, provides an excellent vantage point to see how the principles of Minister Leimena's national plan were to unfold. From its first issue in mid-1950, the newsletter printed several articles exploring various aspects of preventive medicine. It translated entries from English publications on the effects of pregnant women's diet on the fetus,[125] and on "educative medicine"[126] and environmental awareness[127] as pillars of public health; it advertised a new course at the Hygiene Educator School;[128] it stressed the role of schools in fostering physical and emotional health;[129] and it promoted general efforts towards "People's Health Education" (Pendidikan Kesehatan Rakjat).[130]

All of this was articulated as crucial to the advancement of the nation,[131] and quite consistently the newsletter suggested various ways for the fledgling government and its physicians to support the quest of Indonesians for good health. But it often seemed to remain at the theoretical level, in the realm of policy, aspiration, and potentiality, rather than effective change through action. It is all the more striking, then, that the sole *Berita Hygiene* article focusing on the actual implementation of a policy would absolve the government of its responsibilities, and instead narrow its focus on the women's "duty" to "help develop our country" through MCH.[132] Women and their social organizations were the most effective agents of change and national progress, through their promotion of hygienic birthing and healthy infant care.

Once again, health was not an end in itself, but a cornerstone of national development. The Republican government called on people to take health into their own hands, as had the Dutch in years before. It tied bodily wellbeing to "progress," and it placed the responsibility for limiting infant deaths on mothers. In this broad-ranging article on mass organizations, public health, and national development, "**the duty** to improve the level of [people's] health" was placed explicitly and exclusively on women, who as mothers bore the responsibility of caring for infants.[133]

Thinking beyond patriarchal visions of maternalism, I have explored this transformation as a possibly subversive expansion of gendered expectations of domestic caregiving that enabled the creation of a space of autonomy and public political relevance for Indonesian women from a variety of backgrounds. Food and children were seen as "womanly matters" but nutrition and MCH emerged as pillars of nation-building and cornerstones of a labor-intensive economy. In the early-to-mid-1950s, these women saw their activities of care work (domestic or professional, in urban or rural settings) as contributing to the projection of national strength, and in most cases the (male) political establishment acknowledged and accepted them as such.

Sukarno had sought, in *Sarinah*, to separate women from social reproduction, and frame their nationalist contribution as constituting only political awareness, economic production, and biological reproduction. But nonetheless MCH and nutrition policies promoted during his presidency— mostly devised by women who had been involved in political activism during the war—advanced a recognition of social reproductive labor, and women's leading role therein, as key to national development.

This reality was not to last. Sukarno's personal political power increased with the declaration of Martial Law in 1957, and eventually the establishment of Guided Democracy in 1959; his political stance of self-reliance and labor-intensive agriculture became further entrenched. As I reflect on in the Epilogue, Sukarno's nativism clashed with the emergence of birth spacing as the new frontier of maternal health, food security, and overall prosperity. Family planning became the realm where Sukarno asserted that claims for the better health of his citizens did not align with national priorities, at the dire expense of women. Such staunch condemnation of family planning closed the doors for women's agency, and erased the recognition of political relevance for their quotidian gendered activities.

EPILOGUE

IN THE EARLY YEARS OF Indonesia's independence, women's domestic activities of care work were integral to national progress, as modernization relied on a primarily rural population engaged in manual subsistence farming. Even though in the pages of *Sarinah* Sukarno had blamed the "double shift" for women's lack of emancipation, the Indonesian government's policies in the early-to-mid-1950s doubled down on their labor, promoting development through home-based MCH and nutrition. This was different, for example, from Egypt, where despite many commonalities with Indonesia,[1] Nasser chased postcolonial modernity through industrialization, urbanization, and secularization. There the ideal woman-citizen was imagined as belonging to the middle class, employed in an office, and with access to household appliances in support of her domestic duties. She was expected to manage work outside of the home in concert with a small, nuclear family.

Indonesia's and Egypt's strategies were structurally and ideologically different, yet both focused on one common subject of policy: women's reproductive choice. I conclude this book's elaboration of "domestic nationalism" laying bare the limits of my emancipatory reading of women's labor of social reproduction as an acknowledged cornerstone of Indonesia's development. With the end of warfare and other external threats to Indonesia's survival, opportunities for women to exercise their politically relevant public roles *with agency* narrowed amid Sukarno's intensified nationalistic rhetoric.

In a process that would lead to the emergence of hyper-masculine authoritarianism and militarization, in both Indonesia and Egypt, women's social and biological reproductive labor was increasingly treated as an expected duty that ought to conform to nationalist economic priorities. The first arena to reveal the intrinsic exploitative nature and discursive artifice of centering women in nation-building was women's reproductive freedoms. Nasser deployed the imagery of the mother to rally national consciousness, but at once encouraged women to enter the economically productive workforce, introducing birth-control policies and socio-cultural paradigms that turned women's social reproductive efforts into signs of backwardness. As argued by Mai Taha and Sara Salem, Nasser's promotion of women as symbols of the new nation required first of all the "efface[-ment of mothers'] labour at home."[2] Egyptian women's domestic toiling in their second or third shift reminded people of the conservative, Islamic, backward countryside, too far removed from the imagined modern industrializing nation-state.

In Indonesia, instead, Sukarno's focus on labor-intensive agriculture had shaped a discursive environment in which both biological reproductive labor and care work were considered productive. But all the same, it would deprive Indonesian women of their bodily autonomy, as advocates of spaced birthing were publicly chastised. Dr. Julie Saroso Sulianti, who at the time was acting head of the Office for Maternal and Child Welfare, was the first to attract the wrath of the Sukarno-Hatta regime when in 1952 she promoted family planning on public radio.[3] Sulianti had just returned from a WHO-sponsored study trip to several countries, including Sweden—a country which at the time was pursuing an aggressive (and since the 1970s much criticized) eugenicist policy of pregnancy control. While eugenics does not seem to have resonated with Indonesians, some physicians, women journalists, and Islamic scholars, each expressed support in favor of contraception as a strategy to improve women's health and the overall socio-economic wellbeing of the nascent—and admittedly impoverished—nation.

Sukarno and Hatta ignored—or openly rebuked—all suggestions to limit births, whether it was advocated for the benefit of maternal health, national-level food security, or overall socio-economic prosperity. These views were rejected as manifestations of the political agenda of foreign, capitalist, and neo-imperialist institutions such as the Rockefeller Foundation, the Ford Foundation (and their joint venture, the Population Council), and the International Planned Parenthood Federation, as well as aid organizations such as the WHO and USAID.[4] While I do not question the fact that some of these institutional actors did come from a eugenicist milieu, and certainly had their own agendas beyond the putative wellbeing of impoverished Indonesians, it is worth pointing out that the Sukarno government's outright rejection of *any* family-planning measures similarly belied a political agenda that did not place the wellbeing of Indonesian citizens at the forefront. This was the other facet of the exhortation printed in the 1953 *Berita Hygiene* newsletter (already discussed in the previous chapter), which invoked the duty of women to advance national development.

———

Calls for delayed and spaced birthing had been voiced in the archipelago before. In the late 1800s, Dutch physicians noted that *dukuns* were regularly enlisted by indigenous and European women to pursue uterine manipulations to prevent pregnancies.[5] In the 1920s, Malthusian analyses of overpopulation and Europe's problems with increasingly disenfranchised lower classes were concurrently disseminated in the Malay language by Dutch authors,[6] and the Eugenics Society of the Netherlands-Indies was established in 1927.[7] But as argued by Ann Stoler, when eugenics travelled to the Indies, its "elitist, racist, and misogynist" imperialist values came to focus on European colonials themselves, rather than coercively controlling the reproduction of "degenerate" colonized subjects.[8] The work of the Eugenics Society "aimed to increase public awareness of eugenics while disavowing any political implications" for the colonized, and as pointed out by Hans Pols, the Society included representatives of the Javanese aristocracy, too.[9]

In the second half of the 1930s, the rhetoric of ensuring healthy offspring and a "perfect" national progeny surfaced occasionally in the Indies,[10] with the conversation about birth control focusing primarily on matters of familial wellbeing (economic and affective) and overpopulation.[11] Even when discussing matters of heredity the—admittedly scant—sources available suggest that non-European physicians in the Indies were not interested in the common eugenic concern for "what kind of people" would constitute the future nation.[12]

When the Islamic scholar and politician Haji Agus Salim offered a lecture on "Islam and birth control" at the NIAS medical school in Surabaya in 1937, the Dutch press advertised it and reported it in some detail,[13] as the administration had been keenly aware of Java's rapidly increasing population.[14] After laying out his exegetical approach to the scriptures, Salim concluded that whereas limiting the number of children for a married couple was "discouraged" (*makruh*), and not allowed just for "fear of poverty," neither was it in fact expressly forbidden. In addition to the implicit permissibility of spaced birthing implied in the Qur'anic requirement to breastfeed infants for at least twenty-four, and up to thirty, months, Salim asserted that a religiously "permissible intention" (*niyah*) would have made contraception itself permissible.[15] Salim's lecture came shortly after the Mufti of Egypt had released a *fatwa* supporting birth control;[16] conversely, at around the same time the Nahdlatul Ulama—Java's largest Islamic organization then as now—issued a *fatwa* forbidding the prevention of pregnancies.[17]

The issue of "intention" was still central after the transfer of sovereignty. Ahmad Ramali, who had been active in the colonial department of public health (and reportedly had been the first to open the conversation on Islam and birth control in the 1930s),[18] argued that contraception was not forbidden, and its allowability was determined by an individual's intentions. Such were his concluding thoughts to the chapter on contraception and the limiting of births as included in the doctoral dissertation he defended at the Faculty of Medicine of Gadjah Mada University, in Yogyakarta, in December 1950. With the title "Rules for Healthcare in Islamic Law," this book soon became a well-circulated manual for the care of Muslim patients. For Ramali, the only clear limits to contraception were a woman's vanity, the desire for sexual intercourse "for sheer pleasure," desire for wealth (note, no longer "fear of poverty" as had been previously argued by Salim), and family-planning propaganda. While explicitly stating that considerations based on health and socio-economic priorities by individuals would not stain a Muslim's good intention, publicly advocating (*mempropagandakan*) for "the birth of only one or two" children was "certainly wrong."[19] By 1967, religious opinions would further shift to support Jakarta's pilot project for Suharto's New Order policy encouraging—and at times coercively enforcing—a two-children policy.[20]

Ramali was creating a discursive space that could enable birth control as a choice embraced by individuals—he specified that familial consensus was not necessary—while also pushing back against increasing global pressures to contain Asia's perceived "overpopulation."[21] When reporting on his 1948 trip to Java, Marshall Balfour of the Rockefeller Foundation praised the former Dutch colonial regime for their "ability to maintai[n] peace and order, introduc[e] public health measures, [and] spread elementary notions of hygiene and improved agricultural techniques."[22] However, this colonial "enlightened administration" had "failed to develop the administrative, professional and technical skills and the experience" needed for the country's advancement, ultimately leading to an "essentially primitive, although somewhat rationalized, subsistence agriculture" unable to meet the needs of an expanding population.[23]

Balfour's trip had reinforced fears among western observers that in the whole region of Asia, food production had not kept up with population growth. In the midst of the Cold War, supporters of the Western Bloc argued that impoverished peoples would be more likely attracted to communism, echoing President Truman's rationale for the Point Four program. The problem of overpopulation framed assistance and interventions in various fields pertinent to food production, but in fact it was "maternal health" that emerged as a shoehorn for birth control.

While Sukarno continued to argue that the solution to Indonesia's "population problem" lay in the transfer of people out of overcrowded Java and onto less-populated islands (known as transmigration),[24] Balfour saw it in birth control. He concluded:

> In the long run economic development, improved health, and expanded educational opportunities, may lead to an altered position of the Indonesian woman and a lessened emphasis on numbers of children. This has happened in other cultures. In fact, Indonesia's educated groups have accepted the small family pattern of the West. The pressure of numbers is so great, though, that Indonesia cannot afford the long centuries that would be required to stabilize numbers if no direct approach were taken. . . .
>
> Cooperation in the research necessary to find the answer to the most practical of all questions, the limitation of the fertility of the women in the peasant villages, would seem to approach a moral responsibility for a West that will offer freely of its technical knowledge in the fields of economic development and public health.[25]

Balfour was anticipating the 1950s push to deliver medical and agricultural technical assistance to Indonesia. And it might have been this logic connecting international aid to "the most practical of all questions, the limitation of the fertility of the women in the peasant villages," that echoed in Sukarno's ears when Sulianti enthusiastically spoke of birth spacing for the benefit of maternal health, and which Sukarno saw as an obstacle to his vision of development.

The stories of *Pak* Pontjodarmo and *Pak* Mertani presented in Chapter 5, were written in this contested arena, between a national economic strategy that rested on further expanding an already sizable agrarian population on the one hand, and a more muted, emergent health practice that centered the wellbeing of women and their families. The contrast between the prosperous Pontjodarmos, with an intellectually entrepreneurial *Ibu* and only two children, and the "poor" *Pak* Mertani, who did not appear to have a strong wife and rarely consumed the recommended nutritional intake but had four children anyway, obliquely indicated the advantages of having fewer children.[26]

After her exploit in 1952, Sulianti would refrain from further promoting birth control in public, but the idea was now in circulation, ready for Indonesians to adopt. Sulianti promoted family planning in her clinic; the Institute for Family Welfare in Yogyakarta provided tools and information about birth spacing;[27] and in 1953 the Jakarta Central Hospital launched a postnatal program for mothers, where they often recommended spaced births and various family-planning methods for the benefit of maternal health.[28] When Hildred Geertz was doing fieldwork in Central Java, she was asked by an undereducated "poor urban market woman," who at twenty-six years of age had already had three children and three more miscarriages, "if there was some sort of pill she could take in order to space out her children." The same question was often asked by "Western-influenced, educated [women] with intense desires to advance the[ir] status." Piety-oriented men might have thought of it as "a sin against God," at least according to Hildred Geertz, but birth spacing was nonetheless a noteworthy topic of conversation in 1952–1954 for women across classes, even in the "overgrown village" of Modjokuto.[29]

In the meantime more booklets and magazines broaching the topic were printed, even though rarely, if ever, touching upon the matter of population density. Women's magazines published articles about the pros and cons of limiting births, occasionally quoting eugenicists and European physicians, but mostly focusing on the need to promote women's health and its compliance to Islam. In 1955, the publishing house Djambatan—which was active in the field of health and social matters, printing, for example, Poorwo Soedarmo's books on nutrition—published "Building a Family According to a Plan." There, Mrs. Raden Adiwinata presented several contraceptive methods that "did not conflict with Islamic teaching"—as stated by Ahmad Ramali's endorsement in the preface.[30] A year later, a publishing house based in Medan printed another book on the topic; Muhammad Nuh Hudawi's "Planning Children's Birth" drew from a number of sources, duly listed, to

> give information according to Islamic laws. . . . Neglecting or abandoning Islamic law in a matter of life is very detrimental because Islamic law does not only discuss matters of worship alone, but also fulfills all the needs of life and living, from trivial matters to major ones.[31]

Both books were reprinted several times in the late 1950s and into the 1960s. By then, family planning had become a common topic of publication,[32] and a practice advocated by several Planned Parenthood centers across the archipelago—even though it would still be excluded from public policy.

Clarence J. Gamble—scion of the Procter & Gamble industrial empire, and a major actor in the birth-control movement in the US and globally—saw early on that Indonesia should be part of his work. In 1954 he was already corresponding regularly with Sulianti, Leimena, Soedarmo, and several other high-ranking physicians in the Indonesian government. Understanding that arguments grounded in economic prosperity and food security would not win any support, his focus was on women's health.[33] Gamble exchanged letters with various clinics in Java, and explored ways to ship contraceptive supplies to them; by the end of the 1950s, Indonesia had entered the global network of Planned Parenthood.

Margaret Roots had become Gamble's first "fieldworker" through the National Committee on Maternal Health, and in the mid-1950s she had relocated to Southeast Asia. She spent time visiting and networking in Thailand, Singapore, Malaya, and Pakistan,[34] and eventually Indonesia. After speaking in Jakarta about maternal health and birth spacing in 1957, Roots would spend two months in the country. Clarence Gamble would have liked to see more concrete results, but Roots exhorted him: "Do not be impatient please." The country was poor and overpopulated; it lacked experts "in every department," and was trying to implement multiple plans of international aid. Her take was that the work of Planned Parenthood "will bear good fruit in time. [But t]he set-up will be quite different from other countries."[35] Her hope, as she "watch[ed] a nation being built" was "to get f[amily] p[lanning] into the ground floor of Health work."[36] That was going to be an uphill battle for the time being, but results began to show a decade later.

A Planned Parenthood Association (Perkumpulan Keluarga Berentjana) was established in Jakarta in December 1957, under the leadership of Dr. Hadji Soeharto (incidentally, President Sukarno's personal physician) and of Dr. Hurustiati Subandrio—a physician with political influence and an international network, and wife of the minister of foreign affairs.[37] Notably, Sulianti's name was nowhere to be seen in the organization's charter or in any of the articles that would appear in the months and years to follow. She had, however, a strong presence in the Planned Parenthood correspondence, and can be seen as a key behind-the-scenes facilitator of birth spacing practices in 1950s Indonesia.

It was against these developments that Poorwo Soedarmo had inserted family planning into his vision for national nutrition improvement. Indonesia faced more than just agricultural shortages, and the solution to malnutrition needed to be broader than just hoping for higher crop yields. Speaking to the Faculty of Medicine at Gadjah Mada University in 1958, Soedarmo stressed how the improvement of nutrition hinged on multiple small-scale interventions, thus sidelining Sukarno's "Food Policy"—which for too long had relied on increasing food production, aspiring to self-sufficiency. Peppered with English terms, Soedarmo's speech was at odds with Sukarno's policies, and illustrated a path shaped by "food technology," potential alternative sources of protein, "nutrition education," and "family planning."[38] Mere weeks later Soedarmo would be ousted in a cabinet reshuffle, as Sukarno laid the grounds for Guided Democracy.

On the occasion of Pakistani President Ayub Khan's visit to Indonesia in December 1960, Sukarno reportedly indicated that "there might be a case on health ground [sic] for 'spacing' a family."[39] This was the first hint of a move toward family planning, capping a year of scattered initiatives that, while varied in nature, consistently pointed toward change. On the one hand, the Nahdlatul Ulama central board had issued a new *fatwa* now declaring some forms of birth control "discouraged," and thus no longer *haram*.[40] On the other, as the Minister of Health Maj. Gen. Satrio expressed interest in launching a program for Army wives based on health concerns, Col. Suwardjono—head of gynecology at the Army hospital in Bandung—was said to be a strong supporter of the plan "because dependent allowances for soldiers were very expensive."[41]

Sukarno's socio-economic policies for national self-sufficiency continued to fail, with disastrous political implications piled upon the human tragedy. The 1964 "Operation Nutrition," launched by Maj. Gen. Satrio, had failed to realize a "just and prosperous Socialist society based on the Pancasila."[42] While Indonesians died of starvation, Sukarno continued his political demagoguery, enshrining the idea that Indonesia could "stand on its own feet" in his famous independence speech of August 17, 1965. His regime would collapse in a matter of weeks.

Through an unspeakably violent transition (1965–1967), initiated by a militarized intervention to quash an alleged communist coup on September 30, 1965, Suharto's New Order (1967–1997) would settle into a routine of steady authoritarianism and hyper-masculinity that Sukarno himself had set in motion. As others have pointed out, one of the ways that the so-called "October 1965 events" manifested (for months on end) was through "an unprecedented campaign of sexual slander against Gerwani," the militant women's wing of the Indonesian Communist Party.[43] Against this new landscape, women's political activism was marginalized from public discourse, if not completely obliterated. And while Indonesian women would continue to pursue their care work at home and in their neighborhoods, in hospitals and clinics, through government agencies and women's organizations, "womanly matters" were turned into an exclusively social—and *therefore* apolitical—endeavor.[44] From the late-1950s onwards, then, "domestic nationalism" would fade into what Julia Suryakusuma has called Suharto's state *Ibuism*,[45] as women would lose much, if not all, of their agency in public spaces. And once again, reproductive choices were folded into a clearly delimited arena of nationalist priorities that now barred unmarried women access to contraceptive devices, and required all married women to register for family planning.

Glossary

"4 Sehat, 5 Sempurna": "4 for health, 5 for perfection" nutrition slogan

'adat: customary practices, predating the arrival of Islam

bangsa: people, as in those who recognize a common "nation" (not necessarily a nation-state)

boemipoetera: term indexing indigeneity to the Indonesian archipelago

desa: rural village

dukun / doekoen: traditional healer (almost always men)

dukun bayi / dukun beranak: traditional birth attendant (almost always women)

fatwa: non-binding religious opinion

gezondheid: health (Dutch)

halal: permissible to Muslims (of food or behavior)

haram: forbidden to Muslims (of food or behavior)

hawa: air, bodily desires

ibu / iboe: woman, mother

kain-kebaya: woman's outfit, with a long-sleeved buttoned shirt, and sarong

kampung: peri-urban settlement

kemajuan / kemadjoean / kemadjuan: advancement, progress

kesejahteraan / kesedjahteraan: prosperity, welfare, wellbeing *kodrat*: nature, destiny; used to justify the definition of a women's sphere that differs from men's

maju / madjoe: advanced

mantri: (health) inspector, propagandist

merdeka, kemerdekaan: freedom, independence

Njonja / Nyonya: Mrs.

Pak: Mr.

pasar malam: night fair

penghulu: government-appointed Muslim leader in colonial Java

priyayi: Javanese nobility, aristocracy

Raden: general nobility pre-title (followed by rank- and gender-specific title)

rakjat / rakyat: populace, the masses, public, citizenry

romusha: laborers drafted by the Japanese occupation government, in theory voluntary; joining was the outcome of hard and soft coercion (Japanese)

Roro: title of lower nobility (female, unmarried)

sehat, kesehatan: health, healthy

soetji: pure

susu: milk

wayang kulit: shadow puppet theater

Notes

Introduction

1. Soekarmi, "Sedikit tentang Hal Makanan," *Isteri*, no. 11, March 1931, pp. 15–17; and no.12, April, 1931, pp. 27–29.

2. I borrow the concept of scientific (and "modern") motherhood from Rima Apple. Among many references, see: Rima D. Apple, *Perfect Motherhood: Science and Childrearing in America*, New Brunswick, NJ: Rutgers University Press, 2006.

3. The term "propaganda" is borrowed from the sources, and conveys the sense of outward knowledge dissemination from a center, let that be a government office, a sanitary unit, or a printed text.

4. I use the term "indigenous" to refer to women who claimed to originally hail from Java and Sumatra (and thus did not identify as Chinese, Arab, Eurasian, or European), and who were predominantly Muslim; this translates the Dutch *in-lander* (lit. "native") and the Malay *bumiputera* (lit. "son of the soil") in a (still imperfect) attempt to avoid perpetuating the discriminatory histories embodied in those labels.

5. For an early use of the term in scholarship, see Barbara Welter, "The Cult of True Womanhood: 1820–1860," *American Quarterly*, vol. 18 (no. 2), 1966, pp. 151–174.

6. While I usually separate "tradition" (a place-specific reality, often referred to in the sources as *'adat*) from "Islam" (invoked as a source of authority rooted in interpretations of the Qur'an and *hadith*) as two separate ways of knowing, they often interfaced in similar ways to scientific biomedicine and are thus mentioned in tandem.

7. Directrice, "Permoelaan Kalam," *Perempoean Bergerak*, no. 1, May 15, 1919, p. 1.

8. Amy Kaplan, "Manifest Domesticity," *American Literature*, vol. 70 (no. 3), No More Separate Spheres! September 1998, pp. 581–606, p. 581.

9. Ruth Rogaski, *Hygienic Modernity: Meanings of Health and Disease in Treaty-Port China*, Berkeley, CA: University of California Press, 2004.

10. B.W. Richardson, "Woman as Sanitary Reformer," *Fraser's Magazine*, November 1880, pp. 669–671, quoted in A. Davin, "Imperialism and Motherhood," in Frederick Cooper and Ann L. Stoler (eds.) *Tensions of Empire: Colonial Cultures in a Bourgeois World*, Berkeley, CA: University of California Press, 2009, pp. 87–151, p. 132. See also Alison Bashford, *Purity and Pollution: Gender, Embodiment, and Victorian Medicine*, New York, NY: St. Martin's Press, 1998; Nancy Tomes, *The Gospel of Germs: Men, Women, and the Microbe in American Life*, Cambridge, MA: Harvard University Press, 1998.

11. Too many to cite, but these works span from George Kahin's *Nationalism and Revolution in Indonesia* (Cornell, 1952) to Robert Elson's *The Idea of Indonesia* (Cambridge, 2008), and everything in between, including my own work, Chiara Formichi, *Islam and the Making of the Nation: Kartosuwiryo and Political Islam in Twentieth-Century Indonesia*, Leiden: KITLV Press, 2012; Harry A. Poeze, *Verguisd en Vergeten: Tan Malaka, de Linkse Beweging en de Indonesische Revolutie, 1945–1949*, Leiden: KITLV Uitgeverij, 2007; Kevin W. Fogg, *Indonesia's Islamic Revolution*, Cambridge, UK: Cambridge University Press, 2020.

12. Mary Margaret Steedly, *Rifle Reports: A Story of Indonesian Independence*, Berkeley, CA: University of California Press, 2013; and Jean Gelman Taylor, (ed.) *Women Creating Indonesia: The First Fifty Years*, Clayton, Vic., Australia: Monash Asia Institute, 1997.

13. Frances Gouda, "Discipline Versus Gentle Persuasion in Colonial Public Health: The Rockefeller Foundation's Intensive Rural Hygiene Work in the Netherlands East Indies, 1925–1940," *Research Reports from the Rockefeller Archive Center*, 2009; Hans Pols, *Nurturing Indonesia: Medicine and Decolonisation in the Dutch East Indies*, Cambridge, UK: Cambridge University Press, 2018; Eric A. Stein, "Vital Times: Power, Public Health, and Memory in Rural Java," PhD thesis, Ann Arbor, MI, 2005; Eric A. Stein, "Hygiene and Decolonization: The Rockefeller Foundation and Indonesian Nationalism, 1933–1958," in Bu, Liping, Darwin H. Stapleton, and Ka-che Yip (eds.) *Science, Public Health, and the State in Modern Asia*, London: Routledge, 2012, pp. 51–70; Eric A. Stein, "Colonial Theatres of Proof: Representation and Laughter in 1930s Rockefeller Foundation Hygiene Cinema in Java," *Health and History*, vol. 8 (no. 2), 2006, pp. 14–44; Kees van Dijk and Jean Gelman Taylor (eds.) *Cleanliness and Culture: Indonesian Histories*, Leiden: KITLV Press, 2011.

14. Elizabeth Martyn, *The Women's Movement in Post-Colonial Indonesia: Gender and Nation in a New Democracy*, London: Routledge Curzon, 2005; Susan Blackburn, *Women and the State in Modern Indonesia*, Cambridge, UK: Cambridge University Press, 2004; Charles Sullivan, "Years of Dressing Dangerously: Modern Women, National Identity and Moral Crisis in Sukarno's Indonesia, 1945–1966," PhD dissertation, University of Michigan, Ann Arbor, MI, 2020; Saskia Wieringa, *Sexual Politics in Indonesia*, Basingstoke: Palgrave Macmillan, 2002; Julia I. Suryakusuma, *State Ibuism: The Social Construction of Womanhood in New Order Indonesia = Ibuisme Negara: Konstruksi Sosial Keperempuanan Orde Baru*, Jakarta: Komunitas Bambu, 2011. The text first appeared as Suryakusuma's MA thesis at

the Institute of Social Studies in The Hague in 1988. This implicit reassertion of the "separate spheres" theory has inevitably presented Indonesian women who did not operate in the channels of formal politics—an opportunity accessible to few individuals—as passive subjects of colonizing, patriarchal, and Islamic conservative forces.

15. Maternalism is a well-studied field, although scholarship remains focused on the Global North, British colonies, and the role of white women in disseminating maternalist ideals among colonized subjects. See Floya Anthias and Nira Yuval-Davis, introduction to *Woman—Nation—State*, New York, NY: St. Martin's Press, 1989; Kalpana Ram and Margaret Jolly (eds.) *Maternities and Modernities: Colonial and Postcolonial Experiences in Asia and the Pacific*, Cambridge, UK: Cambridge University Press, 1998; Seth Koven and Sonya Michel (eds.) *Mothers of a New World: Maternalist Politics and the Origins of Welfare States*, New York, NY: Routledge, 1993. For an Indonesian perspective, see Suryakusuma, *State Ibuism*.

16. Padma Anagol, "Agency, Periodisation and Change in the Gender and Women's History of Colonial India," *Gender & History*, vol. 20 (no. 3), 2008, 603–627, p. 615. In the original, the emphasis is on "change"; however, I am more interested in the potential underscored by the "possibility" of it.

17. Afsaneh Najmabadi, "Crafting an Educated Housewife in Iran," in Lila Abu-Lughod (ed.) *Remaking Women: Feminism and Modernity in the Middle East*, Princeton, NJ: Princeton University Press, 1998, pp. 91–125, p. 91.

18. Jasamin Rostam-Kolayi, "Foreign Education," in Nikki R. Keddie and Rudolph P. Matthee (eds.) *Iran and the Surrounding World: Interactions in Culture and Cultural Politics*, Seattle, WA: University of Washington Press, 2002, p. 198.

19. Beth Baron, *The Women's Awakening in Egypt: Culture, Society, and the Press*, New Haven, CT: Yale University Press, 1994; Laura Bier, *Revolutionary Womanhood: Feminisms, Modernity, and the State in Nasser's Egypt*, Stanford, CA: Stanford University Press, 2011; Lisa Pollard, *Nurturing the Nation: The Family Politics of Modernizing, Colonizing and Liberating Egypt (1805/1923)*, Berkeley, CA: University of California Press, 2005.

20. Mary Hancock, "Home Science and the Nationalization of Domesticity in Colonial India," *Modern Asian Studies*, vol. 35 (no. 4), October 2001, pp. 871–903, pp. 879–880.

21. Helen M. Schneider, *Keeping the Nation's House: Domestic Management and the Making of Modern China*, Contemporary Chinese Studies Series, Vancouver: UBC Press, 2011.

22. Jordan Sand, *House and Home in Modern Japan: Reforming Everyday Life 1880–1930*, Cambridge, MA: Harvard University Press, 2005, p. 62.

23. Nancy Berlage has shown that home economists transformed "housewifery" into a scientific profession, i.e., home economics, and thus created a space for women in the public sphere: Nancy Berlage, "The Establishment of an Applied Social Science: Home Economists, Science and Reform at Cornell University, 1870–1930," in Helene Silverberg (ed.) *Gender and American Social Science: The Formative Years*, Princeton NJ: Princeton University Press, 1998.

24. Omnia Shakri, Afsaneh Najmabadi, Lila Abu-Lughod, and other contributions to Lila Abu-Lughod (ed.) *Remaking Women*; Bier, *Revolutionary Womanhood*; Pollard, *Nurturing the Nation*. While these scholars I cite—and my own analysis—point at ways in which the interplay of local and western knowledge empowered women, others have highlighted the oppositional and gendered relation between these epistemologies.

25. Hancock, "Home Science."

26. For a recent study of girls' education in the Dutch East Indies, see Kirsten Kamphuis, "Indigenous Girls and Education in a Changing Colonial Society: The Dutch East Indies, c. 1880–1942," dissertation, European University Institute, 2019.

27. I am indebted to the work of many scholars for reaching this understanding of care work. Among them are Silvia Federici, Sandy Grande, Shenila Khoja-Moolji; Nicole Barnes; and the collective analysis by Burnett, Ritchey, and Thomas. Because of the overbearing implications of inhabiting a racialized socio-political space of oppression, I am particularly drawn to theorizations of care work emerging from Black and other minoritized feminist scholars (ranging from Dani McClain to Angela Garbes), although I do recognize the limits of such borrowing. See Silvia Federici, "Social Reproduction Theory: History, Issues and Present Challenges," *Radical Philosophy*, no. 2.04, Spring 2019, pp. 55–57; Sandy Grande, "12. Care," in The Keywords Feminist Editorial Collective (ed.) *Keywords for Gender and Sexuality Studies*, New York, NY: New York University Press, 2021, pp. 43–46; Shenila Khoja-Moolji, *Rebuilding Community: Displaced Women and the Making of a Shia Ismaili Muslim Sociality*, New York, NY: Oxford University Press, 2023; Shenila Khoja-Moolji, *Forging the Ideal Educated Girl: The Production of Desirable Subjects in Muslim South Asia*, Oakland, CA: University of California Press, 2018; Nicole Elizabeth Barnes, *Intimate Communities: Wartime Healthcare and the Birth of Modern China, 1937–1945*, Oakland, CA: University of California Press, 2018; Kristin Burnett, Sara Ritchey, and Lynn M. Thomas, "Introduction: Health, Healing and Caring," *Gender & History*, vol. 33 (no. 3), October 2021, pp. 583–593; Dani McClain, *We Live for the We: The Political Power of Black Motherhood*, 1st ed., New York, NY: Bold Type Books, 2019; Angela Garbes, *Essential Labor: Mothering as Social Change*, 1st ed., New York, NY: Harper Wave, an imprint of HarperCollins Publishers, 2022.

28. Paula Baker, "The Domestication of Politics: Women and American Political Society, 1780–1920," *The American Historical Review*, vol. 89 (no. 3), 1984, 620–647, p. 622.

29. This subject has not yet received due attention in scholarship. See Hans Pols, "Eugenics in the Netherlands and the Dutch East Indies," in Alison Bashford and Philippa Levine (eds.) *The Oxford Handbook of the History of Eugenics*, Oxford Handbooks, 2010; Guo-Quan Seng, *Strangers in the Family: Gender, Patriliny, and the Chinese in Colonial Indonesia*, Ithaca, NY: Southeast Asia Program Publications, an imprint of Cornell University Press, 2023; Ann Laura Stoler, *Carnal Knowledge and Imperial Power: Race and the Intimate in Colonial Rule*, Berkeley, CA: University of California Press, 2010.

30. Edward Said's *Orientalism* remains the foundational text for this. For an excellent exposition of Orientalist visions of non-European non-Christian territories, with a focus on Japan and the Ottoman Empire, see Cemil Aydin. For a reflection from the vantage point of the Dutch East Indies, see Sumit Mandal. Edward W. Said, *Orientalism*, New York, NY: Vintage Books, 2003; Cemil Aydin, *The Politics of Anti-Westernism in Asia: Visions of World Order in Pan-Islamic and Pan-Asian Thought*, New York, NY: Columbia University Press, 2007; Sumit Kumar Mandal, *Becoming Arab: Creole Histories and Modern Identity in the Malay World*, Cambridge, UK: Cambridge University Press, 2018.

31. For a short yet excellent read on veiling and unveiling, and the politics of it across the twentieth century (and into the twenty-first), see Lila Abu-Lughod, "Do Muslim Women Really Need Saving? Anthropological Reflections on Cultural Relativism and Its Others," *American Anthropologist*, vol. 104 (no. 3), 2002, pp. 783–790.

32. Elora Shehabuddin, *Sisters in the Mirror: A History of Muslim Women and the Global Politics of Feminism*, Oakland, CA: University of California Press, 2021, p. 84.

33. Sally Jane White, "Reformist Islam, Gender and Marriage in Late Colonial Dutch East Indies, 1900–1942," PhD dissertation, Australian National University, 2004, pp. 1–2.

34. Shehabuddin, *Sisters in the Mirror*.

35. Deniz Kandiyoti, "Islam and Patriarchy: A Comparative Perspective," in Nikki R. Keddie and Beth Baron (eds.) *Women in Middle Eastern History: Shifting Boundaries in Sex and Gender*, New Haven, CT: Yale University Press, 2017, pp. 23–42, p. 24. Lila Abu-Lughod has also expanded this proposition to the politics of "modernity": Lila Abu-Lughod, introduction to *Remaking Women*, pp. 3–31.

36. Jean Gelman Taylor, "The Sewing-Machine in Colonial-Era Photographs: A Record from Dutch Indonesia," *Modern Asian Studies*, vol. 46 (no. 1), 2012, pp. 71–95, quote p. 94. On the importance of visual materials as a needed and "neglected" source for Indonesian history, see also Jean Gelman Taylor, "Visual History: A Neglected Resource for the Long Durée," in David Henley and Henk Schulte Nordholt (eds.) *Environment, Trade and Society in Southeast Asia*, Leiden: Brill, pp. 181–202; Karen Strassler, *Refracted Visions: Popular Photography and National Modernity in Java*, Durham, NC: Duke University Press, 2010.

Chapter 1

1. Sardjito and R.A. Wongsosewojo, *Dari Hal Mentjari Kesehatan*, Batavia: Balai Poestaka, 1930, pp. 3–4. The book was reprinted again in 1950.

2. In the 1910s to 1920s, Sardjito had studied in the Netherlands first and the United States next (with a Rockefeller Foundation fellowship). He would later become the founding president of the Gadjah Mada University in Yogyakarta. Pols, *Nurturing Indonesia*, p. 153.

3. For an overview of the Ethical Policy, see Merle C. Ricklefs, *A History of Modern Indonesia Since c.1200*, Basingstoke: Palgrave Macmillan, 2008; specifically on economic improvements, Suzanne Moon, *Technology and Ethical Idealism: A*

History of Development in the Netherlands East Indies, Leiden: CNWS Publications, 2007. For a Dutch self-narrative on the perceived impact of Ethicist policies on public health, see the contributions included in the special issue "Indonesia before the War" edited by N.H. Swellengrebel, printed in *Documenta Neerlandica et Indonesica de Morbis Tropicis* ("Quarterly Journal of Tropical Medicine and Hygiene"), vol. 1 (no. 3), September 1949, pp. 193–224.

4. Sangkanningrat. *Iets over Hygiëne: in Verband met Adat, Geloof en Bijgeloof van het Soendaneesche Volk*, Bandoeng: Nix, n.d. This was the tenth volume in a series, and its year of publication was sometime between 1927 and 1931.

5. Ann F. La Berge, *Mission and Method: Early Nineteenth-Century Public Health Movement*, Cambridge, UK: Cambridge University Press, 1992, p. 2.

6. Tomes, *The Gospel of Germs*.

7. William Johnston, *The Modern Epidemic: A History of Tuberculosis in Japan*, Cambridge, MA: Council on East Asian Studies, Harvard University, 1995, n. 45, p. 174.

8. Rogaski, *Hygienic Modernity*, p. 137. See also Hoi-eun Kim, *Doctors of Empire: Medical and Cultural Encounters Between Imperial Germany and Meiji Japan*, Toronto: University of Toronto Press, 2016.

9. Kelvin K. To and Kwok Yung Yuen, "In Memory of Patrick Manson, Founding Father of Tropical Medicine and the Discovery of Vector-Borne Infections," *Emerging Microbes & Infections*, vol. 1 (no. 10), 2012, e31.

10. Lenore Manderson, "Health Services and the Legitimation of the Colonial State: British Malaya 1786–1941." *International Journal of Health Services: Planning, Administration, Evaluation*, vol. 17 (no. 1), 1987, pp. 91–112, p. 104.

11. E. Richard Brown, *Rockefeller Medicine Men: Medicine and Capitalism in America*, Berkeley, CA: University of California Press, 1979, pp. 112–113. Emphasis in original.

12. Warwick Anderson, *Colonial Pathologies: American Tropical Medicine, Race, and Hygiene in the Philippines*, Durham, NC: Duke University Press, 2006, pp. 90–94, quote p. 93.

13. W. Anderson, "Afterword," in Qizi Liang and Charlotte Furth (eds.) *Health and Hygiene in Chinese East Asia: Policies and Publics in the Long Twentieth Century*, Durham, NC: Duke University Press, 2011, p. 275. See also Anderson, *Colonial Pathologies*.

14. Ming-chen Miriam Lo, *Doctors Within Borders: Profession, Ethnicity, and Modernity in Colonial Taiwan*, Berkeley, CA: University of California Press, 2002, pp. 98–99, 112–114.

15. Lo, *Doctors Within Borders*, p. 99. See also Aaron S. Moore, *Constructing East Asia*, Palo Alto, CA: Stanford University Press, 2015, on Japan's hygienism in China.

16. Lo, *Doctors Within Borders*, p. 39.

17. Ruth Rogaski, "Vampires in Plagueland," in Q. Liang and C. Furth (eds.) *Health and Hygiene in Chinese East Asia: Policies and Publics in the Long Twentieth Century*, Durham, NC: Duke University Press, 2011, p. 132.

18. P.K.M. van Roosmalen, "Netherlands Indies Town Planning: An Agent of Modernization (1905–1957)," in Freek Colombijn and Joost Coté, (eds.) *Cars, Conduits, and Kampongs: The Modernization of the Indonesian City 1920–1960*, Leiden: Brill, 2015, p. 91; Maurits Bastiaan Meerwijk, *A History of Plague in Java, 1911–1942*, Ithaca, NY: Southeast Asia Program Publications, an imprint of Cornell University Press, 2022.

19. Freek Colombijn and Martine Barwegen, *Under Construction: The Politics of Urban Space and Housing During the Decolonization of Indonesia, 1930–1960*, Leiden: Brill, 2014, p. 134.

20. Rudolf Mrázek, *Engineers of Happy Land: Technology and Nationalism in a Colony*, Princeton, NJ: Princeton University Press, 2002.

21. M. Kooy and Karen Bakker, "(Post)colonial Pipes: Urban Water Supply in Colonial and Contemporary Jakarta," in Colombijn and Coté (eds.) *Cars, Conduits, and Kampongs*, p. 67.

22. On the emergence of Eurasian elites in Java, and the shift that occurred after the British interregnum, see Jean Gelman Taylor, *The Social World of Batavia: Europeans and Eurasians in Colonial Indonesia*, 2nd ed., Madison, WI: University of Wisconsin Press, 2009. Elsbeth Locher-Scholten notes that in 1880 there were 471 Dutch women for 1,000 Dutch men; in 1900, 636 per 1,000 and in 1930, 884 per 1,000. Elsbeth Locher-Scholten, "Summer Dresses and Canned Food," in Henk Schulte Nordholt (ed.) *Outward Appearances: Dressing State and Society in Indonesia*, Leiden: KITLV Press, 1997," p. 153. She presents even more statistics about employment, living conditions, etc., in Elsbeth Locher-Scholten, *Women and the Colonial State: Essays on Gender and Modernity in the Netherlands Indies, 1900–1942*, Amsterdam: Amsterdam University Press, 2000, pp. 49–84.

23. Ann Laura Stoler, *Race and the Education of Desire: Foucault's History of Sexuality and the Colonial Order of Things*, Durham, NC: Duke University Press, 1995, p. 35.

24. Koloniale School voor Meisjes en Vrouwen (The Hague, Netherlands). *Propagandaboekje van de Koloniale School voor Meisjes nn Vrouwen*. 's-Gravenhage: Koloniale School voor Meisjes en Vrouwen, 1927.

25. This reform had followed the failure of a mandate for European midwives to train others in the profession, including local women. Liesbeth Q. Hesselink, *Healers on the Colonial Market: Native Doctors and Midwives in the Dutch East Indies*, Leiden: KITLV Press, 2011, p. 75ff. (Chapter 5).

26. Cornelis Leendert van der Burg, *De Geneesheer in Nederlandsch-Indië*, Batavia: Ernst & co., 1884, pp. 71–76.

27. Sangkanningrat, *Iets over Hygiëne*.

28. Quoted in Hesselink, *Healers*, p. 23; see pp. 23–25 for an overview of colonial opinions and comments on the *dukun bayi*.

29. Kat De Angelino, Preface to John Lee Hydrick, *Intensive Rural Hygiene Work and Public Health Education of the Public Health Service of Netherlands India*, 1937, p. I.

30. "Oekoeran Air (dengan Wang)," *Pandji Poestaka*, no. 11, February 6, 1925, p. 166.

31. John Lee Hydrick, *Intensive Rural Hygiene Work in the Netherlands East Indies*, New York, NY: Netherlands Information Bureau, 1944, p. 12.

32. "Internationaal Hygiënisch Congres," *Algemeen Handelsblad*, August 16, 1884, p. 2.

33. *Cinquième congrès international d'hygiène et de démographie à La Haye (du 21 au 27 août 1884): Comptes rendus et mémoires (Tome I)*, The Hague: Imprimerie sud hollandaise, 1884, pp. 284–289, p. 285.

34. *Cinquième congres international*, p. 289.

35. Bashford, *Purity and Pollution*; Tomes, *The Gospel of Germs*; Simon Schama, *The Embarrassment of Riches: An Interpretation of Dutch Culture in the Golden Age*, New York, NY: Knopf, 1987.

36. Meerwijk, *A History of Plague*.

37. Brown, *Rockefeller Medicine Men*, pp. 112–113.

38. John Ettling, *The Germ of Laziness: Rockefeller Philanthropy and Public Health in the New South*, Cambridge, MA: Harvard University Press, 1981, p. vii.

39. "Darling to Rose and Heiser," December 12, 1916, p.3; Java, 1916; "Kirk to De Vogel," June 27, 1916; Java, 1916; RG 5, Series 1_02; Subseries 1916_655; Rockefeller Archive Center [RAC].

40. On the Rockefeller Foundation involvement in Java, see, among several, T.H. Hull, "Conflict and Collaboration in Public Health Rockefeller Foundation and Dutch Colonial Government in Indonesia," in Milton James Lewis and Kerrie L. Macpherson (eds.) *Public Health in Asia and the Pacific: Historical and Comparative Perspectives*. Abingdon, UK: Routledge, 2007. See Stein, "Vital Times" for a detailed account of the complex relationship between the Rockefeller Foundation and the Dutch Indies' Health Services.

41. "Heiser to deVogel," October 5, 1918; Java, 1918; RG 5; Series 1_02; Subseries 1918_655; RAC; "Heiser to First Secretary to the Governor General of the Netherlands Indies," April 1, 1915; Java, 1910–1915; RG 5; Series 1_02; Subseries 1915_655; RAC.

42. "Governor General to Heiser," August 14, 1921; Java, 1921; RG 5; Series 1_02; Subseries 1921_655; RAC.

43. "Heiser to van Lonkhuijzen," February 7, 1924; Java – Hydrick, J.L., 1924; RG 5; Series 1_02; Subseries 1924_655; RAC; "Hydrick to Heiser," January 6, 1925, Java – A–Z, 1925; RG 5; Series 1_02; Subseries 1925_655; RAC.

44. "Hydrick to Heiser," December 30, 1924; Java – Hydrick, J.L., 1924; RG 5; Series 1_02; Subseries 1924_655; RAC.

45. John Lee Hydrick, *The Division of Public Health Education of the Public Health Service of the Netherlands East Indies*, Weltevreden: Set up and printed in the Workshop of the Division, 1929.

46. Hydrick, *Intensive* (1944), p. 12, repeated almost verbatim from Kat De Angelino, Preface to Hydrick, *Intensive* (1937), p. I.

47. "Hydrick to Heiser," March 26, 1925; Java – A–Z, 1925; RG 5; Series 1_02; Subseries 1925_655; RAC. On Rockefeller Foundation health work beyond Java, see "Dean to Hydrick," February 18, 1927; Java – A–Z, 1927; RG 5; Series 1_02; Subseries 1927_655; RAC; "Hydrick to Heiser" October 19, 1926; Java – Hydrick, J.P., 1926 October–December; RG 5; Series 1_02; Subseries 1926_655; RAC; "Hydrick to Heiser," November 14, 1929; (Public Health Education), 1928–1941, 1945; RG 1; SG 1.1, Series 300–833; Subseries 655.L; RAC; "De Hygienische Organisatie, Summary for the Year 1935," Java – Public Health Work, Annual Report, 1935; RG 5; Series 3; Subseries 3_655 GEN; RAC.

48. "Hydrick to Russell," February 21, 1935; (Public Health Demonstrations), 1932–1939; Rockefeller Foundation records; RG 1; SG 1.1, Series 300–833; Subseries 655.J; RAC; "Dean to Hydrick," February 18, 1927; RAC.

49. "Hydrick to Heiser," September 17, 1927; Java – De Hass, J.H., 1927; RG 5; Series 1_02; Project Subseries 1927_655; RAC.

50. See also Hans Pols, "Eugenics," pp. 347–362; Hans Pols and Warwick Anderson, "The Mestizos of Kisar: An Insular Racial Laboratory in the Malay Archipelago," *Journal of Southeast Asian Studies*, vol. 49 (no. 3), 2018, pp. 445–463. DOI: 10.1017/S0022463418000358.

51. Amid the Depression, Rockefeller Foundation executives could find "no reason" to extend the Dutch Indies program, arguing instead that the colonial government and local population should be "capable" of doing the work themselves. "Selskar M. Gunn to Mason," October 13, 1933; Java, 1933; RG 2, 1924–1939; Series 1933/655; RAC. Funds continued to flow until 1940, albeit in increasingly diminished amounts. "Hydrick: Trip Batavia – Sumatra – Batavia, 17 September–8 October 1932"; Gunn, Selskar M. "Report on a Visit to Java," 1933; RG 2, 1924–1939; Series 1933/655; RAC.

52. Andries Teeuw, "The Impact of Balai Pustaka on Modern Indonesian Literature," *Bulletin of the School of Oriental and African Studies, University of London*, vol. 35 (no. 1), 1972, pp. 111–127, p. 113.

53. Doris Jedamski, "Balai Pustaka: A Colonial Wolf in Sheep's Clothing," *Archipel*, vol. 44, 1992, pp. 23–46, p. 23.

54. Agus Suwignyo, "The Breach in the Dike: Regime Change and the Standardization of Public Primary-School Teacher Training in Indonesia (1893–1969)." PhD dissertation, University of Leiden, 2012, p. 49. Suwignyo borrows the expression from Hugh Archibald Wyndham, *Native Education: Ceylon, Java, Formosa, the Philippines, French Indo-China, and British Malaya*, London: Oxford University Press, 1933, p. 88.

55. *Algemeen Verslag van het Onderwijs in Nederlandsch-Indië over het Schooljaar 1920*, Batavia, 1921, pp. 36–37.

56. *Algemeen Verslag van het Onderwijs 1927*, Batavia, n.d., part 2, table XI.

57. *Algemeen Verslag van het Onderwijs 1930/1931*, part 2, Batavia, 1933, pp. 8–11; *Algemeen Verslag van het Onderwijs 1935/1936*, part 2, Batavia, 1938, pp. 10–17; *Algemeen Verslag van het Onderwijs 1939–1940*, part 2, Batavia, 1941, table 12. In 1940 there were close to half a million literate women.

58. *Algemeen Verslag van het Onderwijs 1920*, pp. 36–37.

59. *Algemeen Verslag van het Onderwijs 1927*, part 2, table XXVII. In 1927 there were 1,600 indigenous girls enrolled in the ELS and another 16,000 in the HIS.

60. Kees Groeneboer, *Gateway to the West: The Dutch Language in Colonial Indonesia, 1600–1950: A History of Language Policy*, Amsterdam: Amsterdam University Press, 1998, p. 241.

61. Minister of Colonies Ch. J.I.M. Welter, quoted in Groeneboer, *Gateway to the West*, p. 242.

62. S.L. van der Wal, *Het Onderwijsbeleid in Nederlands-Indië, 1900–1940: Een Bronnenpublikatie = Education Policy in the Netherlands-Indies, 1900–1940*, Groningen: J.B. Wolters, 1963, p. 316.

63. Groeneboer, *Gateway to the West*, pp. 241–242. Also, when the advanced elementary schools (MULO, Meer Uitgebreid Lager Onderwijs) were established in 1937, both Dutch and English were taught there as regular subjects in addition to Malay and the local vernacular. The result was that almost all girls receiving an education in the latter half of the 1930s were regularly studying Dutch, Malay, and an additional vernacular.

64. Dutch East Indies. Tijdelijk Kantoor voor de Volkstelling 1930. *Volkstelling 1930: Census of 1930 in Netherlands India*, Batavia: Departement van Landbouw, Nijverheid en Handel, 1933, vol. 8, p. 29, and table 14, p. 111. Indigenous men's literacy rate was enumerated at 10.8%.

65. Groeneboer, *Gateway to the West*, pp. 243–244.

66. Kantoor voor de Volkstelling, *Volkstelling*, vol. 8, p. 30.

67. Jedamski, "Balai Pustaka," p. 27.

68. A 1932 article in *Pandji Poestaka*, for example, reported that a women's group based in Tanjung Pinang, near Medan, taught illiterate village women how to read and write in Malay, as well as in Dutch. "Doenia Isteri: Kaoem Iboe Sepakat di Tandjoeng Pinang," *Pandji Poestaka*, no. 82, October 11, 1932, pp. 1284–1286.

69. Note glued to the inside cover of Muwardi, *Keséhatan (Tentang Hal Sport)*, Solo: Pembatjaan Ra'jat, 1934.

70. G.W.J. Drewes, "D.A. Rinkes: A Note on His Life and Work," *Bijdragen Tot De Taal-, Land- En Volkenkunde*, vol. 117 (no. 4), pp. 417–435.

71. "Auto Balai Poestaka Berkeliling ditanah Djawa," *Pandji Poestaka*, no. 35, May 12, 1925, pp. 570–572; continued in no. 37, May 19, 1925, pp. 603–604. From 1916 to 1924, the number of *volksbibliotheken* increased from 700 to 2,456, and the number of loans increased in those years from 283,000 to 1,500,000. Balai Poestaka, *Resultaten van de Volkslectuur in het Jaar 1925*, Weltevreden: Volkslectuur, 1926, p. 21.

72. William Bradley Horton, "'A Gift of Unlimited Value': Public Health and Colonial Publishing in Indonesia (1910s–1945)," forthcoming.

73. Authored by the Java-born Dutch doctor Frederik Willem van Haeften (1865–1926?), the book was translated by Haji Agus Salim (1884–1954), a prominent leader of the anti-colonial Islamic reformist movement. Translations followed in various local languages, including Javanese and Hata Batak (the latter spoken by

the Toba-Batak people of North Sumatra). Frederik Willem van Haeften, *Hooge Zuigelingensterfte en Zuigelingenzorg—Pemeliharaan Kanak-kanak jang Menjo-eseo*, Indonesia, Serie D.V.G, no. 3, Weltevreden: Balai Poestaka, 1919, bilingual edition.

74. Henry Heinemann and Antonia Zerwer, *Pemimpin Bagi Mengadjar Anak-Anak disekolah dalam Hal Mengoeroes Baji*, Batavia: Balai Poestaka, 1922.

75. Haeften, *Hooge Zuigelingensterfte*, pp. 14/15. For example, *bacil* is introduced on page 23 alongside the term *benih* ("seed" or "germ"), but in subsequent pages only the latter term is used.

76. Heinemann and Zerwer, *Pemimpin Bagi Mengadjar*, p. 3.

77. Heinemann and Zerwer, *Pemimpin Bagi Mengadjar*, pp. 4–5.

78. L.A.S.M. von Römer, *Over Baringen: Een Boekje voor de Doekoen-doekoen Beranak = Pemimpin Doekoen Beranak*, Weltevreden: Balai Poestaka, 1922, pp. 3–5. This booklet was reprinted again in 1928, 1931, and 1933.

79. Von Römer, *Pemimpin Doekoen Beranak*, pp. 3–5.

80. Balai Poestaka, *Resultaten 1925*, pp. 77–90. The Malay version of *Pemimpin bagi Mengadjar* was borrowed 4,657 times in 1924; for comparison, the translation of Charles Dickens' *The Old Curiosity Shop* was borrowed 5,579 times and the traditional *Hikayat Langlang Boeana*, 5,262 times.

81. Horton, "A Gift of Unlimited Value."

82. As reported by Drewes, between 1908 and 1917 the Volkslectuur had published 280 books and pamphlets, while in the following 5 years, under Rinkes, it had added another 500 titles. Drewes, "D.A. Rinkes," p. 433.

83. Balai Poestaka, *Resultaten 1925*, p. 25.

84. Jedamski, "Balai Pustaka," p. 35. As noted by Yamamoto, Rinkes' own comment that *Pandji Poestaka*'s circulation was an "enormous success" should be understood in terms of its influence, rather than sheer numbers. Nobuto Yamamoto, "Print Power and Censorship in Colonial Indonesia, 1914–1942," PhD dissertation, Cornell University, 2011, p. 97, footnote 171. For comparison, it is worth noting that Yamamoto also mentions how *Tjahaja Hindia*, with 4,500–5,000 copies printed daily, was a "best-selling newspaper" that "circulated widely in comparison to other indigenous newspapers at the time." Yamamoto, "Print Power and Censorship," p. 173.

85. "Boekoe Tabib," *Volksalmanak Melajoe 1920*, Weltevreden: Balai Poestaka, 1919, pp. 59–87.

86. "Dari Hal Mendjaga Roemah-tangga," *Volksalmanak Melajoe 1920*, pp. 93–94.

87. "'Kwak' Mendjadi Makanan Orang Banjak," *Volksalmanak Melajoe 1920*, pp. 95–98.

88. "Boekoe Tabib," *Volksalmanak Melajoe 1920*.

89. "Fasal Kepandaian Orang Perempoewan: Dari Hal Air Soemoer," *Volksalmanak Melajoe 1920*, pp. 111–112. The first dictionary to include the word *bacil* (and in fact also *bacteria*) was the 1929 guide for physicians employed in the Indies. H.A. von Dewall, *Hollandsch-Maleische en Maleisch-Hollandsche Gids ten Dienste van*

Geneeskundigen, Utrecht: Kemink, 1929, p. 16. *Bac[c]il, bacteria* and *mikroob* were not included in any of the following dictionaries: A.H.L. Badings and H.L.J. Badings, *Maleisch Woordenboek*, 8th ed., Zwolle: W.E.J. Tjeenk Willink, 1915; A.H.L. Badings, *Nieuw Hollandsch-Maleisch Maleisch-Hollandsch Woordenboek*, 7th ed., Zwolle: W.E.J. Tjeenk Willink, 1901; H. Cornelius Klinkert and Claas Spat, *Nieuw Nederlandsch-Maleisch Woordenboek*, 3rd ed., Leiden: N. V. Boekhandel en Drukkerij Voorheen E.J. Brill, 1926; *Hollandsch-Maleisch en Maleisch-Hollandsch Zakwoordenboek*, 7th ed., Batavia: G. Kolff, 1932. However, the words *bacil* and *bacterie* appear in Javanese and Malay (as well as Dutch) contexts in the trilingual publication L. Kirschner, *De tien Geboden der Hygiëne voor de Tropen*, Bandoeng: Drukkerij Maks & v.d. Klits, 192?

90. "Roekoen Makan," *Volksalmanak Melajoe 1929*, Weltevreden: Balai Poestaka, 1928, pp. 248–249.

91. "Pemeliharaan Roemah Tangga: Menjapoe dan Memboangkan Leboe," *Volksalmanak Melajoe 1922*, Weltevreden: Balai Poestaka, 1921, pp. 93–94.

92. "Keperloean Roemah Tangga," *Volksalmanak Melajoe 1928*, Weltevreden: Balai Poestaka, 1927, p. 263.

93. Richardson, "Woman as Sanitary Reformer."

94. Sand, *House and Home*, p. 57; quotes p. 60 and 62.

95. Beginning at least in 1923, for example, *Bintang Hindia*'s "health" rubric addressed the need to control microbes, bacteria, and human waste, alongside the importance of drinking clean water. Similar articles peppered the Almanac for years to come. "Dari Hal Napas (Ademhaling) dan Pertoekaran Aat (Assimilatie)," *Volksalmanak Melajoe 1922*, pp. 140–142; "Bagi Kesehatan," *Volksalmanak Melajoe 1924*, Weltevreden: Balai Poestaka, 1923, pp. 139–141; "Pendjaga Kesehatan," *Volksalmanak Melajoe 1927*, Weltevreden: Balai Poestaka, 1926, pp. 211–212; "Pendjaga Kesehatan," *Volksalmanak Melajoe 1928*, pp. 221–222; "Dari Hal Kesehatan," *Volksalmanak Melajoe 1929*, pp. 194–195; "Kesehatan," *Bintang Hindia*, no. 24, June 16, 1923, pp. 376–377 (on microbes and prevention); "Kesehatan," *Bintang Hindia*, no. 34, August 21, 1926, pp. 541–542; Parcival, "Kesehatan," *Bintang Hindia*, no. 36, September 4, 1926, p. 572; "Djagalah: Air Minoem!" *Bintang Hindia*, no. 44, October 30, 1926, pp. 694–695; Anna Sjarif, "Doenia Perempoean: Mengoeroes Anak Anak Ketjil," *Bintang Hindia*, no. 13, March 26, 1928, pp. 223–224. *Bintang Hindia* was not a government publication, but it did receive financial support. Yamamoto, "Print Power and Censorship," p. 56.

96. "Pengetahoean Perempoean," *Volksalmanak Melajoe 1924*, pp. 143–151; "Pengetahoean Perempoean," *Volksalmanak Melajoe 1925*, Weltevreden: Balai Poestaka, 1924, pp. 257–269; "Bagi Keperloean Roemah Tangga," *Volksalmanak Melajoe 1926*, Weltevreden: Balai Poestaka, 1925, pp. 222–227; "Pengetahoean Perempoean," *Volksalmanak Melajoe 1926*, pp. 228–232; "Pengetahoean Perempoean," *Volksalmanak Melajoe 1927*, pp. 245–249; "Masak-masakan," *Volksalmanak Melajoe 1928*, pp. 255–262.

97. Pols, "Eugenics," p. 349.

98. J.H.F. Kohlbrugge, "De vragen 94–102 van den Leidraad van het Gewestelijk Onderzoek naar de Oorzaken der Mindere Welvaart van de Inlandsche Bevolking

op Java en Madoera," *Verslagen der Algemeene Vergadering van het Indisch Genootschap*, 1907, pp. 189–218.

99. Arnout van der Meer, *Performing Power: Cultural Hegemony, Identity, and Resistance in Colonial Indonesia*, Ithaca, NY: Cornell University Press, 2020, p. 17. Fairs and exhibits are discussed as sites of negotiation and contestation of "colonial hegemonic power" in his Chapter 6. Hygiene is discussed in pp. 184–185.

100. Van der Meer, *Performing Power*, p. 182.

101. *Programma van den Pasar Gambir, Batavia, 1923*, Batavia: Vereenigin "Het Pasar Gambir-Comité," 1923, p. 11. Hygiene was under the "Nijverheid-, Industrie- en Hygiène-Tentoostellingen" rubric.

102. "De Pasar Gambir," *Bataviaasch Nieuwsblad*, August 23, 1927.

103. "Nuttige en Doeltreffende Propaganda," *Algemeen Handelsblad voor Neder- landsch-Indië*, September 5, 1933.

104. "De Hygiënische Afdeeling," *Programma van den Pasar Gambir, 28 Augustus–9 September 1925*, pp. 16–17. In its early years, the Dutch press discussed the benefits of "consultation centers" established in the Netherlands to help lower-class mothers. "Moedercursussen te Amsterdam," *Deli Courant*, May 15, 1920; "De Zuigelingensterfte in Limburg," *Deli Courant*, June 28, 1917; "De Gemeente," *De Sumatra Post*, July 29, 1920; "De Goede Invloed der Consultatie-Bureaux van den G.G.D.," *Deli Courant*, October 29, 1932. "De Zorg voor Zuigelingen," *De Preanger-bode*, December 12, 1921; "Nederland: Kleuter-congres te Amsterdam," *Het Nieuws van den Dag voor Nederlandsch-Indië*, April 8, 1929; "Nederland: Voor Opbouw van Drente," *Deli Courant*, December 13, 1930.

105. Anna Sjarif, "Oesahanja Dienst Kesehatan," *Bintang Hindia*, no. 37, September 12, 1925, p. 590. On soap as a medium for cleanliness and illness prevention, see *Pandji Poestaka*, no. 95, December 1925, p. 1888.

106. *Programma van den Pasar Gambir, 26 Augustus–6 September 1927*, p. 15.

107. They were featured first at Batavia; see "De Pasar Gambir," August 23, 1927. Later in Semarang, and more locations. See "Pasar Malam Semarang 1928," *De Locomotief*, July 28, 1928. In 1928, Semarang featured EHTINI displays, as did the small center of Klaten (near Yogyakarta), which held then its first *pasar malam* ("night fair"), also inclusive of a substantial hygiene exhibit "De Pasar Malem te Klaten," *De Nieuwe Vorstenlanden*, March 7, 1929; see also "Klaten, de Pasar Malem," *De Locomotief*, March 13, 1928, for the previous year's exhibit, which showcased plates and graphs on malaria, plague, and hookworm; offered lectures, showed movies, and demonstrated the building of latrines. The journalist noted: "It is remarkable how much interest there is." In 1929, Medan's fair similarly added its first hygiene stand. "De Pasar Malam," *De Sumatra Post*, May 31, 1929.

108. "Groep B. Medische Inzendingen van Instituten, Laboratoria, Vereenigingen enz," *Voorloopig Overzicht der Medio Januari 1927 Gereed Zijnde en Definitief Toegezegde Inzendingen op de EHTINI*, pp. 3–4; *Verslag der Eerste Hygiëne-Tentoonstelling in Nederlandsch Indië*, Bandoeng: Vereeniging tot Bevordering der Hygiëne in Nederlandsch-Indië, 1927, p. 10.

109. "Heiser to Russell," January 16, 1926; Java – A–Z, 1926; RG 5; Series 1_02; Subseries 1926_655; RAC; "Neeb to van Wesep," November 9, 1925; Java – Hydrick, J.L., 1925 July–December; RG 5; Series 1_02; Subseries 1925_655; RAC; "Dean to Neeb," December 22, 1925; Java – Hydrick, J.L., 1925 July–December; RG 5; Series 1_02; Subseries 1925_655; RAC; "Neeb to Wesep," July 28, 1927; Java – A–Z, 1927; RG 5; Series 1_02; Subseries 1927_655; RAC.

110. "Hydrick to Heiser," September 17, 1927; RAC.

111. H.M. Neeb, *Rede Uitgesproken Ter Gelegenheed van de Opening der Eerste Hygiëne Tentoonstelling in Nederlandsch-Indië*, Bandoeng: Drukkerij Maks & v.d. Klits, 1927, p. 9.

112. M.A.J. Kelling, "De Eerste Hygiëne-Tentoonstelling in Nederlandsch-Indië," *D'Orient*, no. 6, June 1927, pp. 63–64.

113. M.A.J. Kelling, "De Eerste Hygiëne-Tentoonstelling in Nederlandsch-Indië," *D'Orient*, no. 6, June 1927, pp. 63–64.

114. "Het Abattoir," *De Locomotief*, May 30, 1927; *Verslag der Eerste Hygiëne-Tentoonstelling*. For more on slaughterhouses, see Chiara Formichi, "Bouillon for His Majesty: Healthy Halal Modernity in Colonial Java," *History of Religions*, vol. 62, no. 4 (2023): 373–409.

115. *Officieele Catalogus der 8ᵉ Ned.-Ind. Jaarbeurs en -Markt en der Eerste Hygiëne Tentoonstelling in Ned. Indië*, 1927, pp. 38–39.

116. *Officieele Catalogus der 8ᵉ*, p. 47.

117. *Officieele Catalogus der 8ᵉ*, p. 75.

118. *Officieele Catalogus der 8ᵉ*, p. 95. See also *Verslag der Eerste Hygiëne-Tentoonstelling*, pp. 20, 24, 28.

119. *Officieele Catalogus der 8ᵉ*, p. 128.

120. Neeb, *Rede Uitgesproken*, p. 16.

121. Kelling, "De Eerste," pp. 63–64.

122. Neeb, *Rede Uitgesproken*, p. 4.

123. Kevin E. Ko, "The Non-Immanent Frame: Medicine as Ethics in the Islamic Modernist Movement of Late Colonial Indonesia," *History of Religions*, vol. 58 (no. 4), 2019, 404–431, p. 422. https://doi.org/10.1086/702254.

124. Haeften, *Hooge Zuigelingensterfte*, p. 14/15. In Chapter 3, "Food," "*soetji*" will emerge as a characteristic of a *halal* food product.

125. *Pangkal Kesehatan* was printed by Balai Poestaka in 1925, and reprinted as an insert in *Pandji Poestaka* in February 1926, between numbers 13 and 14.

126. "Bagi Kesehatan: Djagalah Kesehatan," *Volksalmanak Melajoe 1925*, pp. 237–238.

127. Anna Sjarif, "Tjatetan Seorang Isteri," *Bintang Hindia*, no. 2, January 12, 1924, p. 31; Anna Sjarif, "Tjatetan Seorang Isteri," *Bintang Hindia*, no. 3, January 19, 1924, p. 42. For another review, see "Bab Angoepakara Baji," *Pandji Poestaka*, no. 57, July 28, 1925, p. 1012.

Chapter 2

1. The role of women in advancing the sanitary project is shown in many pictures published in Tillema's 1915 *KromoBlanda*, and in John Lee Hydrick's 1937 *Intensive*

Rural Hygiene Work (accounting for just a small selection of all the pictures taken by the Rockefeller Foundation in the 1920s to 1930s), like the photos now held by the National Museum of World Cultures (Nationaal Museum van Wereldculturen, NMVW), Yale University, and many other libraries. See H.F. Tillema, *"Kromoblanda": Over 't Vraagstuk van "het Wonen" in Kromo's Groote Land*, 's-Gravenhage: H. Uden Masman, 1915. Volume 1 especially focuses on hygiene. Tillema's work has been explored, in part, in Mrázek, *Engineers of Happy Land*.

2. Yamamoto, "Print Power and Censorship." Among many on the 1930s political environment, see Formichi, *Islam and the Making of the Nation*.

3. On van Bemmel, see Henk Schulte Nordholt, "Modernity and Middle Classes in the Netherlands Indies. Cultivating Cultural Citizenship," in Susie Protschky (ed.) *Photography, Modernity and the Governed in Late-Colonial Indonesia*, pp. 223–254, Amsterdam: Amsterdam University Press, 2015, p. 241.

4. See Anna Sjarif, "Doenia Isteri: Hati-Hati Pada Doekoen . . . ," *Bintang Hindia*, no. 12, March 21, 1925, pp. 189–190; Anna Sjarif, "Doenia Isteri: Sedikit tentang Demam Beranak," *Bintang Hindia*, no. 50, December 11, 1926, pp. 799–800; Anna Sjarif, "Doenia Isteri: Sedikit tentang Demam Beranak II," *Bintang Hindia*, no. 51, December 2?, 1926, p. 815; "Pemandangan didoenia Anak-anak," *Bintang Hindia*, no. 10, March 5, 1928, pp. 174–175.

5. Frances Gouda, "Teaching Indonesian Girls in Java and Bali, 1900–1942: Dutch Progressives, the Infatuation with 'Oriental' Refinement, and 'Western' Ideas About Proper Womanhood," *Women's History Review*, vol. 4 (no. 1), 1995, pp. 25–62, quote p. 28. DOI: 10.1080/09612029500200072.

6. Dewi Kurniawati Hastuti, "Javanese Women and Islam: Identity Formation Since the Twentieth Century," *Southeast Asian Studies*, vol. 1 (no. 1), 2012, 109–140. https://doi.org/10.20495/seas.1.1_109.

7. See the contributions by Rita Smith Kipp and Frances Gouda, respectively, in Julia Ann Clancy-Smith and Frances Gouda (eds.) *Domesticating the Empire: Race, Gender, and Family Life in French and Dutch Colonialism*, Charlottesville, VA: University Press of Virginia, 1998.

8. Locher-Scholten, *Women and the Colonial State*, Chapter 2.

9. The economically productive engagement of women in Java and Sumatra has been singled out by several scholars of the region. Anthony Reid argued that a "common pattern of relatively high female autonomy and economic importance" characterized Southeast Asia as a region. While cautioning against such broad generalization, Barbara Watson Andaya has noted that women in Java and Sumatra had a strong public presence. Jeff Hadler has discussed how in West Sumatra, Minangkabau women retained a hold on public life within a Muslim society despite pressures from religious reformists and colonial officials. In Java, scholars have recurrently noted how women spent most of their time working in the fields, travelling to markets outside of their villages, at the river, or tending to children (their own offspring, or their younger siblings) and the house. Suzanne Brenner's ethnographic work has recuperated urbanized women's central role as entrepreneurs as well as brokers of spiritual wellbeing in 1990s Central Java. Defining a "domestic economy" that encompassed all the above, Brenner argued that "the market is a

woman's world," and the home was a center of cultural and material production, making the domestic sphere part and parcel of the public. Locher-Scholten has documented Javanese women's employment in the coffee, tea, and rubber plantations. Similarly, Elise van Nederveen Meerkerk has shown that they were "remarkably economically active" beyond their participation in formalized industries, as their labor included the unpaid work conducted in the household, which ranged from cleaning and cooking to subsistence agriculture and food making for plantation workers. Javanese women's "industriousness" was not just a trope of European narratives that berated men as "lazy." We see this in the title art of the economics insert to *Pandji Poestaka* printed in 1939, which depicts a woman making batik, a woman with a basket walking along the paddy fields followed by a child, and two men sitting in the shade of a shed watching the rice grow. See Anthony Reid, *Southeast Asia in the Age of Commerce, 1450–1680*, volume 1, New Haven: Yale University Press, 1988, p. 146; Barbara Watson Andaya, introduction to *The Flaming Womb: Repositioning Women in Early Modern Southeast Asia*, Honolulu: University of Hawai'i Press, 2006; Jeffrey Alan Hadler, *Muslims and Matriarchs: Cultural Resilience in Indonesia Through Jihad and Colonialism*, Ithaca, NY: Cornell University Press, 2008; Suzanne April Brenner, *The Domestication of Desire: Women, Wealth, and Modernity in Java*, Princeton, NJ: Princeton University Press, 1998 (quote from p. 135, citing a Solonese proverb); Locher-Scholten, *Women and the Colonial State*; Elise van Nederveen Meerkerk, *Women, Work and Colonialism in the Netherlands and Java: Comparisons, Contrasts, and Connections, 1830–1940*, 1st ed., Cham: Springer International Publishing, 2019, p. 1; *Perekonomian Ra'jat*, no. 1, January 1939 (see also no. 26, December 20, 1939).

10. Anna Sjarif, "Pakaian Perempoean," *Bintang Hindia*, no. 10, March 8, 1924, pp. 158–159.

11. "Tanggoengan jang Mendjadi Iboe," *De Vrouw*, no. 11, May 1927, p. 4.

12. Directrice, "Permoelaan Kalam."

13. "Gadis-gadis Toerki – Persatoean Menoelis," *Isteri Soesila – Taman Moeslimah*, no. 3, June 1924, p. 39.

14. "Perempoean di Philippijn – Doenia Isteri," *Isteri Soesila – Taman Moeslimah*, no. 1, January 1925, p. 10.

15. Soewarsih, "Doenia Isteri: Pergerakan Perempoean di Filipina," *Bintang Hindia*, no. 4, January 24, 1925, pp. 63–64. The comment on Filipina women being politically aware (*sedar*) is also made in 1926, in contraposition to the Indonesian women's movement that is seen as lagging. Anna Sjarif, "Doenia Isteri: Gerakan Perempoean di Loear Negeri," *Bintang Hindia*, no. 13, March 27, 1926, pp. 207–208.

16. For more see Mina Roces, "Filipino Elite Women and Public Health in the American Colonial Era, 1906–1940," *Women's History Review*, vol. 26 (no. 3), 2017, 477–502. DOI: 10.1080/09612025.2016.1194076.

17. Soewarsih, "Pergerakan Perempoean di Filipina." Similar considerations were offered for China, see Anna Sjarif, "Doenia Isteri: Pergerakan Perempoean di Tiongkok," *Bintang Hindia*, no. 13, March 28, 1927, pp. 173–174.

18. Chan Leang Nio, "Doenia Isteri: Kepentingannja Orang Merawat Baji," *Bintang Hindia*, no. 24, June 13, 1925, pp. 382–384. Chan Leang Nio had just published her first novel—incidentally, "the first novel emanating from a woman writer"—in which she criticized traditional arranged marriages, and societal concerns over friendly bonds between unmarried men and women, expressing what has been labeled a "radical" viewpoint. Claudine Lombard-Salmon, "Chinese Women Writers in Indonesia and Their Views of Female Emancipation," *Archipel*, 1984, pp. 149–171, pp. 156–157.

19. "Perkoempoelan Palang Doewa," *Pandji Poestaka*, no. 42, May 25, 1928, pp. 758–759.

20. "Perkoempoelan Palang Doewa."

21. Gerald E. Thomson, "'A Baby Show Means Work in the Hardest Sense': The Better Baby Contests of the Vancouver and New Westminster Local Councils of Women, 1913–1929," *BC Studies*, no. 128, 2000, pp. 5–36, pp. 7–8.

22. Margaret Mih Tillman, "Measuring Up: Better Baby Contests in China, 1917–45," *Modern Asian Studies*, vol. 54 (no. 6), 2020, pp. 1749–1786, p. 1751. DOI: 10.1017/S0026749X19000258. For another example, see Jean Allman, "Making Mothers: Missionaries, Medical Officers and Women's Work in Colonial Asante, 1924–1945," *History Workshop*, no. 38, 1994, pp. 23–47, http://www.jstor.org/stable/4289318.

23. Thomson, "Baby Show Means Work," p. 6.

24. Tillman, "Measuring Up," p. 1763.

25. Yuehtsen Juliette Chung, *Struggle for National Survival: Eugenics in Sino-Japanese Contexts, 1896–1945*, New York, NY: Routledge, 2002, Chapter 3; quote p. 62.

26. Anna Sjarif, "Schooneidswedstrijd voor Kinderen van 5 tot 11 Jaar," *Bintang Hindia*, no. 49, December 6, 1924, pp. 761–762.

27. Anna Sjarif, "Doenia Isteri: Dari Red. – Pergerakan Perempoean di Filipina," *Bintang Hindia*, January 24, 1925, p. 64. Commentary to Soewarsih.

28. "Bandung Jaarboer," *Doenia Isteri*, no. 1, May 15, 1928, p. 7; "Congress Program," *Soeara Moehammadijah*, no. 11, November 29, 1928, p. 175.

29. On baby contests in the Philippines, see Frauke Scheffler, "Producing Citizens: Infant Health Programs in the Philippines, 1900–1930," PhD dissertation, University of Cologne, 2019.

30. "Seteleng Baji di Solo," *Pandji Poestaka*, no. 16, February 22, 1929, pp. 243–244.

31. "Seteleng Baji."

32. Chan Leang Nio, "Doenia Isteri: Kepentingannja."

33. In the following decade, there were never more than two indigenous women doctors at any one time. *Regeerings-Almanak voor Nederlandsch-Indië 1930*, vol. 2, pp. 517–521; *Regeerings-Almanak 1938*, vol. 2, pp. 541–547.

34. Among many articles reporting on this, see *Isteri*, no. 5, September 1929, p. 2; *Bintang Hindia*, no. 31, August 10, 1929, p. 508. Two other women from the Indies had already graduated as physicians from the STOVIA (School tot Opleiding van Inlandsche Artsen) medical school in Weltevreden in years past. They were both Christian Minahasan from North Sulawesi, and their names were Marie

Joesoef-Thomas (obstetrician) and Anna Karamoy-Warouw (otorhinolaryngologist), *De Locomotief*, July 24, 1929.

35. *De Indische Courant*, July 20, 1929.

36. *De Indiër*, June 7, 1918.

37. *De Indische Courant*, May 22, 1923.

38. Sjarif, "Hati-hati pada Doekoen . . ."

39. Prof. Dr. J.J. Van Loghem, "Geneeskundige Hulp. Een Goede Opleiding Noodig voor het Inlandsch Verplegend Personeel," *De Locomotief*, February 12, 1929. By then, Loghem was head of the Institute for Tropical Hygiene in Amsterdam; previously he had been a bacteriologist at the Medan laboratory, in Sumatra.

40. "De NIAS te Soerabaia," *De Indische Courant*, May 22, 1929; "De NIAS-Examens," *De Indische Courant*, May 28, 1930; "NIAS de Overgangen," *De Soerabajasch Handelsblad*, June 16, 1936; Japan Rikugun, *Orang Indonesia Yang Terkemuka di Jawa*, Yogyakarta: Gadjah Mada University Press, 1986, p. 366.

41. "Doenia Isteri: Nona Moedinem, Arts," *Pandji Poestaka*, no. 100, December 14, 1937, p. 1985; Japan Rikugun, *Orang Indonesia*, p. 333.

42. "Mutaties – D.V.G.," *De Koerier*, February 2, 1934.

43. "Geneeskundige Praktijk," *De Indische Courant*, February 6, 1935.

44. "Akte von Toelating," *De Koerier*, February 20, 1936. Sapartinah had graduated a year earlier, "Examens," *De Locomotief*, January 18, 1935.

45. Japan Rikugun, *Orang Indonesia*, p. 333.

46. "Akte von Toelating," *De Locomotief*, May 4, 1938.

47. "N.I.A.S.," *De Soerabajasch Handelsblad*, September 26, 1941.

48. *Algemeen Handelsblad voor Nederlandsch-Indië*, February 8, 1936; *Bataviaasch Nieuwsblad*, July 15, 1936.

49. Marshall C. Balfour, *Public Health and Demography in the Far East: Report of a Survey Trip, September 13–December 13, 1948*, New York, NY: Rockefeller Foundation, 1950, p. 92.

50. *Bataviaasch Nieuwsblad*, June 7, 1935.

51. "Examen voor Vroedvrouw," *De Locomotief*, August 5, 1938; "Personalia," *De Locomotief*, October 20, 1939.

52. Diary of John Lee Hydrick [JLH Diary], August 24, 1938, in 1938–1939, p. 63; RG 12, F-L; Hydrick, John L.; RAC.

53. *De Indische Courant*, July 20, 1929; *De Indische Courant*, October 1, 1931.

54. She worked there until at least 1939. Japan Rikugun, *Orang Indonesia*, p. 312.

55. "Solo," *De Locomotief*, December 4, 1931.

56. "Perawatan Anak Baji," *Sin Tin Po*, December 7, 1931.

57. Patricia Fara, *A Lab of One's Own: Science and Suffrage in the First World War*, Oxford, UK: Oxford University Press, 2018.

58. Miss H.J. Buddingh had also been appointed as an analyst in Surabaya, since 1917. *Regeerings-Almanak 1918*, part 2, p. 404 lists them all. However, the list of all personnel employed by the medical laboratories from 1888 to 1938, appended to the 1938 *Mededeelingen van den Dienst der Volksgezondheid in Nederlandsch-Indië*,

indicates that Miss M. Noordink was the first woman employed in the Indies' medical laboratories. *Mededeelingen DVG*, XXVIII, 1938 (1–2), p. 272.

59. Miss Carpentier Alting, member of one of the most prominent Dutch families in the colony, upon marriage had transitioned first to working as a pharmacist, and then to teaching at the elite Batavia school named after her family's patriarch; by 1923 she was out of the spotlight, back to private life. *Regeerings-Almanak 1919*, part 2, p. 421; *Regeerings-Almanak 1920*, part 2, p. 445. She is not mentioned in the 1921 volume. *Regeerings-Almanak 1922*, part 2, p. 350; *Regeerings-Almanak 1923*, part 2.

60. *Regeerings-Almanak 1924*, part 2, p. 446.

61. J.K. Baars, "De Chemische Afdeeling van het Geneeskundig Laboratorium Gedurende het Tijdvak 1916–1936," *Mededeelingen DVG*, XXVIII, 1938 (1–2), p. 57.

62. Several commercial products mentioned in their advertisements that they were being certified by the colonial laboratory.

63. Steven Paul Palmer, *Launching Global Health: The Caribbean Odyssey of the Rockefeller Foundation*, Conversations in Medicine and Society, Ann Arbor: University of Michigan Press, 2010, p. 107.

64. Willem De Vogel, "De Rol van het Geneeskundig Laboratorium te Batavia, in de Gezondheidszorg voor Nederlandsch-Indië," *Mededeelingen DVG*, XXVII, 1938, pp. 4–14, p. 8.

65. *Mededeelingen DVG*, XXV, 1936, 3, pp. 212–213. In 1937 another course was established in Bandung for "Auxiliary Analysts" with broader admissions and a shorter training period ("Hulp Analysten-cursus," *De Locomotief*, May 6, 1938), but no women participated there ("Onderwijs. Examen voor Hulp-Annalyst [*sic*]. Alle Candidaten Geslaagd," *De Indische Courant*, January 13, 1939). In the late 1930s, "sanitary inspectors" might also be trained in the examination of milk, to expand the reach of its monitoring. JLH Diary, May 12, 1939, in 1938–1939, p. 268; RAC.

66. *Mededeelingen DVG*, XXVIII, 1939 (2–3), p. 137.

67. Ny. Lily Gamar Sutantio, Arsip Nasional Republik Indonesia, *Di bawah Pendudukan Jepang: Kenangan Empat Puluh Dua Orang Yang Mengalaminya*. Penerbitan Sejarah Lisan, no. 4, Jakarta: Arsip Nasional Republik Indonesia, 1988, p. 38.

68. Hydrick, *The Division of Public Health Education*, 1929.

69. Hydrick, *Intensive* (1937), p. 18, emphasis in original. This was a highly impactful report worldwide. First published in Dutch in 1936, it was soon after translated in several languages: English in 1937 (and more later), French in 1938, Japanese in 1942, and Spanish in 1944.

70. John Lee Hydrick, *Intensive Rural Hygiene Work in the Netherlands East Indies*, New York, NY: Netherlands Information Bureau, 1942, p. 12.

71. Hydrick, *Intensive* (1937).

72. Hydrick, *Intensive* (1937), caption to plate before p. 19.

73. Hydrick, *Intensive* (1937), caption to plate after p. 18.

74. Hydrick, *Intensive* (1937), p. 18, emphasis in original.

75. "De Hygiënische Organisatie, Summary for the Year 1935," p. 41; RAC.

76. Hydrick, *Intensive* (1937), p. 16, emphasis in original.

77. "Dean to Hydrick," February 18, 1927; RAC; "Hydrick to Heiser" October 19, 1926; RAC; "Hydrick to Heiser," November 14, 1929; RAC; "De Hygienische Organisatie, Summary for the Year 1935"; RAC.

78. Stein, "Vital Times," p. 82, quote marks in original.

79. "1933 3rd Quarter Report," p. 11; Reports – Java (Indonesia); 1933; RG 5; Subseries 3_655 GEN; RAC.

80. "De Pasar Gambir," *Bataviaasch Nieuwsblad*, August 25, 1931.

81. "Nuttige en Doeltreffende Propaganda," *Algemeen Handelsblad voor Nederlandsch-Indië*, September 5, 1933.

82. "Tentoonstelling 'De Zuigeling,'" *Het Nieuws van den Dag voor Nederlandsch-Indië*, August 28, 1933. This was in stark contrast with the 1927 EHTINI Exhibition in Bandung where Lactogen had been able to showcase its products.

83. "Hydrick to Miss Beard," March 13, 1934, p. 2, SG 1.1, Series 300–833, Subseries 655.L. After many years as a nurse, administrator, and nursing educator, Mary Beard (who graduated in 1903 from New York Hospital School of Nursing, which later became Cornell University New York Hospital School of Nursing) had become Associate Director of the IHD in 1931, and in 1938 assumed the directorship of the American Red Cross Nursing Services.

84. Anne-Emmanuelle Birn, "Skirting the Issue: Women and International Health in Historical Perspective," *American Journal of Public Health*, vol. 89 (no. 3), 1999, pp. 399–407, citation p. 400.

85. Java – Public Health Work, 1st Quarterly Report 1934, 1934, p. 14; RG 5; Subseries 3_655 GEN; RAC.

86. "Hydrick to Miss Beard," March 13, 1934, pp. 3–4; RAC.

87. "1934 3rd Quarter Report," "1935 2nd Quarter Report," p. 18. Reports – Java (Indonesia); 1933; RG 5; Subseries 3_655 GEN; RAC.

88. "1935 3rd Quarter Report," p. 11; Reports – Java (Indonesia); 1933; RG 5; Subseries 3_655 GEN; RAC.

89. JLH Diary, July 19, 1938, in 1938–1939, p. 20; RAC.

90. JLH Diary, July 5, 1938, in 1938–1939, p. 5; RAC.

91. "Hydrick to Dr. Russell," March 26, 1935, SG 1.1, Series 300–833, Subseries 655.L; RAC.

92. "Hydrick to Dr. Sawyer," September 19, 1935, SG 1.1, Series 300–833, Subseries 655.L; RAC.

93. "Hydrick to Dr. Sawyer," October 1, 1935, SG 1.1, Series 300–833, Subseries 655.L; RAC.

94. "Hydrick to Dr. Sawyer," September 19, 1935.

95. "Hydrick to Miss Beard," March 13, 1934.

96. "Hydrick to Dr. Russell," March 26, 1935; RAC.

97. "The Organization of Hygiene Work, Summary for the Year 1938," p. 73; Java – Public Health Work, Annual Report 1938, 1938; RG 5; Subseries 3_655 GEN; RAC.

98. "Intensive Hygiene Work in Netherlands India, a Brief Summary for 1936," p. 21; Java – Public Health Work, Annual Report 1936, 1936; RG 5; Subseries 3_655 GEN; RAC.

99. JLH Diary 1938–1939, December 20, 1938, in 1938–1939, p. 152; RAC.

100. JLH Diary 1938–1939, August 24, 1938, in 1938–1939, p. 63; RAC.

101. "Examen voor Vroedvrouw," August 5, 1938, *De Locomotief.*

102. JLH Diary 1938–1939, December 22, 1938, in 1938–1939, p. 154; RAC.

103. JLH Diary 1938–1939, March 16, 1939, in 1938–1939, p. 217; RAC.

104. JLH Diary 1938–1939, April 14, 1939, in 1938–1939, p. 240; RAC.

105. JLH Diary 1938–1939, April 13, 1939, in 1938–1939, p. 239; RAC.

106. André G. Van Veen, "'De Voeding' op de Conferentie van Landelijke Hygiëne, van 3–13 Augustus, te Bandoeng," *Geneeskundig Tijdschrift voor Nederlandsch-Indië*, vol. 77, no. 46, November 16, 1937, pp. 2805–2817.

107. "The Organization of Hygiene Work, Summary for the Year 1938," pp. 236 and 77; RAC.

108. "The Organization of Hygiene Work, Summary for the Year 1938," pp. 23–24; RAC.

109. "The Organization of Hygiene Work, Summary for the Year 1938," p. 77; "The Organization of Hygiene Work, January–June 1939," p. 3; Java – Public Health Work, 1st Semi-Annual Report 1939, 1939; RG 5; Subseries 3_655 GEN; RAC.

110. "Perkoempoelan Palang Doewa."

111. Hydrick, *Intensive*, 1937, p. 36.

112. Hydrick, *Intensive*, 1937, p. 35.

113. Hydrick, *Intensive*, 1937, p. 37.

114. JLH Diary 1938–1939, July 7, 1938, in 1938–1939, p. 8; RAC.

115. JLH Diary 1938–1939, August 1, 1938, in 1938–1939, pp. 36–37; RAC.

116. Birn, "Skirting the Issue," p. 404. See also Susan Lynn Smith, *Sick and Tired of Being Sick and Tired: Black Women's Health Activism in America, 1890–1950*, Philadelphia, PA: University of Pennsylvania Press, 1995; and Margaret Charles Smith and Linda Janet Holmes, *Listen to Me Good: The Life Story of an Alabama Midwife*, Columbus, OH: Ohio State University Press, 1996.

117. "Doenia Isteri: Perempoean di Philippijn"; Soewarsih, "Doenia Isteri."

118. Chan Leang Nio, "Doenia Isteri: Kepentingannja."

119. "Perkoempoelan Palang Doewa."

120. JLH Diary, April 22, 1939, RCH archives, 1938–1939, p. 248; see also May 15, 1939, p. 270; RAC.

121. "The Organization of Hygiene Work, January–June 1939," p. 3; RAC.

Chapter 3

1. Amir, and Burgerlijke Geneeskundige Dienst (BGD), *Vliegen en Vliegenverdelging = Dari Hal Lalat (Langau) Serta Ichtiar akan Memoesnahkannja*, Weltevreden: Drukkerij Volkslectuur, 1921, p. 33.

2. Burg, *De Geneesheer*; Cornelis Leendert van der Burg, *Persoonlijke Gezondheidsleer voor Europeanen*, Amsterdam: J.H. de Bussy, 1895; W.F. Donath, *Opmerkingen over de Inheemsche Voeding*, Buitenzorg: Archipel, 1931.

3. Burg, *De Geneesheer*, p. 144.

4. Burg, *De Geneesheer*, p. 149.

5. Burg, *De Geneesheer*, p. 155–156.

6. E.g., *Deli Courant*, September 25, 1886; *Deli Courant*, July 3, 1889; *De Loco-motief*, November 11, 1890; *Soerabaijasch Handelsblad*, February 16, 1899.

7. Burg, *Persoonlijke Gezondheidsleer*, pp. 38–42.

8. Adel P. den Hartog, "Diffusion of Milk as a New Food to Tropical Regions: The Example of Indonesia, 1880–1942," PhD dissertation, Stichting Voeding Nederland Proefschrift Wageningen, 1986, p. 85; W. van den Akker, "Over de Taak van den Veterinair-hygiënist bij de Indische Gemeente," *Nederlandsch-Indische Bladen voor Diergeneeskunde*, no. 4, 1929, pp. 201–215.

9. Burg, *Persoonlijke Gezondheidsleer*, pp. 28–31, 95–98.

10. Burg, *De Geneesheer*, pp. 144–147.

11. Susie Protschky, "The Colonial Table: Food, Culture and Dutch Identity in Colonial Indonesia," *Australian Journal of Politics & History*, vol. 54 (no. 3), 2008, 346–357. https://doi.org/10.1111/j.1467-8497.2008.00501.x.

12. Burg, *Persoonlijke Gezondheidsleer*, p. 27.

13. See De Vogel, "De Rol van het Geneeskundig Laboratorium," quote p. 5.

14. Amir, *Vliegen en Vliegenverdelging*, p. 29.

15. Formichi, "Bouillon for His Majesty."

16. Paul Christiaan Flu, *Tropenhygiëne: Populaire Voordrachten*, Batavia: Javasche Boekhandel & Drukkerij, 1917.

17. Local companies were present in Medan, Batavia, and Surabaya, e.g., advertisement for Jasmilico (Java Sterilized Milk Company), *Bintang Hindia*, no. 20, May 19, 1923, p. 312; advertisement for Jasmilico, *Bintang Hindia*, no. 24, June 16, 1923, p. 370. News about dairy production abroad: see, among others, "Peroesahan Pemerahan Soesoe di Amerika," *Pandji Poestaka*, no. 6, January 18, 1929, p. 88; "Kroniek," *Pandji Poestaka*, no. 23, March 19, 1929, p. 372. Similar concerns were widespread also in Singapore, for example throughout the 1910s to 1930s, and China. See Nicole Tarulevicz, "Untouched by Human Hands: Making and Marketing Milk in Singapore, 1900–2007," in Cecilia Leong-Salobir (ed.) *Routledge Handbook of Food in Asia*, London: Routledge, 2019, pp. 193–206; François Sabban, "The Taste for Milk in Modern China (1865–1937)," in Jakob A. Klein and Anne Murcott (eds.) *Food Consumption in Global Perspective. Essays in the Anthropology of Food in Honour of Jack Goody*, Basingstoke: Palgrave Macmillan, 2014, pp. 182–208.

18. Baars, "De Chemische Afdeeling," p. 47.

19. Baars, "De Chemische Afdeeling," p. 46.

20. Flu, *Tropenhygiëne*; Paul Christiaan Flu, *Kesehatan didalam Kampoeng*, Batavia: Balai Poestaka, 1922.

21. See, for example, "Pemerahan Soesoe dikampoeng-kampoeng dalam Gemeente Betawi," *Pandji Poestaka*, no. 1, January 2, 1925, p. 6.

22. Amir, *Vliegen en Vliegenverdelging*, quote p. 27; "Boekoe Tabib," *Volksalmanak Melajoe 1920*; "Fasal Kepandaian Orang Perempoewan"; Pierre Peverelli and F. van Bemmel, *Blyf Gezond!: Platenatlas Ten Behoeve Van Het Onderwijs in De Gezondheidsleer Op De Indische Lagere Scholen = Sehatlah Selaloe! Boekoe Gambar*

jang Dipergoenakan Oentoek Mengadjarkan Ilmoe Kesehatan disekolah Rendah di-tanah Hindia, Groningen: Wolters, 1933, plate #10.

23. The *Geneeskundig Tijdschrift Nederlandsch Indië* regularly published research on nutrition; the number of articles surged from 1933 onwards. Van Veen also wrote about this in 1950. He identified three phases in scientific production on nutrition, namely: 1885 to 1918, dominated by research on beriberi and rice, and culminating in the discovery of vitamins; 1918 to 1932, reflecting the expansion of knowledge on vitamins and focusing on foods' components rather than their consumption; 1933 onwards, when the focus shifted to dietary surveys and the conditions that affect them. André Van Veen, "Nutrition Studies in Indonesia 1850–1950," *Documenta Neerlandica et Indonesica de Morbis Tropicis*, vol. 2 (no. 4), 1950, pp. 374–383.

24. "Moesoeh Kita," *Isteri*, no. 12, April 1930, p. 3; it indicates it is "from G.B. no. 3," which I read to be the *Gezondheid Brigades* newsletter (printed in both Indonesian and Dutch), curated by Peverelli for children (both European and Malay) enrolled in the Brigades. Its symbol was of two blond children defending themselves from a gigantic fly by holding a shield engraved with crosses.

25. Among many pertinent sources, see "Hydrick to Heiser," August 20, 1930 (Public Health Education), 1928–1941, 1945; RG 1; SG 1.1, Series 300–833, Subseries 655.L; RAC; "Java - Public Health Work, Report for the 3rd quarter - 1930, Narrative and Statistical" Java - Public Health Education, 3rd Quarterly Report, 1930, 1930; RG 5; Subseries 3_655 L; RAC.

26. "De Hygiënische Tentoonstelling," *Het Nieuws van den Dag voor Nederlandsch-Indië*, August 29, 1931.

27. "De 11ᵉ Pasar Gambir. De Hygiënische Tentoonstelling," *Het Nieuws van Den dag voor Nederlandsch-Indië*, September 2, 1931.

28. See Chapter 2, "Labor," for a note on how nutrition found its way at Purwokerto in the late 1930s.

29. With milk priced at 50 cents per liter, a civil-servant family would have allocated just under a fifth of their daily income to milk, but those employed as laborers in European firms would have not been able to spend 40% of their daily wage. Hartog, "Diffusion of Milk," pp. 92–95, fn 72.

30. The Association and newsletter appeared first in 1931 in Batavia, and shortly branches mushroomed across the archipelago, each issuing its own newsletter too (in Surabaya and Semarang, and eventually Bandung and Deli [Medan]); all regularly printed articles on nutrition and vitamins.

31. *De Huisvrouw in Indië*, no. 1, November 1931, back cover.

32. *De Huisvrouw in Indië*, no. 1, November 1931, p. 8.

33. *Officieel Orgaan van de Vereeniging van Huisvrouwen Soerabaja*, February 1932, Milk Report for December 1931.

34. "Dari Hal Kesehatan."

35. "Roekoen Makan."

36. Soekarmi, "Sedikit tentang Hal Makanan."

37. Haeften, *Hooge Zuigelingensterfte*.

38. Heinemann and Zerwer, *Pemimpin Bagi Mengadjar.*

39. Haeften, *Hooge Zuigelingensterfte*, pp. 14/15.

40. For news on such cases see, e.g., "Diratjoen," *Pandji Poestaka*, no. 91, November 13, 1928, p. 1531.

41. Haeften, *Hooge Zuigelingensterfte*, pp. 51–59.

42. Haeften, *Hooge Zuigelingensterfte*, p. 19.

43. Heinemann and Zerwer, *Pemimpin Bagi Mengadjar*, p. 3.

44. How breastfeeding could have been achieved is not clear. Extensive perusal of colonial photograph collections has not uncovered any images of women at work in the rice fields, tea, or tobacco plantations, or any factory, with their baby on the hip. To me, this was quite obviously an Ethicist projection that assumed that a mother who didn't have access to clean water did not work. There is however a remote possibility, documentation of which I have so far not seen, that new mothers were employed in tasks that allowed them to keep their infant with them. Another exception was the setting up of a maternity ward at the Holland American Plantation Company in Kisaran, Sumatra; starting in 1918, female labourers employed there were given three months of paid "maternity leave" to care for their newborns ("Stadnieuws," *Deli Courant*, December 7, 1921; see also N.C. Keukenschrijver and W.B. Doorenbos, "Eenige Statistische Gegevens naar Aanleiding van een Duizend Bevallingen in de Kraaminrichring van de Holland-Amerikaansche Platagemaatschappij te Kisaran," *Geneeskundig Tijdschrift*, vol. 61, 1921, pp. 488–499). This estate was characterized as "the cleanest and best-kept plantation in the East. . . . One of the features . . . is a large hospital which is regarded as the best in the Asiatic tropics." ("The Sumatra Plantation of the United States Rubber Plantations, Inc.," *The India Rubber World*, vol. 60, August 1919, pp. 611–613, quote p. 612. See also Shakila Yacob, "Model of Welfare Capitalism? The United States Rubber Company in Southeast Asia, 1910–1942," *Enterprise and Society*, vol. 8 (no. 1), 2007, pp. 136–174).

45. Davin, "Imperialism and Motherhood." For a Dutch example, "De Zuigelingensterfte in Limburg."

46. Thomas Stamford Raffles, *The History of Java*, London: Oxford University Press, [1830] 1965, Chapter 2, p. 78.

47. Padmasusastra, *Tata Cara*, Jakarta: Departemen Pendidikan dan Kebudayaan, Proyek Penerbitan Buku Bacaan Sastra Indonesia dan Daerah, 1980 [1907], p. 45.

48. Burg, *Persoonlijke Gezondheidsleer*, pp. 103–105.

49. This is an interesting intervention by H.A. Salim, who translated Haeften's original statement that "mother's milk is the best food for babies *als regel*" with *'adat*, implying customs and tradition, as opposed to mere "practice" (the Dutch wording would literally translate "as a rule"). For the role of translators as cultural filters, see Tom Hoogervorst, "Gained in Translation: The Politics of Localising Western Stories in Late-Colonial Indonesia," in Grace Chin (ed.) *Translational Politics in Southeast Asian Literatures: Contesting Race, Gender and Sexuality*, pp. 100–131, New York, NY: Routledge, 2021.

50. European narratives often berated indigenous men as "lazy." See Van Nederveen Meerkerk, *Women, Work and Colonialism*, p. 5, citing Daendels' observations published in 1814, and colonial reports from the 1910s and 1930s.

51. Kohlbrugge, "De vragen 94."

52. Henry Heinemann, *Practische Wenken voor Moeders*, Medan: Typ. Köhler and Co., 1928; A.G. Klift-Snijder, *Moeder-cursus in Mowewe (z.o. Selebes)*, Zeist: SIMAVI, 1936.

53. Heinemann, *Practische Wenken*, pp. 23, 28.

54. Hildred Geertz, *The Javanese Family: A Study of Kinship and Socialization*, New York: Free Press, 1961, p. 107; James L. Peacock, *Muslim Puritans: Reformist Psychology in Southeast Asian Islam*, Berkeley, CA: University of California Press, 1978, p. 60.

55. Hartog, "Diffusion of Milk," pp. 77–78.

56. Similar approaches had been pursued by the French colonial order in Indochina; there, *métis* children were removed from their mothers and "raised . . . as modern French citizens," fluent in the French language and comfortable in a French cultural social environment. Christina Firpo, "Modernity and the Body: Franco-Vietnamese Children in the Colonial Era and Beyond," in Susie Protschky, Tom van den Berge, and Timothy P. Barnard (eds.) *Modern Times in Southeast Asia, 1920s–1970s*, Leiden: Brill, 2018, pp. 191–210; quote p. 193.

57. Ann Laura Stoler, "A Sentimental Education: Native Servants and the Cultivation of European Children in the Netherlands Indies," in Laurie J. Sears (ed.) *Fantasizing the Feminine in Indonesia*, pp. 71–91, p. 79, New York, NY: Duke University Press, 2020. https://doi.org/10.1515/9780822396710-005.

58. Stoler, "A Sentimental Education," p. 72.

59. Locher-Scholten, "Summer Dresses," p. 171.

60. Quote from: "Kindersterfte in Verband met Voeding," *De Locomotief*, June 3, 1908; "Zuigelingenvoeding," *Bataviaasch Nieuwsblad*, May 6, 1903; "Over Kindersterfte," *Soerabaijasch Handelsblad*, November 26, 1904; "Van Vreemden en Eigen Bodem," *Bataviaasch Nieuwsblad*, October 14, 1908; "De Zuigelingensterfte in Limburg"; "Onze Voeding," *De Preanger-Bode*, December 19, 1906; and many more.

61. Schulte Nordholt, "Modernity and Middle Classes," p. 231. For a comparative reading, see Raquel A.G. Reyes, "Modernizing the Manileña: Technologies of Conspicuous Consumption for the Well-to-Do Woman, Circa 1880s–1930s," *Modern Asian Studies*, vol. 46 (no. 1), 2012, pp. 193–220. http://www.jstor.org/stable/41330659.

62. I draw these conclusions based on the newspaper collection included on delpher.nl. The Ovomaltine advertisement appeared thirteen times between July 30, 1926, and October 11, 1927 (and reappeared again briefly in 1938–1939). Glaxo's advertisement appeared close to fifty times in 1931 and 1932.

63. Articles by Prof. Dr. E. Gorter (who wrote in support of breastfeeding) and Dr. Enklaar (whose writings focused on alternative forms of infant feeding) appeared in *De Locomotief* (and from there were reprinted in the *Deli Courant* and *De Indische Courant*) between March 1930 and February 1931 (with follow-ups in 1934 and 1938, respectively).

64. A. Kolping and H. Mosmans, *Huwelijk en Huisgezin*, reviewed in "Recensies," *De Koerier*, March 16, 1932.

65. "Tentoonstelling voor de Huisvrouw," *Soerabaijasch Handelsblad*, May 5, 1934. These examples simply reinforced extant trends, e.g., "De Jonge Moeder, Verpleging en Voeding van het Kind. II," *De Sumatra Post*, August 28, 1925.

66. "Nestlé and Anglo Swiss Condensed Milk Co.," *Pandji Poestaka*, no. 93, November 18, 1932, p. 1458.

67. *Asjraq*, Oct–Nov 1926, pp. 217–218. Until February 1928, *Asjraq* glossed itself as the magazine of the Perhimpoenan Pergerakan Perkoempoelan Perempoean Soematera, or Sumatra's women's movement association. From March 1928 onwards it identified itself with the organization SKIS, Soeara Kaoem Iboe Soematera.

68. "Pemandangan didoenia Anak Anak," *Bintang Hindia*, no. 10, March 5, 1928, pp. 174–175.

69. *Isteri*, no. 1, May 1929, p. 2.

70. Iboe, "Iboe dan Anak," *Isteri*, no. 6–7, Oct–Nov 1931, pp. 133–137. A similar narrative would still be held onto in the 1950s by *Suara 'Aisjijah*, the magazine published by the women's branch of the Islamic organization Muhammadiya; see "Makanan Baji," *Suara 'Aisjijah*, June 4, 1953, pp. 100–102.

71. "Merawat Anak2," *Soeara Iboe*, no. 3, July 1932, pp. 1–2.

72. Iboe, "Iboe dan Anak."

73. "Merawat Anak2."

74. "Lactogen" milk powder, *D'Orient*, 1926.

75. "Lactogen" milk powder, *Pandji Poestaka*, no. 1–2, January 7, 1927, cover page.

76. "Sebabnja Si Sarip Terlambat Masoek Sekolah," *Volksalmanak Melajoe 1929*, pp. 207–210.

77. Kelling, "De Eerste," pp. 63–64.

78. Henk Schulte Nordholt, "Modernity and Cultural Citizenship in the Netherlands Indies: An Illustrated Hypothesis," *Journal of Southeast Asian Studies*, vol. 42 (no. 3), 2011, pp. 435–457.

79. "Hygiëne & Economie Gas," *D'Orient*, June 1927, p. 59.

80. "Servel Fridge," *De Indische Courant*, March 2, 1928.

81. "General Electric," *Officieel Orgaan van de Vereeniging van Huisvrouwen Soerabaja*, April 1932.

82. "General Electric," *De Huisvrouw in Indië*, January 1932.

83. "General Electric," *De Huisvrouw in Indië*, April 1932.

84. "General Electric," *De Huisvrouw in Indië*, July 1932.

85. "Westinghouse," *De Mode-Revue*, April 1933.

86. "Frigidaire," *De Huisvrouw in Indië Semarang*, December 1936.

87. "Frigidaire," *Pemimpin*, October 1935, p. 102; "Frigidaire," *Pandji Poestaka*, no. 84, October 21, 1938, n.p.; "Westinghouse," *Pemimpin*, November 1939, p. 105.

88. One article noted that "the Indies are at a turning point with regards to economic policy" as in the 1930s "exports suffered great losses, and hence indigenous consumers have come at the center of interest" as buyers. "Hollandsche Bladzijden:

Keperloan Roemah Tangga," *Pedoman Isteri*, no. 4, April 1936, p. 57. Another article stated, "the world of Indonesian women is already ripe, just like the world of women of other nationalities. There are already Indonesian housekeepers who use appliances and décor in their homes according to the needs of the time, and according to the needs of hygiene and practicality. // Not all among our women still only eat salted fish and shrimp paste, cooking in a wood or coal stove." "Tentoonstelling dan Demonstratie Keperloean Roemah Tangga," *Pedoman Isteri*, June 1936, pp. 74–76.

89. A women's column argued that "after five or six months, breast milk may be slowly replaced" by a "weak broth." The author was quick to add, however: "Do not be alarmed, mother . . . this doesn't mean you have to make broth every day: a Maggi cube will give you the desired liquid in an instant, and that for almost no money!" "Maggi," *Algemeen Handelsblad voor Nederlandsch-Indië*, June 9, 1933.

90. "Not only is the consumption of salt greatly reduced as a medical prescription, but the followers of modern nutrition also use as little salt as possible" ("Maggi," *Het Nieuws van den Dag voor Nederlandsch-Indië*, September 11, 1935). Another article on "hygiene" pointed at Maggi as a tasty addition to raw spinach—an important combination to provide the teeth with the minerals they need to stay healthy ("Hygiëne," *Algemeen Handelsblad voor Nederlandsch-Indië*, November 23, 1934).

91. In 1938 a Maggi advertisement asserted: "Scientific experiments and practical experiences in hospitals, clinics, and the like, conclusively prove the good and health-promoting properties of Maggi"; in the background a man dressed in a white coat (a doctor, one is led to think) stands in front of a chart. "Maggi," *De Sumatra Post*, January 19, 1938.

92. E.g., "Maggi, " *Het Nieuws van den Dag voor Nederlandsch-Indië*, January 3, 1939.

93. "Maggi," *Het Nieuws van den Dag voor Nederlandsch-Indië*, January 20, 1939.

94. "Maggi," *Bataviaasch Nieuwsblad*, January 4, 1938.

95. "Maggi en Nestlé," *De Indische Courant*, October 10, 1934.

96. "Maggi," *Pandji Poestaka*, no. 24, March 22, 1932, cover.

97. "Maggi," *Pandji Poestaka*, no. 60, July 29, 1939, p. 1116. For more details on *halal* advertising in the 1930s Dutch East Indies, see Formichi, "Bouillon for His Majesty."

98. "Maggi," *Pemimpin*, February 1938, p. 181, bold in original. The same Maggi advertisement was also printed in *Pandji Poestaka* no. 16, February 25, 1938, p. 303. It is worth mentioning that although today Maggi is part of the Unilever conglomerate (of which Van den Bergh was an initial participant), Maggi was not bought until 1947.

99. See *Pemimpin* issues for February, July, November, and December 1938, as well as January, February, and June 1939; and *Pandji Poestaka*, July 29, 1939. In August the message had returned to its "strengthening" and "healing" properties, especially for those men who "worked hard" (see *Pemimpin*, August 1939, plus January and February 1940).

100. "Hoog Bezoek aan de Maggistand," *De Locomotief*, May 6, 1939.

101. "De Maggi-Stand," *De Indische Courant*, October 2, 1939.

102. "Blue Band," *Pemimpin*, February 1938, p. 173.

103. Merle C. Ricklefs, *Polarizing Javanese Society: Islamic and Other Visions, c. 1830–1930*, Honolulu: University of Hawai'i Press, 2007, pp. 2, 11, 53, 97; all indicate that even the "most lax" of Java's Muslims abhorred pork.

104. "Blue Band," *Pemimpin*, February 1938, p. 173.

105. E.g., "Palmboter" in *De Huisvrouw in Indië*, no. 12, October 1933, p. 32.

106. "Blue Band," *De Huisvrouw in Indië*, September 1934, p. I; "Blue Band," *Vereeniging van Huisvrouwen Medan*, October 1934.

107. "Blue Band," *De Indische Courant*, February 8, 1936.

108. Angela Amico, Margo G. Wootan, Michael F. Jacobson, Cindy Leung, A. Walter Willett, "The Demise of Artificial Trans Fat: A History of a Public Health Achievement," *Milbank Quarterly*, vol. 99 (no. 3), 2021, pp. 746–770.

109. The advertisements' claim that the product was "nutritious" was made on its association with butter, rather than scientific data. In 1931, Dr. Van Marle's report on the analysis of Blue Band margarine mentioned that the name "fine kitchen butter" was misleading. *Mededeelingen DVG*, XXI, 1932, p. 169. At around the same time, margarine producers in the Netherlands, including Van den Bergh, had gotten into major legal trouble for their continued use of the tagline "freshly churned," since it projected the image of butter without having anything, really, to do with butter. See Algemeen Rijksarchief, "Tweede Afdeling, Rikszuivelinspectie 1900–1944," The Hague: Nationaal Archief Nederland [NAN].

110. "Archa," *Officieel Orgaan van de Vereeniging van Huisvrouwen Soerabaja*, October 1938, p. 6.

111. "Blue Band," *De Huisvrouw in Indië*, December 1938, p. 635; *Officieel Orgaan van de Vereeniging van Huisvrouwen Soerabaja*, November 1938, p. 10.

112. T.M. Oesman, "Gemoek Babi dalam Kunst Mentega dan Minjak Sapi?" *Pertja Selatan*, August 2, 1938, p. 1.

113. Abdoel Moeid and Haji Mohammad Hassan, "Soerat Keterangan," *Pedoman Isteri*, August 1938, p. 95. Abdoel Moeid was identified as "penghoeloe [of] Mangga Besar Batavia-Centrum"; Imam Haji Mohammad Hassan as "Hoofd-penghoeloe Landraad di Batavia." The statement is dated August 1. I was not able to determine any direct connection between this statement (released in Batavia) and Oesman's challenge to the overall claim printed in Palembang a day later. I am inclined to think of them as not directly connected, but reflective of similar anxieties and concerns.

114. "Blue Band," *Pedoman Isteri*, October 1938, p. 114.

115. "Blue Band," *Doenia Kita*, November 1938, n.p.; Haji A. Salim, "Margarine dan Minjak Samin," *Doenia Kita*, November 1938, p. 28; "Laboratory Certificate," *Doenia Kita*, November 1938, p. 29.

116. "Planta," *Pandji Poestaka*, no. 88, November 4, 1938, n.p.

117. "Planta," *Pandji Poestaka*, no. 90, November 11, 1938, n.p.

118. "Planta," *Pandji Poestaka*, no. 92, November 18, 1938, n.p. The same advertisement would still be printed in *Keoetamaan Isteri*, no. 4, April 1940, p. 17.

119. "Planta" and "Blue Band," *Pandji Islam*, December 1938, pp. 2972–2973.

120. Haji Agus Salim, "Apa Tjampoerannja? Bagaimana Bikinannja?," *Pandji Islam*, December 5, 1938 (Nomor Lebaran ke-II), p. 2972.

121. Salim, "Apa Tjampoerannja?"

122. Haji Agus Salim, "Margarine dan Minjak Samin," *Pedoman Masjarakat*, no. 49, December 7, 1938, p. 1000.

123. "Lactogen," *De Mode-Revue*, March 1933, p. 27.

124. On the subsequent page, three models with bobbed hair, painted lips, sensual legs, and breasted bodies posed provocatively in nightgowns next to an advertisement for Cocomalt, a "healthy" chocolate drink for children. *De Mode-Revue*, March 1933, p. 26, see Figure 3.8, left page.

125. E.g., "Maggi," *Pemimpin*, September 1939, n.p.

126. "Het Blue Band Meisje Komt Zelf naar Indië," *De Indische Courant*, November 5, 1936.

127. "Maggi," *Het Nieuws van den Dag voor Nederlandsch-Indië*, January 3, 1939.

128. "Maggi" and "Blue Band," *Bataviaasch Nieuwsblad*, January 25, 1930.

129. "Maggi," *De Sumatra Post*, January 19, 1938.

130. "Verkade," *Pandji Poestaka* no. 44–45, June 3, 1927, p. 743.

131. "Verkade," *Pandji Poestaka*, no. 97, December 6, 1935, p. 1903. See also "Verkade," *Pemimpin*, no. 7, January 1936, p. 193.

132. "Kodak," *Pemimpin*, no. 5, November 1935, p. 138.

133. "Philips," *Pemimpin*, no. 7, January 1939, n.p.

134. "Balsem tjap Matjan," *Pemimpin*, no. 4, October 1936, cover.

135. Alys Eve Weinbaum and Modern Girl Around the World Research Group, *The Modern Girl around the World: Consumption, Modernity, and Globalization*, Durham, NC: Duke University Press, 2008.

136. "Quaker Oats," *Pandji Poestaka*, no. 43, May 31, 1939, n.p.

137. "Quaker Oats," *Isteri Indonesia*, no. 3, March 1941, p. 19.

138. Instituut voor Voedsvoeding, *Makanan jang Moerah Tetapi Baik*, Batavia: Balai Poestaka, 1941.

139. Jean Gelman Taylor, "Official Photography," in Taylor (ed.) *Women Creating Indonesia*, pp. 91 and 122.

140. E.g., "Delfia," *Wanita*, no. 2, January 31, 1950, n.p.

141. "Seni Dapur," *Wanita*, no. 8, November 30, 1949, p. 86.

142. "Sehari dengan Ibu Rapih di Dapur Tionghoa," *Wanita*, no. 15, August 1951, p. 312. Moira Field and San-chao Chung, *Easy Chinese Dishes for Today*, London: John Lane, 1943.

143. For example, "Delfia Tanggung Halal!," *Wanita*, no. 10, May 25, 1957; "Delfia Tanggung Halal!," *Suara Perwari*, no. 10, December 1958, p. 31.

144. This emerges in Apple's first book, and remains a thread in most of her subsequent publications. Rima D. Apple, *Mothers and Medicine: A Social History of Infant Feeding, 1890–1950*, Madison, WI: University of Wisconsin Press, 1987.

Chapter 4

1. Z., ". . . Boekan Oeroesan Perempoean," *Keoetamaan Isteri*, no. 10, October 1939, pp. 5–7.

2. *Pandji Poestaka*, no. 42, May 27, 1939, p. 775; *Pandji Poestaka*, no. 5, January 1940.

3. "Doenia Isteri: Pekerdjaan Kaoem Iboe dalam Waktoe Mobilisatie, Pidato Raden Ajoe Abdoerrachman dimoeka Microfoon Betawi," *Pandji Poestaka*, no. 101, December 20, 1939, n.p.

4. Steedly, *Rifle Reports*, p. 94.

5. S. Dnl., "Kaoem Iboe Indonesia di Zaman Perang," *Isteri Indonesia*, December 1941, p. 2.

6. Formichi, *Islam and the Making of the Nation*; Fogg, *Indonesia's Islamic Revolution*.

7. White, "Reformist Islam," p. 131.

8. For an example, see "Koedoenghandel Ta: Astinia & Co.," *Soeara 'Aisjijah*, no. 1, January 1941, n.p.

9. Katharine E. McGregor, *Systemic Silencing: Activism, Memory, and Sexual Violence in Indonesia*, Madison, WI: University of Wisconsin Press, 2023.

10. See Wieringa, *Sexual Politics*, p. 112 on new employment opportunities.

11. Kelly A. Hammond, *China's Muslims & Japan's Empire: Centering Islam in World War II*, Chapel Hill, NC: The University of North Carolina Press, 2020, p. 6.

12. See also Louise P. Edwards, *Women Warriors and Wartime Spies of China*, Cambridge, UK: Cambridge University Press, 2016.

13. McGregor, *Systemic Silencing*, Chapter 2.

14. Shigeru Satō, *War, Nationalism, and Peasants: Java Under the Japanese Occupation, 1942–1945*, Armonk, NY: M.E. Sharpe, 1994, p. 158.

15. Paul H. Kratoska, *The Japanese Occupation of Malaya and Singapore, 1941–45: A Social and Economic History*, 2nd ed., Singapore: NUS Press, 2018.

16. Ethan Mark, *Japan's Occupation of Java in the Second World War: A Transnational History*, London: Bloomsbury Academic, 2018, p. 261.

17. M. Ullfah [*sic*] Santoso, "Kewadjiban Kaoem Wanita dalam Masjarakat Baroe," *Djawa Baroe*, no. 7, April 1, 1943, pp. 4–5; "Berbaris dengan 'Mompe,'" *Djawa Baroe*, no. 3, February 1, 1944, pp. 20–21; "Melatih Pemimpin Wanita," *Djawa Baroe*, no. 11, June 1, 1944, pp. 12–13.

18. See also Anton Lucas, "Images of the Indonesian Woman During the Japanese Occupation 1942–45," in Taylor (ed.) *Women Creating Indonesia*, pp. 52–90.

19. McGregor, *Systemic Silencing*, p. 70.

20. Lucas, "Images," pp. 70–77.

21. McGregor, *Systemic Silencing*, p. 5.

22. McGregor, *Systemic Silencing*, pp. 70–71.

23. Lucas, "Images," p. 78.

24. Lucas, "Images," p. 52.

25. Arsip Nasional, *Di bawah Pendudukan*.

26. Kementerian Penerangan RI, *Republik Indonesia: Kotapradja Djakarta Raya*, Jakarta: Kementerian Penerangan, Indonesia, 1952, pp. 401–402.

27. Pols, *Nurturing Indonesia*, p. 174.

28. Kementerian Penerangan, *Republik Indonesia: Kotapradja*, pp. 401–402.

29. Anne Booth, *The Indonesian Economy in the Nineteenth and Twentieth Centuries*, Basingstoke: Palgrave, 1998, p. 48.

30. Mark, *Japan's Occupation*, p. 217.

31. "Pelapoeran tentang Pengobatan Pertama Kali Oentoek Penjakit Framboesia," *Djawa Baroe*, no. 17, September 1, 1944, p. 7; "Penjakit Koelit Disebabkan Tiada Pengatahoean dan Koerang Berhati-hati," *Djawa Baroe*, no. 10, May 15, 1945, p. 33.

32. "Oesaha Mentjegah Penjakit Malaria di Malaka," *Djawa Baroe*, no. 3, February 1, 1943, pp. 20–21; "Penjelidikan tentang Malaria," *Djawa Baroe*, no. 17, September 1, 1943, pp. 16–17; "Kampoeng-model di Tjirebon," *Djawa Baroe*, no. 17, September 1, 1943, pp. 14–15; "Sedjarah Djawa Baroe dalam Tahoen 2603," *Djawa Baroe*, no. 24, December 15, 1943, pp. 3–8; "Pengaroeh Moesim kepada Penjakit," *Djawa Baroe*, no. 4, February 15, 1944, pp. 8–9.

33. "Menjehatkan Bangsa," *Berita Ketabiban*, no. 1-2-3, months 1, 2, 3, 1944, p. 59.

34. "Rantjangan Pekerjaan," *Berita Ketabiban*, no. 1-2-3, months 1, 2, 3, 1944, p. 33.

35. T. Sato, "Pendirian Djawa Sehat dan Ketetapan Hati Pendoedoek," *Pandji Poestaka*, no. 4-5, 1944, pp. 134–135.

36. "Laboratorioem Pasteur," *Djawa Baroe*, no. 16, August 15, 1943, pp. 16–17.

37. "Obat2 jang Dibikin di Djawa," *Djawa Baroe*, no. 2, January 15, 1944, pp. 14–15.

38. Ny. Hajjah Aminah Roezin, Arsip Nasional, *Di bawah Pendudukan*, p. 42.

39. Dr. Ali Akbar, Arsip Nasional, *Di bawah Pendudukan*, pp. 42–43.

40. "Djamoe-djamoe Djawa (I)," *Djawa Baroe*, no. 13, July 1, 1944, pp. 8–10.

41. "Djamoe-djamoe Djawa (I)"; "Djamoe-djamoe Djawa (II)," *Djawa Baroe*, no. 14, July 15, 1944, pp. 7–9.

42. Hans Pols, "European Physicians and Botanists, Indigenous Herbal Medicine in the Dutch East Indies, and Colonial Networks of Mediation," *East Asian Science, Technology and Society: An International Journal*, vol. 3 (no. 2), 2009, pp. 173–208.

43. Pols, *Nurturing Indonesia*, p. 157.

44. Pols, *Nurturing Indonesia*, p. 157.

45. "Jang Terpenting Sampai Hari Ini," illustration, *Djawa Baroe*, no. 8, April 15, 1943, p. 28. The reopening of the school is mentioned in a caption to the image of two female and one male *mantri* sitting at a table, looking through microscopes. The article, listing the "most important things" happening between late March and early April, shows the picture but does not mention the reopening of the school.

46. "Sekolah Tabib Tinggi Djakarta," *Djawa Baroe*, no. 11, June 1, 1943, pp. 20–21.

47. "Jang Terpenting Sampai Hari Ini," i; cover page, *Djawa Baroe*, no. 11, June 1, 1943; "Sekolah Tabib Tinggi Djakarta"; "Obat2 jang Dibikin di Djawa."

48. "Latihan Pertolongan Pertama oleh Wanita," *Djawa Baroe*, no. 17, September 1, 1943, pp. 18–19.

49. "Djoeroe Rawat Wanita Berlatih Dengan Giat," *Djawa Baroe*, no. 19, October 1, 1944, pp. 12–13.

50. "Djoeroe-Rawat Peladjar-Wanita," *Djawa Baroe*, no. 17, September 1, 1944, pp. 24–25.

51. "Tegoeh Ketetapan Hati Djoeroerawat Wanita Indonesia dibawah Bendera 'Palang-Merah,'" *Djawa Baroe*, no. 3, February 1, 1945, pp. 22–23.

52. "Ada Soemoer, Ada Telpon," September 1, 1944, pp. 12–13; "Kampoeng Model di Tjirebon," September 1, 1943, pp. 14–15.

53. Cover page, *Djawa Baroe*, no. 11, June 1, 1943; cover page, *Djawa Baroe*, July 1, 1944.

54. "Odopharm," *Djawa Baroe*, July 15, 1945; and August 1, 1945; "Moethalib," *Djawa Baroe*, August 1, 1945; "Wahido Shoten," *Djawa Baroe*, February 1, 1945.

55. Ny. Baheram Iskandar, Arsip Nasional, *Di bawah Pendudukan*, p. 43.

56. For a comparative study centered on the United States, see Amy Bentley, *Eating for Victory: Food Rationing and the Politics of Domesticity*, Urbana, IL: University of Illinois Press, 1998.

57. "Mekar-semekar disekitar Goentoer," *Djawa Baroe*, no. 3, February 1, 1945, pp. 20–21.

58. Wieringa, *Sexual Politics*, pp. 81–82; Steedly, *Rifle Reports*, p. 181. See also Martyn, *Gender and Nation*, pp. 70–71; Mutiah Amini, *Sejarah Organisasi Perempuan Indonesia (1928–1998)*, Jakarta: Gadjah Mada University Press, 2021, pp. 63–66; "Kegiatan Fujinkai di dalam Kota," Arsip Nasional, *Di bawah Pendudukan*, pp. 48–53.

59. Arsip Nasional, *Di bawah Pendudukan*, p. 48.

60. Arsip Nasional, *Di bawah Pendudukan*, p. 51.

61. Lucas, "Images," pp. 52–57.

62. Santoso, "Kewadjiban Kaoem Wanita."

63. "Makan dan Penjakit: Jang Haroes Kita Takoeti, Ialah Ketiadaan Pengetahoean," *Djawa Baroe*, no. 8, April 15, 1945, p. 33.

64. "Dapoer dan Kesehatan," *Djawa Baroe*, no. 7, April 1, 1945, p. 32.

65. "Masakan Djawa dan Tjara Memperbaikinja, Baiklah Kita Ichtiarkan Lagi," *Djawa Baroe*, no. 6, March 15, 1945, p. 33.

66. Aulia, "Beberapa Pikiran tentang Terapi atau Pengobatan dengan Makanan Mentah," *Berita Ketabiban*, no. 1–3, Jan–Mar 1944, pp. 68–77; Japan Rikugun, *Orang Indonesia*, p. 305.

67. Aulia, *"Makanan jang Séhat" dan Beberapa Ichtiar jang Lain Boeat Memeliharakan Keséhatan dan Menolong Menjemboehkan Penjakit*, 2nd ed., Djakarta: Djawa Goenseikanboe, Balai Poestaka, 2603.

68. "Doea Matjam Tjara Menanak Nasi," *Djawa Baroe*, no. 3, February 1, 1945, pp. 32–33.

69. "Apakah Toean Soedah Tahoe Atoeran Mentjoetjokkan Bibit Oebi Djalar Tjara Nippon?," *Djawa Baroe*, no. 8, April 15, 1945, pp. 24–25; "Tjara Menanam Oebi Djalar jang Benar," *Djawa Baroe*, no. 8, April 15, 1945, p. 31; "Tjara Memakan Oebi Djalar," *Djawa Baroe*, no. 8, April 15, 1945, p. 32.

70. *Ubi* would still be praised in 1952 as a valuable source of nutrients. S.K.T., "Berita Dapur," *Wanita*, no. 1, January 1952, pp. 20–21.

71. Ny. Barkah Alganis Baswedan, Arsip Nasional, *Di bawah Pendudukan*, p. 35.

72. Ny. Barkah Alganis Baswedan, Arsip Nasional, *Di bawah Pendudukan*, 1988, p. 27.

73. Ny. Hafni Zahra Abu Hanifa, Arsip Nasional, *Di bawah Pendudukan*, p. 28.

74. Ny. Hafni Zahra Abu Hanifa, Arsip Nasional, *Di bawah Pendudukan*, p. 45.

75. "Perbaikan Makanan dimasa Peperangan," *Djawa Baroe*, no. 1, January 1, 1945, pp. 24–25.

76. "Pidato Toean Ir. Soekarno (30-VIII-2603)," *Berita Ketabiban*, no. 1–3, January–March 1944, p. 28.

77. For an overview, see Morris Low (ed.) *Building a Modern Japan: Science, Technology, and Medicine in the Meiji Era and Beyond*, New York, NY: Palgrave Macmillan, 2005.

78. The 1940 manuscript does not appear to be publicly available. But that book was said to be forthcoming (and available for pre-orders) from Penerbit Tjerdas, in Medan ("Ir Soekarno! Sarinah, Bagaimana Engkau," *Pandji Masjarakat*, no. 16, April 17, 1940, p. 315). Tjerdas printed the second edition of *Sarinah* in 1948, which appeared with the subtitle "Soal Perempoean." This did not match the proposed chapter outline advertised in 1940, but instead matched the first half of the now standard *Sarinah: Kewadjiban Wanita* published in Yogyakarta in 1947. Soekarno, *Sarinah: Soal Perempoean, Laki dan Perempoean, dari Goea ke Kota*, T. Tinggi: Tjerdas, 1948. It is worth mentioning that based on the available list of contents, the first iteration scheduled to be printed in 1940 appeared to focus mostly on Islam, reflecting Sukarno's concurrent studies first in Flores and then in Bengkulu. Sukarno spent much of his time as an internee studying Islam, as documented in his collected correspondence with Ahmad Hassan, leader of the Bandung-based Persatoean Islam between 1936 and 1938 (see *Surat-surat dari Endeh*), and continued his engagement with the subject when he was moved to Bengkulu in 1938; there he studied with Muhammadiyah teacher Hassan Dini, also father of Sukarno's wife-to-be, Fatmawati.

79. Redactie, "Pidato Ir. Soekarno pada Tanggal 1 Agustus 1929 di P.N.I. Vergadering," *Isteri*, no. 5, September 1929, p. 1. Male representatives of conservative organizations thought that "the kitchen" was indeed the "women's only place" (as cited in Martyn, *Gender and Nation*, p. 64).

80. Sukarno, *Sarinah: Kewadjiban Wanita dalam Perdjoangan Republik Indonesia*, Jakarta: Panitya Penerbit Buku-buku Karangan Presiden Sukarno, 1963 [1947], p. 328.

81. Sukarno, *Sarinah: Kewadjiban*, p. 323.

82. Sukarno, *Sarinah: Kewadjiban*, p. 321.

83. Sukarno, *Sarinah: Kewadjiban*, p. 312.

84. Sukarno, *Sarinah: Kewadjiban*, p. 325.

85. Sukarno, *Sarinah: Kewadjiban*, pp. 324–325.

86. Sukarno, *Sarinah: Kewadjiban*, e.g., pp. 25, 79.

87. Sukarno, *Sarinah: Kewadjiban*, pp. 87–88, 156, 202.

88. Sukarno, *Sarinah: Kewadjiban*, pp. 37, 75–82.

89. Sukarno, *Sarinah: Kewadjiban*, pp. 9, 229–237.

90. So-called regional rebellions swept across the archipelago for years, when not decades. The most dramatic cases involved Aceh, Irian Jaya/Papua, and East Timor (which would remain a Portuguese colony until 1975, after which Suharto's New Order regime claimed it should be part of the Indonesian republic, starting a war that would end only in the year 2000 with a UN-brokered referendum). Many more areas attempted to assert their independence, including West Java, Sumatra, Sulawesi, and South Borneo.

91. "Sitsen to Sawyer," March 24, 1943, Indonesia, 1943; RG 2, 1940–1946; Series 1943/652; RAC.

92. For a detailed account of the events, see Kahin, *Nationalism and Revolution*.

93. "Republic of Indonesia Office, NYC PR#33," October 8, 1948, Java, 1948; RG 2, 1947–1951; Series 1948/655; RAC.

94. Gregg Huff, "The Great Second World War Vietnam and Java Famines," *Modern Asian Studies*, vol. 54 (no. 2), 2000.

95. Marwati Djoened Poesponegoro and Nugroho Notosusanto, *Sejarah Nasional Indonesia*, vol. VI, Jakarta: Departemen Pendidikan dan Kebudayaan, 1993, pp. 222–223.

96. Poesponegoro and Notosusanto, *Sejarah Nasional*, vol. VI, pp. 100, 225. See also Sebastiaan Broere, "Auto-Activity: Decolonization and the Politics of Knowledge in Early Postwar Indonesia, ca.1920–1955." *Lembaran Sejarah*, vol. 16 (no. 2), 2020, p. 143. https://doi.org/10.22146/lembaran-sejarah.66956.

97. E.F. Vloeker, "An Outsider's View on Red Cross Work in Indonesia," *Officieel Orgaan van het Nederlandse Rode Kruis Afdeling Indonesië*, no. 6, August 1947, p. 12. Vloeker was the former head of the Foreign Broadcasting Department of Radio Batavia.

98. Nederlandse Rode Kruis Feeding Team, *Report on Nutritional Survey in Netherlands East Indies, Conducted During Oct. 1945 till June 1946*, The Hague: Van Loon, 1948, p. 7.

99. Steedly, *Rifle Reports*, p. 49; on women fighters, see also pp. 73, 169, and especially 179–196; Wieringa, *Sexual Politics*, pp. 83–84, 142, 144.

100. Steedly, *Rifle Reports*, pp. 168–169.

101. Steedly, *Rifle Reports*, p. 47; repeated on p. 286. See also p. 168: "new skills and forms of knowledge, like shooting a rifle and reading a newspaper; and on ordinary activities that took on a new significance when illuminated by the spirit of struggle, like cooking and pounding rice."

102. Steedly, *Rifle Reports*, pp. 42; 54–55; 139; especially 168–169; 173; 179; 183; 190–191; 255–258.

103. Steedly, *Rifle Reports*, p. 165.

104. Steedly, *Rifle Reports*, p. 51; see also p. 171 and Chapter 4 in general.

105. Steedly, *Rifle Reports*, p. 202. During the war, certain groups of women (married, financially precarious, rural) suffered greatly under the double duties of supporting their families *and* the nationalist struggle (Steedly, *Rifle Reports*, pp. 192–203).

106. Kementerian Penerangan, *Republik Indonesia: Kotapradja*, p. 154.

107. Kementerian Penerangan, *Republik Indonesia: Kotapradja*, p. 155.

108. Among many, see these references to the Bulletin of the Dutch Red Cross Indonesia Branch, *Nederlandse Rode Kruis Afdeling Indonesië = Palang Merah Belanda Tjabang Indonesia*: "Kerstvieringen in de Ziekenhuizen," February 1947, no. 2–3, pp. 11–12; "Batavia," February 1947, no. 2–3, p. 24 (includes the quantities of food and clothes sent to each city in the archipelago); "Mobile Teams," April 1947, p. 3; "Onder de Vanen van het Rode Kruis," December 1947, pp. 11–12; "Gaarkeuken," January 1948, p. 5, cover image, February 1948; "Mobile Teams: Sumatra," May 1948, p. 9, cover, June 1948; "Serang Ditolong," June 1949, pp. 14–15; "Kamp Pelarian dekat Padang," February 1949, pp. 6–7; "Sumatra setelah 19 Desember," February 1949, p. 13; "De Excursie naar Rustenburg en Tangerang," Congress Nummer, pp. 3–4; "Peminta2 di Djakarta," August 1949, pp. 16–17; "Bantuan Makanan disekolah," Kerstnummer 1949, p. 49; E.H. Ramaer-Sibinga Mulder archive, NAN.

109. "Dapur Makanan," *Madjallah Resmi Palang Merah Tjabang Indonesia*, June 1948, p. 11, E.H. Ramaer-Sibinga Mulder archive, NAN.

110. Kementerian Penerangan, *Republik Indonesia: Kotapradja*, p. 153. This is an exception, as women were often marginalized in official historiography. Jean Gelman Taylor, "Official Photography," in Taylor (ed.) *Women Creating Indonesia*, pp. 98–99.

111. Steedly, *Rifle Reports*, pp. 168–169.

112. Mohd. Sjatrie, "Beras Ada Mengandung Zat untuk Penolak Penjakit Biri2," *De Huisvrouw in Indonesië*, no. 6, October 1949, pp. 22–23 and no. 7, November 1949, pp. 22, 24.

113. Mohd. Sjatrie, "Afschrift: 'Kebersihan Pangkal Kesehatan,'" *De Huisvrouw in Indonesië*, June 1949, no. 2, p. 14.

114. "Pendidikan Rakjat Menoeroet Ahli Hygiene," *Nederlandse Rode Kruis Afdeling Indonesië = Palang Merah Belanda Tjabang Indonesia*, November 1949?, pp. 13–14, E.H. Ramaer-Sibinga Mulder archive, NAN.

115. The new women's magazine *Wanita* printed a double entry, one titled "Flies: Our Enemy," and the other, "Our Kitchen." R., "Lalat Musuh Kita," *Wanita*, no. 4, September 30, 1949, p. 34; P., "Dapur Kita," *Wanita*, no. 4, September 30, 1949, p. 35. *Wanita*, a widely circulated magazine in the postwar period, focused far more on nutrition than infant care, marking a stark contrast with colonial-era Malay-language publications. While *Wanita* sprinkled information about nutrition and conveyed the message of food as a vehicle for health in several guises, *Karya* printed only one article under the "Health" rubric, with the straightforward title "On the Benefits of Vitamins." "Kesehatan: Tentang Faedahnja Vitamin," *Karya*, no. 3,

March 1949, pp. 19–20; Dr. Soeharto, "Kesehatan: Pemeliharaan Perempuan jang Hamil dan Baji," *Karya*, no. 6, September 1948, pp. 13–19.

116. Sullivan, *Years of Dressing*, pp. 115–116.

117. Redaksi, "Merdeka!," *Wanita*, no. 1, August 1949, pp. 1–2.

118. Redaksi, "Merdeka!"

119. *Wanita*, no. 1, January 1950, p. 1.

120. *Wanita*, no.1, 1950.

121. *Wanita*, no.1, 1950.

122. On the *dhalang* and *wayang kulit* in Javanese history, as well as reflections on Sukarno, see Laurie J. Sears, *Shadows of Empire: Colonial Discourse and Javanese Tales*, Durham, NC: Duke University Press, 1996.

123. *Wanita*, no.1, 1950.

124. Benedict R.O'G. Anderson, *Java in a Time of Revolution: Occupation and Resistance, 1944–1946*, 1st Equinox ed., Jakarta: Equinox Publishing, 2006.

125. "Blue Band," *Karya*, no. 4, April 1950, p. 7; "Blue Band," *Wanita*, no. 7, special issue ("Hari Kartini"), April 1, 1950, p. 125. Pusaka, a local competitor produced by Procter & Gamble, was marketed as being "from Indonesian ingredients, by Indonesian laborers, for Indonesian households" (*Wanita*, no. 19, October 1951, back cover), also underscoring its patriotism and nationalism. This specific Blue Band advertisement ran regularly at least until mid-1951 in *Karya*, but was more sporadic in *Wanita*, where Blue Band advertisements ceased altogether in late 1950. By 1956 the tagline had changed to "Sehat-Kuat," with an exclusive focus on children and the disappearance of any nation-building references (see *Wanita*, no. 14, July 25, 1956, p. 403). For women, see e.g.: *Karya*, no. 7, July 1950, p. 12; *Karya*, no. 8, August 1950, p. 12; *Karya*, no. 9, September 1950, p. 12; *Karya*, no. 9, September 1950, p. 13; *Karya*, no. 12, December 1950, p. 18; more in 1951.

126. The first appearance I found was in *Dunia Wanita*, March 15, 1951, back cover, followed by *Wanita*, no. 7 ("Hari Kartini"), April 1951, n.p. (insert between p. 135 and p. 136), and *Suara Perwari*, May 1951, back cover. Back in 1941, Blue Band also made a connection between building and bodily strength, as it compared cement used to make strong walls to Blue Band used to make strong bodies (*Koeoetamaan Isteri*, no. 6, June 1941, p. 25).

127. N. Stokvis-Cohen Stuart and H. Subandrio, *Sang Baji Datang: Sebuah Buku untuk Para Istri dan Ibu Muda*, Djakarta: Djambatan, 1950. This was the second volume in the series.

128. Johannes Leimena, *Membangun Kesehatan Rakjat*, Djakarta: Noordhoff-Kolff, 1952, p. 41. (Authored in 1951, printed in 1952.)

129. Caption to the illustration accompanying the article: Nj. Soemarmo, "Sedikit tentang Pemeliharaan Baji," *Suara Perwari*, no. 8, May 1951, pp. 13–16 (illustration on p. 13).

130. S.K.T., "Petunjuk Djalan kearah Kesehatan," *Wanita*, no. 24, December 1951, pp. 519–520.

131. *Wanita* continued to educate its audience about the principles of nutrition in theoretical and practical terms, explaining the science, and proposing menus and

dishes that satisfied its demands. In two entries in the "Seni Dapur" rubric in 1950, for example, the magazine offered recipes that "alternat[ed] vitamins and important substances" as much as possible, and encouraged readers to make things such as *tautjo* (Indonesian miso) and *tempeh* at home for economic and hygienic reasons. S.K.T., "Tjara Menjimpan Bahan-bahan Makanan," *Wanita*, no. 19, October 1951, pp. 398–399; Niza Hamid, "Resep Membuat Tautjo," *Wanita*, no. 20, October 1950, p. 365; S.K.T., "Sayuran Mentah dalam Makanan kita Sehari-hari," *Wanita*, no. 24, December 1950, pp. 448–449; S.K.T., "Buah-buahan," *Wanita*, no. 7, April 1951, pp. 142–143; S.K.T., "Buah-Buahan jang Dibuat Tahan Lama," *Wanita*, no. 13, July 1951, pp. 269–271; see also S.K.T., "Resep-resep dari Kelapa," *Wanita*, no. 21, November 1951, p. 442, on coconut; S.K.T., "Katul: Sumber Protein dan Vit. B1, jang Tidak Terkenal," *Wanita*, no. 8, April 1951, pp. 165, 168; S.K.T., "Sekali Lagi: Katul," *Wanita*, no. 11, June 1951, pp. 223–224; S.K.T., "Apakah jang Dapat Dibuat dari Katjang Kedele?," *Wanita*, no. 20, October 1951, pp. 422–424; Setiawati Wahab, "Seni Dapur," *Wanita*, no. 1, January 15, 1950, pp. 14, 16. For a similar approach in the Dutch-language press, see also: "Menu," *De Huisvrouw in Indonesië*, no. 2, June–July 1950, p. 5. The Islamic reformist *Suara 'Aisjijah* joined in later. See Mudjaeni, "Kerumah Tanggaan: Kesehatan Adalah Pangkal Kebahagian," *Suara 'Aisjijah*, no. 2, April 1953, pp. 34–36; Nj. Sumarmo, "Hal Dapur," *Suara 'Aisjijah*, no. 10, December 1953, pp. 193–?; "Kebersihan Makanan," *Suara 'Aisjijah*, no. 6, October 1955, pp. 19–22; S.K.T., "Makanan jang Berfaedah," *Wanita*, no. 23, December 1950, pp. 431–432; S.K.T., "Berita Dapur"; S.K.T., "Makanan Berchasiat Keluarga Sehat," *Wanita*, no. 20, October 1952, pp. 470–472; W. Warnani, "Pilihlah Makanan jang Bermanfaat!," *Wanita*, no. 9, May 1952, pp. 209, 212. It was not only "S.K.T" who argued in this direction; see also Fatma, "Sedikit tentang Ilmu Kesehatan," *Wanita*, no. 2, January 1952, pp. 34–36.

132. Wieringa, for example, has suggested that the inclusion of articles on care work in *Api Kartini* was nothing more than "bait" for middle-class readers. Wieringa, *Sexual Politics*, p. 273.

133. "17 Agustus – Wanita – 1 Tahun," *Wanita*, no. 15, August 15, 1950, inside-cover page.

134. Zainab, "Wanita dan Pembangunan Negara," *Suara 'Aisjijah*, vol. 17 (no. 6), April 1952, pp. 83–86 (quote pp. 84–85).

135. Siti Isnadijah Aly Semarang, "Tjermin Teladan Wanita Islam," *Suara 'Aisjijah*, vol. 18 (no. 1), March 1953, pp. 21–23.

136. Sukarno writes about this in *Sarinah*, discussed above. For a recent scholarly interpretation, see Sullivan's dissertation that, for example, discusses 1942 *Asia Raya* coverage of Mother's Day (Hari Ibu) celebrating infant health and the role of mothers in raising healthy families as social issues connected to *kodrat wanita* rather than questions of Indonesian political autonomy and sovereignty. Sullivan, "Years of Dressing," fn. 13 p. 224.

137. Elleke Boehmer, *Stories of Women: Gender and Narrative in the Postcolonial Nation*, Manchester, UK: Manchester University Press, 2009, p. 23.

138. P.C., "Instituut voor Volksvoeding," *De Huisvrouw in Indonesië*, no. 1, May 1950, pp. 1–2; "Lembaga Makanan Rakjat," p. 7.

139. Taylor Soja, "Kitchen Window Feminism: Sarah Macnaughtan, Wartime Care and the Authority of Experience in the South African and First World Wars," *Gender & History*, vol. 33 (no. 3), October 2021, pp. 668–682. See also Karen Hagemann, Stefan Dudink, and Sonya O. Rose (eds.) *The Oxford Handbook of Gender, War, and the Western World since 1600*, Oxford Academic, 2020. https://doi.org/10 .1093/oxfordhb/9780199948710.001.0001.

Chapter 5

1. Suwardjo, *Menudju ke Kemakmuran Desa*, Djakarta: Kementerian Pertanian, 1950? The booklet does not indicate the year of publication; however, Suwardjo was appointed *kepala pusat djawatan pertanian rakjat* in 1952 (see *Madjallah Berkala Pertanian*, no. 3, 1952, p. 8), and sometime in 1957 the position was occupied by Hardjoamodjojo (see *Almanak Tani 1956* and *Madjallah Berkala Pertanian*, no. 2, 1958, p. 55). Thus, *Menudju* was printed between 1952 and 1957.

2. A chapter in the book is dedicated to a gathering of the women of the village, led by *Ibu* Pontjodarmo, dedicated to discussing nutrition. See Suwardjo, *Menudju*, pp. 32–34.

3. The poor sanitary conditions of Indonesians' homes were also a trope in postwar assessments of the country's conditions, as opposed to those of the Europeans and Chinese. See, for example, Quang Đán Phan, *Public Health in Indonesia and Principles of Technical Assistance in the Field*, 1953, p. 9; T. Sujud, "Masjarakat Desa," *Wanita*, July 10, 1958, pp. 386–387.

4. Hardja Sadeli, "Pengalaman Sehari-hari: Sket Kehidupan Tani Miskin," *Madjallah Berkala Pertanian*, no. 2, 1958, pp. 76–80, p. 80.

5. Sadeli, "Pengalaman Sehari-hari," p. 80.

6. Sadeli, "Pengalaman Sehari-hari," p. 80.

7. Sadeli, "Pengalaman Sehari-hari," p. 77.

8. Sadeli, "Pengalaman Sehari-hari," p. 78.

9. "Lembaga Makanan Rakjat," *De Huisvrouw in Indonesië*, no. 3, August 1950, p. 7 (previously published as "Instituut voor Volksvoeding," *De Huisvrouw in Indonesië*, no. 1, May 1950, pp. 1–2).

10. Leimena, *Membangun*, p. 5.

11. Johannes Leimena, *Public Health in Indonesia: Problems and Planning*, The Hague: Van Dorp, 1956, p. 10.

12. "Lembaga Makanan Rakjat."

13. "Laporan Tahunan Ke II Panitia Negara Perbaikan Makanan diachiri pada 1 Juni 1954," p. 5, Archief Jan Adam Nijholt, International Institute of Social History, Amsterdam (IISG).

14. *Berdiri di kaki sendiri*, "to stand on its own feet."

15. Sunil Amrith, *Decolonizing International Health: India and Southeast Asia, 1930–65*, Basingstoke: Palgrave Macmillan, 2006, p. 14.

16. United Nations Women, *A Short History of the Commission on the Status of Women*, New York, NY: United Nations, 2019, p. 7.

17. A. Margaret McArthur, *Report to the Government of Indonesia on the Central Java Nutrition Project*, FAO CEP Report, Rome 1962, p. 1.

18. "Lembaga Makanan Rakjat."

19. Booth, *The Indonesian Economy*, p. 116.

20. For a detailed overview of the economic situation, see Anne Booth, *Economic Change in Modern Indonesia: Colonial and Post-Colonial Comparisons*, Cambridge, UK: Cambridge University Press, 2016, pp. 35–62. See also Booth, *The Indonesian Economy*, pp. 53–63.

21. This is supported by the available statistical data. In 1958, 85% of Java's population was considered rural; of that, 76% of those above 12 years of age belonged to the labor force, as noted by Widjojo Nitisastro: "Particularly in the rural areas the majority of females are both home-houseworkers and are at the same time engaged in economic activity." According to the 1961 census, 23.9% and 30.4% of the labor force in urban and rural areas, respectively, were women nationwide (with Java at 29.1% and Sumatra at 33.4% across settings). In agriculture, laboring men and women represented, respectively, 73% and 69% of the population. Widjojo Nitisastro, *Population Trends in Indonesia*, Ithaca, NY: Cornell University Press, 1970, pp. 136–189, quote p. 183.

22. "Notes on Technical Assistance for Indonesia—Nutrition, from Thelma J. Morris, Nutr Div to Dr. Karl Olsen," August 23, 1950, David Lubin Memorial Library, Food and Agriculture Organization of the United States, Archives, Rome, Italy [FAO].

23. Suwardjo, *BPMD (Balai Pendidikan Masjarakat Desa—Village Educational Center)*, Djakarta: Pusat Djawatan Pertanian Rakjat, 1953, pp. 3–11.

24. S.K.T., "Petunjuk Djalan Kearah Kesehatan."

25. "Lembaga Makanan Rakjat."

26. Nick Cullather, *The Hungry World: America's Cold War Battle against Poverty in Asia*, Cambridge, MA: Harvard University Press, 2010; see p. 64 for an explicit reference, the entire book for the bigger picture and argument.

27. "Memorandum by the Technical Cooperation Administration (Bennett) to the Director of the Management Staff (Heneman)," Washington, April 20, 1951. Foreign Relations of the United States, East Asia and the Pacific, Volume VI [FRUS EAP VI], 890.00r/3-1650.

28. E. Ross Jenney, "Technical Assistance for Public Health in the Republic of Indonesia," *Public Health Reports*, vol. 68 (no. 7), July 1953, pp. 707–713.

29. "Memorandum by the Officer in Charge of Economic Affairs, Office of Philippine and Southeast Asian Affairs (Shohan), to the Deputy Assistant Secretary of State for Far Eastern Affairs (Merchant)," [WASHINGTON,] March 16, 1950. FRUS EAP VI, 890.00R/3-1650.

30. "The Ambassador in Indonesia (Cochran) to the Secretary of State, Jakarta, March 23, 1950—6 p. m." FRUS EAP VI, 756D.00/3-2350: Telegram.

31. "The Ambassador in Indonesia (Cochran) to the Secretary of State, Jakarta, March 14, 1951—6 p. m." FRUS EAP VI, PART 1, 756D.00/3-1451: Telegram.

32. "The Ambassador in Indonesia (Cochran) to the Secretary of State, Jakarta, December 5, 1951, 3 p. m." FRUS EAP VI, PART 1, 756D.5–MSP/12–551: Telegram.

33. "The Ambassador in Indonesia (Cochran) to the Secretary of State, [Jakarta,] June 1, 1951." FRUS EAP VI, PART 1, 883.00–FA/6–151: Telegram. "The Ambassador in Indonesia (Cochran) to the Secretary of State, Jakarta, December 5, 1951, 3 p. m." FRUS EAP VI, PART 1, 756D.5–MSP/12–551: Telegram.

34. Bradley R. Simpson, *Economists with Guns: Authoritarian Development and U.S.-Indonesian Relations, 1960–1968*, Stanford, CA: Stanford University Press, 2008, p. 9.

35. "Kremlin's Point Four Program," *The New York Times*, November 7, 1954.

36. "Ichtisar Perdjalanan dan Penindjauan di Sovjet Russia," *Berita Kementerian Kesehatan Republik Indonesia*, no. 6, April 1955; R. Mochtar, "Dr. R. Mochtar: Laporan tentang Fellowship untuk Beladjar di U.S.A.," *Berita Kementerian Kesehatan Republik Indonesia*, no. 2, April 1952, pp. 7–16.

37. *Almanak Tani 1958*, p. 131.

38. S.K.T., "Petunjuk Djalan kearah Kesehatan."

39. Dutch East Indies, *Regeerings-Almanak 1941*, p. 489. Van Veen was appointed head of department of the Batavia Eijkman Institute in 1936, and he still held the position in 1941. He returned to the Netherlands after the war, and after a short stint as professor at a Dutch university, he begun working at the FAO. He was instrumental to the organization of the Nutrition Division. After over a decade working for the FAO, he joined Cornell University as professor of international nutrition (1962). https://hdl.handle.net/1813/19181.

40. "Laporan Tahunan 1951 dan 1952," pp. 1–2.

41. Van Veen ratified Indonesia's agreement with the FAO, and advised Soedarmo in a number of programs. First, two new fellowships were made available for study in the US, one in medical nutrition and the other in home economics; secondly, a new agreement was drafted, for the assignment of another advisor to lead a dietitians' course; thirdly, plans were laid out to introduce nutrition in lower domestic-science schools; lastly, they agreed on the establishment of the Dewan Perbaikan Makanan, or the Board/Council for the Improvement of Nutrition. "Indonesia Supplemental Agreement no. 5, from Van Veen to Wahlen," n.d., FAO.

42. On the Commission, see "Laporan Tahunan 1951 dan 1952," p. 1. For biographical data, see Kementerian Penerangan, *Republik Indonesia: Kotapradja*, p. 153–156; Wieringa, *Sexual Politics*, pp. 84–85, p. 113, p. 121; Liberty P. Sproat, "Nurturing Transitions: Housewife Organizations in (Colonial) Indonesia, 1900–1972," PhD dissertation, Purdue University, 2015, p. 66; Locher-Scholten, *Women and the Colonial State*, fn. 51 p. 251; "Lid-Lid Boemipoetera Gemeenteraad Semarang jang Baroe," *Pandji Poestaka*, no. 83, October 18, 1938, pp. 1576–1578.

43. For a full list as of January 1952, see Organization for Scientific Research in Indonesia, *Guide of Scientists in Indonesia*, 3rd ed., Bulletin no. 11, Djakarta, January 1952.

44. "Laporan Tahunan Ke II." It is likely in relation to this report that Soedarmo launched a "blitz survey" on food and health. Purwo Sudarmo, "Uraian," *Berita Kementerian Kesehatan Republik Indonesia*, no. 4, April 1954, pp. 150–157.

45. The Indonesian establishment was fully aware of the challenge provided by the Dutch departure, especially since the efforts of the Japanese military authority to shape a local professional leadership had fallen short of enabling the envisioned leap. Health, nutrition, and agriculture were all fields that had been dominated by the Dutch in the colonial period, and as articulated by the Minister of Education Dr. Abu Hanifa in the early 1950s, "The Indonesian people are very, very backward [*terbelakang*] in the technical knowledge that is needed by the modern world [*dunia modern*]. General knowledge is considered important, but technical knowledge is given top priority because it is considered the key to progress [*kunci kemajuan*]." Poesponegoro and Notosusanto, *Sejarah Nasional*, vol. VI, p. 258.

46. "Letter no. 15 – Landed at Djakarta on March 19, 1952," Mr. N.E. Dodd – Trip to Near East and Far East, FAO.

47. "Lembaga Makanan Rakjat."

48. According to information contained in S.K.T., "Petunjuk Djalan kearah Kesehatan," p. 519, the school was opened sometime in mid-1950.

49. https://sehatnegeriku.kemkes.go.id/baca/rilis-media/20190125/5329219/sejarah-hari-gizi-nasional/. Last accessed December 14, 2023. A 1954 report suggests that the school opened as late as February 1953 ("Laporan Tahunan Ke II," p. 5), but the April 1952 issue of *Berita Kementerian Kesehatan Republik Indonesia* indicates that a first course was launched in 1952 itself ("Pendidikan-pendidikan jang Diselanggarakan Kementerian Kesehatan," *Berita Kementerian Kesehatan Republik Indonesia*, no. 2, April 1952, pp. 98–99).

50. Indonesia Departemen Kesehatan, *Sejarah Kesehatan Nasional Indonesia*, Jakarta: Departemen Kesehatan RI, 1980, vol.2, p. 35.

51. The SGKP in Yogyakarta had suspended activities during the Dutch occupation, but upon its reopening in August 1949, pupils eager to become teachers had returned; the school graduated on average thirty teachers at each of the three exam sessions held between January 1951 and September 1952, while that same year Jakarta's SGKP enrolled a whopping 370 pupils. Numbers would first decrease slightly, but overall increased: there were 260 young women enrolled in Jakarta in 1954–1955 (29 of which graduated in 1955), and 310 in 1956–1957. The SKP had enrolled 340 pupils in 1952, 450 in 1954–1955 (50 of which graduated in 1955), and almost 1,000 the subsequent year. Across the archipelago, there were over 9,000 girls enrolled in the Girls' Domestic Schools in 1953–1954, and over 500 in the teachers' schools. (*Republik Indonesia: Daerah Istimewa Jogjakarta*, Bandung: Kementerian Penerangan, 1952, pp. 777, p. 453; *Pengadjaran (Sekolah Rendah dan Sekolah Landjutan) 1954/1955*, Djakarta: Biro Pusat Statistik, Statistik Sosial, Kulturil dan Umum, Seksi Pengadjaran, 1958, p. 9, pp. 182–185, 64–65; *Pengadjaran (Sekolah Rendah dan Sekolah Landjutan) 1956/1957*, Djakarta: Biro Pusat Statistik, Statistik Sosial, Kulturil dan Umum, Seksi Pengadjaran, 1959, pp. 2, 6–7, 10–11; Kementerian Penerangan, *Republik Indonesia: Kotapradja*, p. 453). These numbers reflected a broader trend

towards literacy. Differently from the Dutch era, literacy rates were now growing. In the postwar independence era, the numbers of girls enrolled in both secondary and elementary schools increased at a much faster pace than boys. In Jakarta in 1949, a little over 500 young girls were in the graduating class of the six-year basic school, the same number as in 1951. (*Statistik Pengadjaran Rendah di Indonesia 1949*, Djakarta: Penerbitan Kantor Pusat Statistik, 1951, p. 116; *Statistik Pengadjaran Rendah di Indonesia 1951*, Djakarta: Penerbitan Kantor Pusat Statistik, n.d., pp. 127–128). At the national level there were 17,000 girls in the Indonesian-language-medium sixth grade, and a total of 350 thousand enrolled across the elementary school grades in 1951 (*Statistik Pengadjaran Rendah di Indonesia 1951*, p. 117)—a number lower than those recorded in the mid-1930s. (*Algemeen Verslag Van Het Onderwijs in Neder-landsch-Indië over het Schooljaar 1935/1936*, part 2, Batavia, 1938, pp. 10–17.) But by the school year 1954–1955, there were over two million girls enrolled in elementary schools across the archipelago. (*Pengadjaran Sekolah Rendah dan Sekolah Land-jutan) 1954/55–1955/56*, Djakarta: Biro Pusat Statistik, Statistik Sosial, Kulturil dan Umum, Seksi Pengadjaran, 1957, p. 42.) At the same time, enrolled boys grew from one million in 1949 to four million in 1954–1955 (*Statistik Pengadjaran Rendah 1949*, p. 116; *Pengadjaran 1954/55–1955/56*, p. 42).

52. The first course for dietitians, started in 1950, had enrolled fifteen pupils; in 1951, there were twenty-nine students enrolled. Graduation rates were low, though, as only ten pupils were expected to finish in 1953 and possibly as few as three in 1954. The Vocational School for Nutrition Outreach had twenty-seven students. "Pendi-dikan-pendidikan jang Diselanggarakan Kementerian Kesehatan," pp. 98–99.

53. Reflecting on the low number of applications to the School for Nutritionists, Miss Visser—in 1952 an FAO dietitian advisor—argued that the main challenge was administrative, since teachers of Girls' Domestic Schools admitted to the course were not granted study leave to attend the school. "Visit to Indonesia by Dr. S.S. De, 9 June? 1952," n.d., Asia and Far East Regional Office Trips and Tours by Staff, FAO.

54. These were all women: C.F. Guillaume, W. Pranger, and J.W.B. Visser. Poorwo Soedarmo and Arjatmo Tjokronegoro, *Gizi dan Saya*, Jakarta: Fakultas Kedokteran, Universitas Indonesia, 1995, pp. 38–39. The first exam session was held in August 1951; the second one, in August 1953. After that, the LMR was able to run its own courses.

55. A further discrepancy was noted for assistant dieticians: while the goal was to have at least two of them for each regency (for a total of 320), and one for each of the 100 hospitals with a capacity of at least 150 beds, by 1953 there had been only 30 graduates from the Vocational School for Nutrition Outreach. See Azir, "Health in Indonesia," *Berita Kementerian Kesehatan Republik Indonesia*, December 1957, pp. 5–15, p. 11. His proposed numbers of graduates, 30 from the lower-level school, and 14 for the School for Nutritionists, are consistent with the expectations of the Ministry of Health. Leimena, *Public Health in Indonesia*, pp. 89–90.

56. McArthur, *Report to the Government*, p. 1.

57. McArthur, *Report to the Government*, p. 8.

58. André Van Veen, "Indonesia – Nutrition – Report to the Government," FAO Report NU-EPTA 3 TA/182/S/5, 1951.

59. "Indonesia Field Report no. 4, JWB Visser – Dietician," January 1952, FAO.

60. In the second half of the decade, Soekamto participated in several other international events, including the FAO's home economics meeting held in Tokyo in 1956, and the seminar on home economics held in Bogor (Indonesia) in 1957. By then, Indonesia was firmly on the map of international circuits of development and aid, within which home economics had staked a position alongside public health, agriculture, etc. I discuss that in a separate article.

61. Soedarmo, *Gizi dan Saya.*

62. S.K.T., "Makanan jang Berfaedah."

63. The masthead was not always published; Soekamto must have joined at some point between March and June 1951. She appeared listed in *Wanita*, no. 11, June 1951, and from then on until no. 18, September 1952, p. 403, the last issue to list all names of those officially involved in the magazine. From no. 19, October 1952, the magazine would only state the editor in chief.

64. C.M. Schaap, "Preliminary Bibliography on Nutrition Research in Indonesia," *OSR News*, vol. III (no. 12), December 1951, pp. 261–268.

65. Seno, "Pertimbangan Buku," *Madjalah Kedokteran Indonesia*, vol. 2 (no. 10), October 1952, pp. 426–427. In 1952, in Jakarta, 10 liters of rice would have cost 17.82 Indonesian rupiah. Hence, the book cost about as much as a person's supply of rice for about 10–14 days. *Dapur Indonesia* itself suggested a consumption of 700 grams of rice per day for an adult man doing heavy manual labor (p. 40); another publication recommended 400 grams of rice a day for an adult man employed as a clerk. Poorwo Soedarmo, *Pedoman untuk Membuat Menu dan Kumpulan Menu untuk Pelbagai Golongan dan Umur,* 's-Gravenhage: Van Goor, 1952, p. 63. See G.F. Papanek and D. Dowsett, "The Cost of Living. 1938–1973," *Economics and Finance in Indonesia*, Faculty of Economics and Business, University of Indonesia, vol. 23, 1975, pp. 181–206, p. 204.

66. Soedarmo, *Dapur Indonesia*, p. VII.

67. Steedly notes that *sandiwara* were usually politically charged agit-prop dramas aimed at instilling commitment to the struggle for independence, and were accompanied by political songs (including the national anthem) and speeches. Steedly, *Rifle Reports*, pp. 139–141.

68. Seno, "Pertimbangan Buku."

69. Soedarmo, *Dapur Indonesia*, p. 16.

70. "Lembaga Makanan Rakjat."

71. Dutch colonial administrators had argued that the indigenous population needed to be educated so as to foster feelings of responsibility and desire for self-directed initiative; this was often conveyed in agricultural extensions through "personal contact." Broere, "Auto-Activity," p. 145. See also Suzanne Moon on colonial-era extension services. Moon, *Technology and Ethical Idealism*.

72. Van Veen, "Indonesia – Nutrition," p. 5.

73. In the context of famine and reduced production, the effort toward "better nutrition" seemed inadequate to some, and funding for public health gradually faded. In 1947, for example, the Rockefeller Foundation's International Health Division had already recognized that improved health conditions and disease prevention had lowered death rates. The Rockefeller Foundation took this observation to signify the need to move away from "health," with the eventual disbandment of the IHD in 1951. These changes had already been underway since before the war, as exemplified by the Mexico Agricultural Project, which had begun in 1941. Relying on the same format of demonstration units and extension work, the Rockefeller Foundation and USAID launched programs dedicated to agricultural innovation across Latin America and Asia, promoting the "Green Revolution" in the 1950s and 1960s; Indonesia would be one of the last countries to join in—in the 1970s—but not for lack of trying on the part of such international actors. Marcos Cueto and Steven Paul Palmer, *Medicine and Public Health in Latin America: A History*, New York, NY: Cambridge University Press, 2015, p. 139. John Farley, *To Cast out Disease: a History of the International Health Division of the Rockefeller Foundation (1913-1951)*, Oxford, UK: Oxford University Press, 2004, p. 275-277.

74. As laid out by Walt W. Rostow, in true Cold War logic, modernization was going to ensure the success of capitalism, too. An excellent elaboration on this point is Cullather, *The Hungry World*.

75. Broere, "Auto-Activity."

76. Suzanne M. Moon, "Takeoff or Self-Sufficiency? Ideologies of Development in Indonesia, 1957–1961," *Technology and Culture*, vol. 39 (no. 2), 1998, pp. 187–212.

77. Amrith, *Decolonizing International Health*, p. 84.

78. Victoria De Grazia, *Irresistible Empire: America's Advance Through Twentieth-Century Europe*, Cambridge, MA: Belknap Press of Harvard University Press, 2005, p. 453. Much has been written on "the kitchen" in the Cold War, primarily because of the famous "Kitchen Debate" between Nixon and Khrushchev in 1959, but more broadly, on the kitchen as a space of Americanization and development. See Ruth Oldenziel and Karin Zachmann (eds.) *Cold War Kitchen: Americanization, Technology, and European Users*, Cambridge, MA: MIT Press, 2009; Sibel Bozdogan, "Democracy, Development, and the Americanization of Turkish Architectural Culture in the 1950s," in Sandy Isenstadt and Kishwar Rizvi (eds.) *Modernism and the Middle East: Architecture and Politics in the Twentieth Century*, Seattle, WA: University of Washington Press, 2008, pp. 116–138; and Diana Cucuz, *Winning Women's Hearts and Minds: Selling Cold War Culture in the US and the USSR*, Toronto: University of Toronto Press, 2023.

79. Nancy Berlage, *Farmers Helping Farmers: The Rise of the Farm and Home Bureaus, 1914–1935*, Baton Rouge, LA: Louisiana State University Press, 2016, pp. 124–126.

80. K. Soewardjo, "Extension Methods (in Indonesia)," paper presented at the "Workshop on Extension Program and Plan of Work," Bhopal, India, December 1955, p. 7.

81. See among several, *Madjallah Berkala Pertanian*, no. 10, cover image; no. 3, 1952, p. 23; no. 4, 1952, p. 8. Also, women were recurrently featured in several of the pictures included in *Tjermin Masjarakat: Hal-Hal jang Patut Diketahui oleh Masjarakat*, Djakarta: Kementerian Pertanian, Pusat Djawatan Pertanian Rakjat, Bag. Publikasi Urusan Penerbitan, 1953.

82. Hildred Geertz, *The Javanese Family: A Study of Kinship and Socialization*, New York, NY: Free Press of Glencoe, 1961, pp. 44–46, 122–128.

83. Writing in the 1970s, Boserup noted that in fact international development in the 1950s and 1960s had deteriorated women's public position and role. Ester Boserup, *Woman's Role in Economic Development*, New York, NY: St. Martin's Press, 1970.

84. Soewardjo, "Extension Methods," p. 11.

85. *Report of the Technical Meeting on Home Economics for South and East Asia*, Tokyo, Japan, 5–12 October 1956. Rome: Food and Agriculture Organization of the United Nations, 1957.

86. Soesiah Sardjono, "Peranan Wanita dalam Pembangunan Masjarakat Desa," *Suara Perwari*, no. 12, December 1958, pp. 16–17, 24.

87. See Clifford Geertz's 1956 paper "The Development of the Javanese Economy: A Socio-Cultural Approach" (later expanded in the monograph *Agricultural Involution*) and *Peddlers and Princes*. (See also Cossu, "Talcott Parsons," p. 265.) Clifford Geertz, *Peddlers and Princes: Social Change and Economic Modernization in Two Indonesian Towns*, Chicago, IL: The University of Chicago Press, 1963. Clifford Geertz, *Agricultural Involution: The Process of Ecological Change in Indonesia*, Berkeley, CA: Published for the Association of Asian Studies by University of California Press, 1994. Considering that Clifford and Hildred Geertz did fieldwork at the same time, in the same place, one wonders whether awareness of the different role of women, for example, played any part in Clifford Geertz's "ambivalence and a certain degree of reluctance" toward modernization theory. Andrea Cossu, "Talcott Parsons and Clifford Geertz: Modernization, Functionalism, and Interpretive Social Science," in A. Javier Treviño and Helmut Staubmann (eds.) *The Routledge International Handbook of Talcott Parsons Studies*, Abingdon, UK: Routledge, 2022, pp. 261–271, quote p. 265. For an illustration of Geertz's work, and interrelation with policy-making through university affiliations, see Simpson, *Economists with Guns*, pp. 21–23.

88. United States Department of State. *Foreign Service List*. Washington: For sale by the Supt. of Docs., U.S. Govt. Print. Off, 1957 (3); Irene Roberts (1957–1958). This mirrored ICA staffing in a handful of other countries, among them the Philippines (1953), India (1954), and Colombia (1955).

89. *Foreign Service List*, 1960 (1).

90. The work of US Foreign Service advisors was amplified through international cooperation, as various land-grant universities across the US were matched with counterparts in the "third world." The University of Kentucky was tasked with supporting Indonesia, and in the nine years between 1957 and 1966, professors and technicians rotated at the Bogor Institute of Agriculture, tending to experimental

stations and training local experts. Nicholas M. Rice, *Kentucky at Bogor: A Final Report to the United States Agency for International Development*, Institute Pertanian Bogor and University of Kentucky Center for Developmental Change, 1968, pp. 54–55.

91. Howard W. Beers, *An American Experience in Indonesia: The University of Kentucky Affiliation with the Agricultural University at Bogor*, Lexington, KY: University Press of Kentucky, 1971, p. 83. By the time Beers had arrived at Bogor, extension education was no longer taught (Rice, *Kentucky at Bogor*, p. 54).

92. Rice, *Kentucky at Bogor*, pp. 54–55.

93. "While the basic idea of the agricultural extension model might be sound, a lack of sensitivity to inconsistencies between the US and third world contexts made the application of the model in less developed countries far less effective and satisfactory than it might have been." Everett M. Rogers, J.D. Eveland, Alden S. Bean, "Extending the Agricultural Extension Model. Preliminary Draft," Stanford University, 1976, p. 100.

94. Malnutrition was not an exclusively rural or class-defined problem in the early years of independence. Awareness of such circumstances led to a widespread effort in nutritional health propaganda that targeted the urban poor who struggled to absorb the calories and nutrients needed for their labor, as well as the upper-class urbanites who were putatively unaware of what constituted good nutrition. "Goed Gevoed – Toch Ondervoed," *Maandblad van de Vereniging van Huisvrouwen Bandoeng*, no. 5, May 1950, pp. 14–16, p. 20.

95. "Lembaga Makanan Rakjat."

96. Soedarmo, *Pedoman*.

97. Sudarsono, "Vitamin," *Wanita*, no. 4, February 1953, n.p.

98. Poorwo Soedarmo, "Keluarga dan Makanannja," *Keluarga*, no. 3, March 1953, pp. 7–9; Poorwo Soedarmo, "Keluarga dan Makanannja II," *Keluarga*, no. 4, April 1953, pp. 11, 26.

99. Mudjaeni, "Kerumah Tanggaan: Kesehatan Adalah Pangkal Kebahagian"; Nj. Sumarmo, "Kerumah Tanggaan: Makanan Baji," *Suara 'Aisjijah*, no. 4, June 1953, pp. 100–101; Nj. Sumarmo, "Kerumah Tanggaan: Mendjaga Makanan Sehat," *Suara 'Aisjijah*, no. 5, July 1953, pp. 123–124.

100. Phan, *Public Health in Indonesia*, p. 11.

101. United States, *National Wartime Nutrition Guide*, Washington, DC: United States Department of Agriculture, War Food Administration, Nutrition and Food Conservation Branch, 1943.

102. Soedarmo, *Pedoman*, p. 14.

103. Soedarmo, *Dapur Indonesia*.

104. "Kinderwagen," *Koeoetamaan Isteri*, March 1939, p. 31.

105. "Van Veen," September 1955, Nutr. Div. – Technology – Milk, Vol III (Jan 1954–Dec 1956), FAO.

106. "Van Veen to Burgess on Local Foods in Child Feeding," April 1953; "Van Veen on Fish Flour and Saridele," November 25, 1955, Nutr. Div. – Technology – Milk, Vol III (Jan 1954–Dec 1956), FAO.

107. "Laporan Tahunan Ke II," p. 4. *Berita Kementerian Kesehatan Republik Indonesia*, vol. 3 (no. 5), October 1954. Among many instances in the Rockefeller Archives, see "1934 3rd Quarter Report," Reports – Java (Indonesia); 1933; RG 5; Subseries 3_655 GEN; RAC; "De Hygienische Organisatie, Summary for the Year 1935," p. 41; RAC.

108. "McNaughton to Aykroyd," October 9, 1956; "Marjorie L. Scott to Dr. Aykroyd," October 17, 1956; Nutr. Div. – Technology – Milk, Vol III (Jan 1954–Dec 1956), FAO.

109. *Keluarga Sedjahtera: People's Welfare*, Semarang: Lembaga Perbaikan Makanan Rakjat Daerah DjaTeng, cover image, September to October 1957.

110. "Kursus Ibu," *Berita Hygiene*, no. 1, January 1953, pp. 1–4, quote p. 2.

111. Julie Sulianti, "Pelaksanaan Pemerintah Terhadap Tjita2 Pergerakan Wanita dalam Lapangan Kesehatan," *Suara Perwari*, no. 3, December 1953, pp. 11–12.

112. "Kursus Ibu," p. 2.

113. Sulianti, "Pelaksanaan Pemerintah," pp. 11–12.

114. The bottom half of the second page of the article was taken up by an advertisement for the March 1952 School for Nutritionists course. "Kemanterian Kesehatan RI," *Wanita*, no. 24, December 1951, p. 520.

115. S.K.T., "Petunjuk Djalan kearah Kesehatan," p. 519.

116. Dr. Sulianti, "Mother and Childcare in Indonesia," *Women's International Club Journal*, vol. 1 (no. 2), 1953, pp. 33–35, quote p. 33.

117. As stated by Agus Suwignyo, "By July 1945, the overall structure of primary education fell into three categories, namely primary schools with three and four years, the people's schools [*Sekolah Rakyat*] of two, four, five and six years, and the so-called complete schools which offered as many as five and six years." (Suwignyo, *The Breach in the Dike*, p. 206). From September 1946 all *Sekolah Rakyat* became four-year programs (*Sejarah Nasional Indonesia*, vol. VI, p. 245), and in July 1950 they were upped to six years of instruction (Suwignyo, *The Breach in the Dike*, p. 285), enrolling children between eight and fourteen years of age (Suwignyo, *The Breach in the Dike*, p. 297).

118. Sulianti, "Mother and Childcare in Indonesia," quote p. 34. The course also covered the care of pregnant women, care of women in labor and delivery, infant feeding (on which occasion breastfeeding was also characterized as a gift of God), infant care (including washing, sleeping, and clothing), and the role of consultation centers for mother and child. "Kursus Ibu."

119. Sulianti, "Mother and Childcare in Indonesia," quote p. 35.

120. Indonesia Departemen Kesehatan, *Sejarah Kesehatan*, vol. 2, p. 35.

121. S.K.T., "Petunjuk Djalan kearah Kesehatan," p. 520.

122. S.K.T., "Petunjuk Djalan kearah Kesehatan," p. 519.

123. She had graduated from the Batavia Medical School in 1942. In the early 1950s she became a leading member of KOWANI. "Saroso, Julie Sulianti," in *Apa dan Siapa Sejumlah Orang Indonesia 1983–1984*, Yogyakarta: Grafiti Pers, 1984, pp. 761–762; Terence H. Hull, *People, Population, and Policy in Indonesia*, Jakarta: Equinox Publishing, 2005, p. 6. She would later become head of the Office for

Village Public Health, where she spearheaded campaigns for family planning and maternal and infant health. In the late 1960s she specialized in infectious diseases at Tulane University. She reached the highest ranks of the WHO and, in recognition of her work in the field, Jakarta's Infectious Diseases Hospital was named after her in 2020.

124. *Berita Kementerian Kesehatan*, no. 1, March 1956, p. 8.

125. "Karangan Kiriman dari Lembaga Makanan Rakjat di Djakarta," *Berita Hygiene*, no. 6, June 1951, pp. 2–3.

126. "Educative Medicine," *Berita Hygiene*, no. 1, January 1952, pp. 1–3. The topic is also continued in the following issue. See also "Pendidikan Kesehatan kepada Rakjat," *Berita Hygiene*, no. 1, January 1951, pp. 1–4.

127. "Menjehatkan Lingkunan Hidup Manusia," *Berita Hygiene*, no. 6, June 1952, pp. 1–3.

128. "Pengumuman tentang Sekolah Pendidik Hygiene," *Berita Hygiene*, no. 4, April 1952, n.p.; reprinted and shortened in *Berita Hygiene*, no. 9, September 1952, p. 3.

129. "Rentjana Pekerdjaan Pemeliharaan Gigi Teratur di Sekolah," *Berita Hygiene*, no. 2, February 1951, p. 1; "Pedoman tentang Kesehatan Gigi untuk Guru dan Organg Tua," *Berita Hygiene*, no. 2, February 1951, pp. 4–6; continued in the following issue. On emotional health: "Pendidikan Kesehatan Rochani dalam Sekolah Pergaulan dalam Masjarakat," *Berita Hygiene*, no. 5, May 1952, pp. 1–4; continued in *Berita Hygiene*, no. 7, July 1952, pp. 1–3.

130. "Pendidikan Kesehatan Rakjat," *Berita Hygiene*, no. 7, July 1952, pp. 3–4, continued in *Berita Hygiene*, no. 8, August 1952, pp. 1–3; *Berita Hygiene*, no. 9, September 1952, pp. 1–3; *Berita Hygiene*, no. 10, October 1952, pp. 1–3; *Berita Hygiene*, no. 11, November 1952, pp. 1–4; *Berita Hygiene*, no. 3, March 1953, pp. 1–4.

131. For explicit references to mothers and children in relation to nation-building and development, see "Organisasi Masjarakat dan Kesehatan," *Berita Hygiene*, no. 12, December 1952, pp. 1–3; "Persediaan Alat2 Bersalin dan Keperluan Pertumbuhan Baji," *Berita Hygiene*, no. 4, April 1951, pp. 1–4.

132. "Organisasi Masjarakat dan Kesehatan."

133. "Organisasi Masjarakat dan Kesehatan." Bold in original.

Epilogue

1. Egypt was also a Muslim-majority, postcolonial, heavily rural, non-aligned country in the emerging Cold War order.

2. Mai Taha and Sara Salem, "Social Reproduction and Empire in an Egyptian Century," Dossier: Social Reproduction Theory, *Radical Philosophy*, vol. 204, (Spring 2019), pp. 47–54, quote p. 49.

3. Hull, *People, Population*, p. 6.

4. In 1956 the USAID (with additional funding from the Ford Foundation) sponsored an Indonesian obstetrician to study family planning in the States. Hull, *People, Population*, p. 9.

5. Burg, *De Geneesheer*, p. 72.

6. A. Ressel, *Pertjintaan jang Tinggal Gelap: Satoe Nasehat Thabib Boewat Menjegah Perkara Hamil*, Weltevreden: Electrische Drukkerij "Favoriet," 192? (n.d.).

7. On eugenics: Pols, "Eugenics"; Seng, *Strangers in the Family*; Stoler, *Carnal Knowledge*.

8. Stoler, *Carnal Knowledge*, pp. 62–64.

9. Pols, "Eugenics," p. 355.

10. See the advice offered by Dr. Aboe Hanifah to the Muhammadiyah and 'Aisyiyah congress of 1939. "Preadvies: Oeroesan Kesehatan dan Bersalin," *Soeara Moehammadijah*, 1939, p. 87.

11. "Uit de Inheemsche Wereld. Rasveredeling en Geboortebeperking," *Soerabaijasch Handelsblad*, November 10, 1936.

12. I speak here in contrast to, for example, India. See Asha Nadkarni, *Eugenic Feminism: Reproductive Nationalism in the United States and India*, Minneapolis, MN: University of Minnesota Press, 2014.

13. "Geboortebeperking Inheemschen," *Soerabaijasch Handelsblad*, May 14, 1937; "Islam en de Kinderbeperking. Lezing van H.A. Salim," *Soerabaijasch Handelsblad*, May 20, 1937; "N.I.A.S.-Vereeniging. Salim over Geboortebeperking," *De Indische Courant*, May 18, 1937; "Islam en Geboortebeperking. Causerie Hadji Salim," *De Indische Courant*, May 19, 1937.

14. "Het Groote Vraagstuk van Java's Overbevolking," *Deli Courant*, February 25, 1937.

15. "Islam en de Kinderbeperking. Lezing van H.A. Salim."

16. "A Mohamedan 'fatwa' on Contraception," *Human Fertility*, vol. 10 (no. 2), June 1945, pp. 45–46.

17. M. Barry Hooker, *Indonesian Islam: Social Change through Contemporary Fatawa*, Crows Nest: Asian Studies Association of Australia, 2003, p. 166; Jeremy Menchik, "The Co-Evolution of Sacred and Secular: Islamic Law and Family Planning in Indonesia," *South East Asia Research*, vol. 22 (no. 3), 2014, pp. 359–378, p. 365. This was the only *fatwa* issued on the topic by either Nahdlatul Ulama or Muhammadiyah until the late 1960s.

18. This is mentioned, with no further details, in "N.I.A.S.-Vereeniging. Salim over Geboortebeperking."

19. Ahmad Ramali, *Peraturan² untuk Memelihara Kesehatan dalam Hukum Sjara' Islam: Sumbangan untuk Penerangan Kepada Orang Muslimin tentang Ilmu Kesehatan*, 2nd ed., Djakarta: Balai Pustaka, 1956 [1950], p. 246.

20. For a critique of New Order family-planning policies and practices, see Leslie Dwyer, "Spectacular Sexuality: Nationalism, Development, and the Politics of Family Planning in Indonesia," in Tamar Mayer (ed.) *Gender Ironies of Nationalism: Sexing the Nation*, London: Routledge, 2000, pp. 25–64; Kathryn Robinson, "Choosing Contraception: Cultural Change and the Indonesian Family Planning Program," in P. Alexander (ed.) *Creating Indonesian Cultures*, Sydney: Oceania Publications, 1989; Betsy Hartmann, *Reproductive Rights and Wrongs: The Global Politics of Population Control*, Boston, MA: South End Press, 1995; Maryani Palupy Rasidjan, "'Kita Habis . . . We Will Be Gone': The Politics of Population, Family

Planning and Racialization in West Papua," *Medical Anthropology Quarterly*, vol. 38 (no. 4), 2024, pp. 407–419.

21. This is evident in publications circulating in the Philippines in the early 1950s targeting students at theological seminaries and teachers, which argued that family planning was a positive aspect of western culture, which the East should embrace. See, for example, McGilvary Theological Seminary Chiangmai, Thailand, and Philippine Federation of Christian Churches, *Christian Family Life: A Course for Theological Student by Chienmai Delegates to the Study and Training Institute on Marriage Guidance and Family Life Education*, Manila: Philippine Federation of Christian Churches, 1958; McGilvary Theological Seminary Chiangmai, Thailand, *Family Life Education: Outline of a Course of Training for Christian Teachers*, Manila: Philippine Federation of Christian Churches, 1958.

22. Balfour, *Public Health and Demography*, p. 90.

23. Balfour, *Public Health and Demography*, p. 95.

24. "Asia and the Far East Seminar on Population, Bandung, 21 November to 3 December 1955, Organized by the United Nations in Cooperation with the Government of Indonesia, with the Collaboration of the International Social Science Council," New York: United Nations, 1957, p. 14.

25. Balfour, *Public Health and Demography*, p. 97.

26. Other images of farming families with only two children had already appeared in earlier years; see, for example, the back cover to *Madjallah Berkala Pertanian*, no. 12, December 1952.

27. Hull, *People, Population*, pp. 7–8.

28. "Country Profiles: Indonesia," *The Population Council*, April 1971, p. 7. See also Sarwono, "Family Planning in Indonesia Under the Old Order," in Anke Niehof and Firman Lubis (eds.) *Two Is Enough: Family Planning in Indonesia under the New Order 1968–1998*, Leiden: KITLV Press, 2003, p. 21.

29. Hildred Geertz, *The Javanese Family*, pp. 84–85 (on contraception), p. 8 (on Modjokuto).

30. S. Adiwinata, *Membina Keluarga Menurut Rentjana: Berdasarkan Kemadjiran Berkala dari Wanita*, Djakarta: Djambatan, 1955.

31. Muhammad Nuh Hudawi, *Merentjanakan Kelahiran Anak*, Medan: Madju, 1956, quote p. 5.

32. These are just the few books available at the Cornell University Library: A. Prasdho, *Mentjegah Hamil: Mengatur Kelahiran Anak untuk Membina Keluarga Sehat, Ekonomi Kuat*, Surabaja: Marfiah, 1961; Rahmah Rijandi, *Membatasi Kelahiran Anak*, 5th ed., Medan: U.P. Segara, 196?; Michael L. Tan, *Pembatasan Penduduk dan Pengendalian Kelahiran I*, Kediri: Interstar, 195?. See also the several articles that appeared throughout the 1950s in *Suara Perwari*, *Dunia Wanita*, and *Wanita*.

33. "C.J. Gamble and R.B. Gamble, Summary of Indonesia, April 1954," Gamble, Clarence J. papers, 1920–1970s (inclusive), 1920–1966 (bulk), H MS c23. Francis A. Countway Library of Medicine, Harvard Medical Library (HML), Boston, MA.

34. Doone Williams and Greer Williams, *Every Child a Wanted Child: Clarence James Gamble, M.D. and His Work in the Birth Control Movement*, edited by Emily

Flint, Boston, MA: Harvard University Press, 1978. See pp. 249–260 on Margaret Roots.

35. "Margaret Roots to C.J. Gamble," June 10, 1957, Pathfinder Fund records, 1948–2019 (inclusive), 1954–1981 (bulk), H MS c635. HML.

36. "Margaret Roots to C.J. Gamble," May 5, 1957, H MS c635. HML.

37. "Perkumpulan 'Keluarga Berentjana,'" *Suara Perwari*, no. 1, January 1958, pp. 15–16.

38. Poorwo Sudarmo, *Perbaikan Makanan di Indonesia*, Djakarta: Kementerian Penerangan, 1958, pp. 20–26.

39. "1960 report to IIPF on visit to Indonesia by George and Barbara Cadbury, Dec.," H MS c23. HML.

40. Menchik, "The Co-Evolution."

41. "1960 report to IIPF on visit to Indonesia by George and Barbara Cadbury, Dec.," H MS c23. HML.

42. Satrio, *Revolusi Makanan Rakjat*, Djakarta: Dept. Kesehatan, 1965. The booklet took the title from a speech Minister of Health Maj. Gen. Satrio gave to the women's group KOWANI in 1965.

43. Wieringa, *Sexual Politics*, pp. 280–281; see also Sullivan, "Years of Dressing."

44. Among several contributions on the New Order's "domestication" of women, see also: Nelly van Doorn-Harder, *Women Shaping Islam: Indonesian Women Reading the Qur'an*, Urbana, IL: University of Illinois Press, 2006; Martyn, *The Women's Movement*; Wieringa, *Sexual Politics*; Kathryn May Robinson, *Gender, Islam, and Democracy in Indonesia*, New York, NY: Routledge, 2009; Blackburn, *Women and the State*.

45. Suryakusuma, *State Ibuism*.

Bibliography

Periodicals

Adil
Algemeen Handelsblad voor Nederlandsch-Indië
Algemeen Verslag van het Onderwijs in Nederlandsch-Indië over het Schooljaar
Almanak Moehammadijah
Almanak Tani
Asjraq
Bataviaasch Nieuwsblad
Berita Hygiene
Berita Kementerian Kesehatan Republik Indonesia
Berita Ketabiban
Bintang Hindia
D'Orient
De Huisvrouw in Indië
De Huisvrouw in Indië Semarang
De Huisvrouw in Indonesië
De Indiër
De Indische Courant
De Koerier
De Locomotief
De Nieuwe Vorstenlanden
De Preanger-bode
De Soerabajasch Handelsblad
De Sumatra Post
De Vrouw
Deli Courant
Djawa Baroe
Doenia Kita

Dunia Wanita
Geneeskundig Tijdschrift voor Nederlandsch-Indië
Guide of Scientists in Indonesia
Het Nieuws van den Dag voor Nederlandsch-Indië
Isteri
Isteri Indonesia
Isteri Soesila – Taman Moeslimah
Karya
Keluarga Sedjahtera: People's Welfare
Keoetamaan Isteri
Maandblad van de Vereniging van Huisvrouwen Bandoeng
Madjallah Berkala Pertanian
Mededeelingen van den Dienst der Volksgezondheid in Nederlandsch-Indië
De Mode-Revue
O.S.R. Publication
Officieel Orgaan van de Vereeniging van Huisvrouwen Soerabaja
Officieel Orgaan van het Nederlandse Rode Kruis Afdeling Indonesië
Pandji Poestaka
Pedoman Isteri
Pemimpin
Perempoean Bergerak
Pertja Selatan
Programma van den Pasar Gambir
Public Health Reports
Regeerings-Almanak voor Nederlandsch-Indië
Sedar
Sin Tin Po
Soeara 'Aisjijah (later *Suara 'Aisjijah*)
Soeara Moehammadijah
Suara Perwari
The New York Times
Tjermin Masjarakat: Hal-hal jang Patut Diketahui oleh Masjarakat
United States Department of State. *Foreign Service List.*
Volksalmanak Melajoe
Wanita
Women's International Club Journal

Books and Journal Articles
Abu-Lughod, Lila. "Do Muslim Women Really Need Saving? Anthropological Re-
flections on Cultural Relativism and Its Others." *American Anthropologist* 104,
no. 3 (2002): 783–790.
Abu-Lughod, Lila, ed. *Remaking Women: Feminism and Modernity in the Middle
East.* Princeton, NJ: Princeton University Press, 1998.

Adiwinata, S. *Membina Keluarga Menurut Rentjana: Berdasarkan Kemadjiran Berkala dari Wanita*. Djakarta: Djambatan, 1955.

Alexander, Paul, ed. *Creating Indonesian Cultures*. Sydney: Oceania Publications, 1989.

Allman, Jean. "Making Mothers: Missionaries, Medical Officers and Women's Work in Colonial Asante, 1924–1945." *History Workshop*, no. 38 (1994): 23–47.

Amico, Angela, Margo G. Wootan, Michael F. Jacobson, Cindy Leung, and A. Walter Willett. "The Demise of Artificial Trans Fat: A History of a Public Health Achievement." *Milbank Quarterly* 99, no. 3 (2021): 746–770.

Amini, Mutiah. *Sejarah Organisasi Perempuan Indonesia (1928–1998)*. Jakarta: Gadjah Mada University Press, 2021.

Amir and Burgerlijke Geneeskundige Dienst (BGD). *Vliegen en Vliegenverdelging = Dari Hal Lalat (Langau) Serta Ichtiar akan Memoesnahkannja*. Weltevreden: Drukkerij Volkslectuur, 1921.

Amrith, Sunil. *Decolonizing International Health: India and Southeast Asia, 1930–65*. Basingstoke: Palgrave Macmillan, 2006.

Anagol, Padma. "Agency, Periodisation and Change in the Gender and Women's History of Colonial India." *Gender & History* 20, no. 3 (2008): 603–627.

Andaya, Barbara Watson. *The Flaming Womb: Repositioning Women in Early Modern Southeast Asia*. Honolulu: University of Hawai'i Press, 2006.

Anderson, Benedict R.O'G. *Java in a Time of Revolution: Occupation and Resistance, 1944–1946*. 1st Equinox ed. Jakarta: Equinox Publishing, 2006.

Anderson, Warwick. *Colonial Pathologies: American Tropical Medicine, Race, and Hygiene in the Philippines*. Durham, NC: Duke University Press, 2006.

Anthias, Floya, and Nira Yuval-Davis. *Woman—Nation—State*. New York, NY: St. Martin's Press, 1989.

Apa dan Siapa Sejumlah Orang Indonesia 1983–1984. Yogyakarta: Grafiti Pers, 1984.

Apple, Rima D. *Mothers and Medicine: A Social History of Infant Feeding, 1890–1950*. Madison, WI: University of Wisconsin Press, 1987.

Apple, Rima D. *Perfect Motherhood: Science and Childrearing in America*. New Brunswick, NJ: Rutgers University Press, 2006.

Arsip Nasional Republik Indonesia. *Di bawah Pendudukan Jepang: Kenangan Empat Puluh Dua Orang yang Mengalaminya*. Penerbitan Sejarah Lisan, no. 4. Jakarta: Arsip Nasional Republik Indonesia, 1988.

"Asia and the Far East Seminar on Population, Bandung, 21 November to 3 December 1955, Organized by the United Nations in Co-operation with the Government of Indonesia, with the Collaboration of the International Social Science Council." New York, NY: United Nations, 1957.

Aulia, *"Makanan jang Séhat" dan Beberapa Ichtiar jang Lain Boeat Memeliharakan Keséhatan dan Menolong Menjemboehkan Penjakit*. 2nd ed. Djakarta: Djawa Goenseikanboe, Balai Poestaka, 2603 [1943].

Aydin, Cemil. *The Politics of Anti-Westernism in Asia: Visions of World Order in Pan-Islamic and Pan-Asian Thought*. New York, NY: Columbia University Press, 2007.

Badings, A.H.L. *Nieuw Hollandsch-Maleisch Maleisch-Hollandsch Woordenboek*. 7th ed. Zwolle: W.E.J. Tjeenk Willink, 1901.

Badings, A.H.L., and H.L.J. Badings. *Maleisch Woordenboek*. 8th ed. Zwolle: W.E.J. Tjeenk Willink, 1915.

Baker, Paula. "The Domestication of Politics: Women and American Political Society, 1780–1920." *The American Historical Review* 89, no. 3 (1984): 620–647.

Balai Poestaka. *Resultaten van de Volkslectuur in het Jaar 1925*. Weltevreden: Volkslectuur, 1926.

Balfour, Marshall C. *Public Health and Demography in the Far East: Report of a Survey Trip, September 13–December 13, 1948*. New York, NY: Rockefeller Foundation, 1950.

Barnes, Nicole Elizabeth. *Intimate Communities: Wartime Healthcare and the Birth of Modern China, 1937–1945*. Oakland, CA: University of California Press, 2018.

Baron, Beth. *The Women's Awakening in Egypt: Culture, Society, and the Press*. New Haven, CT: Yale University Press, 1994.

Bashford, Alison. *Purity and Pollution: Gender, Embodiment, and Victorian Medicine*. New York, NY: St. Martin's Press, 1998.

Bashford, Alison, and Philippa Levine, eds. *The Oxford Handbook of the History of Eugenics*. New York, NY: Oxford University Press, 2010.

Beers, Howard W. *An American Experience in Indonesia: The University of Kentucky Affiliation with the Agricultural University at Bogor*. Lexington, KY: University Press of Kentucky, 1971.

Bentley, Amy. *Eating for Victory: Food Rationing and the Politics of Domesticity*. Urbana, IL: University of Illinois Press, 1998.

Berlage, Nancy. *Farmers Helping Farmers: The Rise of the Farm and Home Bureaus, 1914–1935*. Baton Rouge, LA: Louisiana State University Press, 2016.

Bier, Laura. *Revolutionary Womanhood: Feminisms, Modernity, and the State in Nasser's Egypt*. Stanford, CA: Stanford University Press, 2011.

Birn, AnneEmanuelle. "Skirting the Issue: Women and International Health in Historical Perspective." *American Journal of Public Health* 89, no. 3 (1999): 399–407.

Blackburn, Susan. *Women and the State in Modern Indonesia*. Cambridge, UK: Cambridge University Press, 2004.

Boehmer, Elleke. *Stories of Women: Gender and Narrative in the Postcolonial Nation*. Manchester, UK: Manchester University Press, 2009.

Booth, Anne. *Economic Change in Modern Indonesia: Colonial and Post-Colonial Comparisons*. Cambridge, UK: Cambridge University Press, 2016.

Booth, Anne. *The Indonesian Economy in the Nineteenth and Twentieth Centuries*. Basingstoke: Palgrave, 1998.

Boserup, Ester. *Woman's Role in Economic Development*. New York, NY: St. Martin's Press, 1970.

Brenner, Suzanne April. *The Domestication of Desire: Women, Wealth, and Modernity in Java*. Princeton, NJ: Princeton University Press, 1998.

Broere, Sebastiaan. "Auto-Activity: Decolonization and the Politics of Knowledge in Early Postwar Indonesia, ca. 1920–1955." *Lembaran Sejarah* 16, no. 2 (2020): 143.

Brown, E. Richard. *Rockefeller Medicine Men: Medicine and Capitalism in America*. Berkeley, CA: University of California Press, 1979.

Bu, Liping, Darwin H. Stapleton, and Ka-che Yip, eds. *Science, Public Health, and the State in Modern Asia*. London: Routledge, 2012.

Burg, Cornelis Leendert van der. *De Geneesheer in Nederlandsch-Indië*. Batavia: Ernst & co., 1884.

Burg, Cornelis Leendert van der. *Persoonlijke Gezondheidsleer voor Europeanen*. Amsterdam: J.H. de Bussy, 1895.

Burnett, Kristin, Sara Ritchey, and Lynn M. Thomas. "Introduction: Health, Healing and Caring." *Gender & History* 33, no. 3 (October 2021): 583–593.

Chin, Grace V.S., ed. *Translational Politics in Southeast Asian Literatures: Contesting Race, Gender and Sexuality*. New York, NY: Routledge, 2021.

Chung, Yuehtsen Juliette. *Struggle for National Survival: Eugenics in Sino-Japanese Contexts, 1896–1945*. New York, NY: Routledge, 2002.

Cinquième congrès international d'hygiène et de démographie à La Haye (du 21 au 27 août 1884): comptes rendus et mémoires (Tome I). The Hague: Imprimerie sud hollandaise, 1884.

Clancy-Smith, Julia Ann, and Frances Gouda, eds. *Domesticating the Empire: Race, Gender and Family Life in French and Dutch Colonialism*. Charlottesville, VA: University Press of Virginia, 1998.

Colombijn, Freek, and Martine Barwegen. *Under Construction: The Politics of Urban Space and Housing During the Decolonization of Indonesia, 1930–1960*. Leiden: Brill, 2014.

Colombijn, Freek, and Joost Coté, eds. *Cars, Conduits and Kampongs: The Modernization of the Indonesian City 1920–1960*. Leiden: Brill, 2015.

Connelly, Matthew. *Fatal Misconception: The Struggle to Control World Population*. Cambridge, MA: Belknap Press of Harvard University Press, 2008.

Cooper, Frederick., and Ann L. Stoler. *Tensions of Empire: Colonial Cultures in a Bourgeois World*. Berkeley, CA: University of California Press, 2009.

Cucuz, Diana. *Winning Women's Hearts and Minds: Selling Cold War Culture in the US and the USSR*. Toronto: University of Toronto Press, 2023.

Cueto, Marcos, and Steven Paul Palmer. *Medicine and Public Health in Latin America: A History*. New York, NY: Cambridge University Press, 2015.

Cullather, Nick. *The Hungry World: America's Cold War Battle against Poverty in Asia*. Cambridge, MA: Harvard University Press, 2010.

Davin, A. "Imperialism and Motherhood." In *Tensions of Empire: Colonial Cultures in a Bourgeois World*, edited by Frederick Cooper and Ann L. Stoler, pp. 87–151. Berkeley, CA: University of California Press, 2009.

De Grazia, Victoria. *Irresistible Empire: America's Advance Through Twentieth-Century Europe*. Cambridge, MA: Belknap Press of Harvard University Press, 2005.

Dewall, H.A. von. *Hollandsch-Maleische en Maleisch-Hollandsche Gids ten dienste van Geneeskundigen*. Utrecht: Kemink, 1929.

Donath, W.F. *Opmerkingen over de Inheemsche Voeding*. Buitenzorg: Archipel, 1931.

Doorn-Harder, Nelly van. *Women Shaping Islam: Indonesian Women Reading the Qur'an*. Urbana, IL: University of Illinois Press, 2006.

Drewes, G.W.J. "D.A. Rinkes: A note on His Life and Work." *Bijdragen Tot De Taal-, Land- En Volkenkunde* 117, no. 4 (1961): 417–435.

Dutch East Indies. Tijdelijk Kantoor voor de Volkstelling 1930. *Volkstelling 1930: Census of 1930 in Netherlands India*. Vol. 8. Batavia: Departement van Landbouw, Nijverheid en Handel, 1933.

Edwards, Louise P. *Women Warriors and Wartime Spies of China*. Cambridge, UK: Cambridge University Press, 2016.

Elson, Robert. *The Idea of Indonesia*. Cambridge, UK: Cambridge University Press, 2008.

Ettling, John. *The Germ of Laziness: Rockefeller Philanthropy and Public Health in the New South*. Cambridge, MA: Harvard University Press, 1981.

Fara, Patricia. *A Lab of One's Own: Science and Suffrage in the First World War*. Oxford, UK: Oxford University Press, 2018.

Farley, John. *To Cast out Disease: A History of the International Health Division of the Rockefeller Foundation (1913–1951)*. Oxford, UK: Oxford University Press, 2004.

Federici, Silvia. "Social Reproduction Theory: History, Issues and Present Challenges." *Radical Philosophy* 2.04 (Spring 2019): 55–57.

Field, Moira, and San-chao Chung. *Easy Chinese Dishes for Today*. London: John Lane, 1943.

Flu, Paul Christiaan. *Kesehatan didalam Kampoeng*. Batavia: Balai Poestaka, 1922.

Flu, Paul Christiaan. *Tropenhygiëne: Populaire Voordrachten*. Batavia: Javasche Boekhandel & Drukkerij, 1917.

Fogg, Kevin W. *Indonesia's Islamic Revolution*. Cambridge, UK: Cambridge University Press, 2020.

Formichi, Chiara. "Bouillon for His Majesty: Healthy *Halal* Modernity in Colonial Java." *History of Religions* 62, no. 4 (2023): 373–409.

Formichi, Chiara. *Islam and the Making of the Nation: Kartosuwiryo and Political Islam in Twentieth-Century Indonesia*. Leiden: KITLV Press, 2012.

Garbes, Angela. *Essential Labor: Mothering as Social Change*. 1st ed. New York, NY: Harper Wave, an imprint of HarperCollins Publishers, 2022.

Geertz, Clifford. *Agricultural Involution: The Process of Ecological Change in Indonesia*. Berkeley, CA: Published for the Association of Asian Studies by University of California Press, 1994.

Geertz, Clifford. *Peddlers and Princes: Social Change and Economic Modernization in Two Indonesian Towns*. Chicago, IL: The University of Chicago Press, 1963.

Geertz, Hildred. *The Javanese Family: A Study of Kinship and Socialization*. New York, NY: Free Press, 1961.

Gouda, Frances. "Discipline Versus Gentle Persuasion in Colonial Public Health: The Rockefeller Foundation's Intensive Rural Hygiene Work in the Netherlands East Indies, 1925–1940." *Research Reports from the Rockefeller Archive Center*, 2009.

Gouda, Frances. "Teaching Indonesian Girls in Java and Bali, 1900–1942: Dutch Progressives, the Infatuation with 'Oriental' Refinement, and 'Western' Ideas About Proper Womanhood." *Women's History Review* 4, no. 1 (1995): 25–62.

Groeneboer, Kees. *Gateway to the West: The Dutch Language in Colonial Indonesia, 1600–1950: A History of Language Policy.* Amsterdam: Amsterdam University Press, 1998.

Hadler, Jeffrey Alan. *Muslims and Matriarchs: Cultural Resilience in Indonesia Through Jihad and Colonialism.* Ithaca, NY: Cornell University Press, 2008.

Haeften, Frederik Willem van. *Hooge Zuigelingensterfte en Zuigelingenzorg— Pemeliharaan Kanak-kanak jang Menjoeseo*, Serie D.V.G, no. 3. Weltevreden: Balai Poestaka, 1919.

Hagemann, Karen, Stefan Dudink, and Sonya O. Rose, eds. *The Oxford Handbook of Gender, War, and the Western World since 1600.* Oxford Academic, 2020.

Hammond, Kelly A. *China's Muslims & Japan's Empire: Centering Islam in World War II.* Chapel Hill, NC: The University of North Carolina Press, 2020.

Hancock, Mary. "Home Science and the Nationalization of Domesticity in Colonial India." *Modern Asian Studies* 35, no. 4 (October, 2001): 871–903.

Hartmann, Betsy. *Reproductive Rights and Wrongs: The Global Politics of Population Control.* Boston, MA: South End Press, 1995.

Hartog, Adel P. den. "Diffusion of Milk As a New Food to Tropical Regions: The Example of Indonesia, 1880–1942." Dissertation, Stichting Voeding Nederland Proefschrift Wageningen, 1986.

Heinemann, Henry. *Practische Wenken voor Moeders.* Medan: Typ. Köhler and Co., 1928.

Heinemann, Henry, and Antonia Zerwer. *Pemimpin bagi Mengadjar Anak-Anak Disekolah dalam Hal Mengoeroes Baji.* Batavia: Balai Poestaka, 1922.

Henley, David, and H. Schulte Nordholt, *Environment, Trade and Society in Southeast Asia.* Leiden: Brill, 2015.

Hesselink, Liesbeth. *Healers on the Colonial Market: Native Doctors and Midwives in the Dutch East Indies.* Leiden: KITLV Press, 2011.

Hollandsch-Maleisch en Maleisch-Hollandsch Zakwoordenboek. 7th ed. Batavia: G. Kolff, 1932.

Hooker, M. Barry. *Indonesian Islam: Social Change Through Contemporary Fatawa.* Crows Nest: Asian Studies Association of Australia, 2003.

Horton, William Bradley. "'A Gift of Unlimited Value': Public Health and Colonial Publishing in Indonesia (1910s–1945)." Forthcoming.

Hudawi, Muhammad Nuh. *Merentjanakan Kelahiran Anak.* Medan: Madju, 1956.

Huff, Gregg. "The Great Second World War Vietnam and Java Famines." *Modern Asian Studies* 54, no. 2 (2000).

Hull, Terence H. *People, Population, and Policy in Indonesia.* Jakarta: Equinox
Publishing, 2005.

Hydrick, John Lee. *The Division of Public Health Education of the Public Health
Service of the Netherlands East Indies.* Weltevreden: Set up and printed in the
Workshop of the Division, 1929.

Hydrick, John Lee. *Intensive Rural Hygiene Work and Public Health Education of
the Public Health Service of Netherlands India,* Batavia, 1937

Hydrick, John Lee. *Intensive Rural Hygiene Work in the Netherlands East Indies.*
New York, NY: Netherlands Information Bureau, 1942.

Hydrick, John Lee. *Intensive Rural Hygiene Work in the Netherlands East Indies.*
New York, NY: Netherlands Information Bureau, 1944.

Indonesia Departemen Kesehatan. *Sejarah Kesehatan Nasional Indonesia.* Jakarta:
Departemen Kesehatan RI, 1980.

Instituut voor Voedsvoeding. *Makanan jang Moerah tetapi Baik.* Batavia: Balai
Poestaka, 1941.

Isenstadt, Sandy, and Kishwar Rizvi, eds. *Modernism and the Middle East: Architecture and Politics in the Twentieth Century.* Seattle, WA: University of Washington Press, 2008.

Japan Rikugun. *Orang Indonesia yang Terkemuka di Jawa.* Yogyakarta: Gadjah
Mada University Press, 1986.

Jedamski, Doris. "Balai Pustaka: A Colonial Wolf in Sheep's Clothing." *Archipel* 44
(1992): 23–46.

Johnston, William. *The Modern Epidemic: A History of Tuberculosis in Japan.* Cambridge, MA: Council on East Asian Studies, Harvard University, 1995.

Kahin, George McTurnan. *Nationalism and Revolution in Indonesia.* Ithaca, NY:
Southeast Asia Program Publications, Cornell University, 1952.

Kamphuis, Kirsten. "Indigenous Girls and Education in a Changing Colonial Society: The Dutch East Indies, c. 1880–1942." Dissertation, European University
Institute, 2019.

Keddie, Nikki R., and Beth Baron, eds. *Women in Middle Eastern History: Shifting
Boundaries in Sex and Gender.* New Haven, CT: Yale University Press, 2017.

Keddie, Nikki R., and Rudolph P. Matthee. *Iran and the Surrounding World: Interactions in Culture and Cultural Politics.* Seattle, WA: University of Washington
Press, 2002.

Kementerian Penerangan RI. *Republik Indonesia: Kotapradja Djakarta Raya.* Jakarta: Kementerian Penerangan, Indonesia, 1952.

Khoja-Moolji, Shenila. *Forging the Ideal Educated Girl: The Production of Desirable
Subjects in Muslim South Asia.* Oakland, CA: University of California Press,
2018.

Khoja-Moolji, Shenila. *Rebuilding Community: Displaced Women and the Making
of a Shia Ismaili Muslim Sociality.* New York, NY: Oxford University Press, 2023.

Kim, Hoi-eun. *Doctors of Empire: Medical and Cultural Encounters Between Imperial Germany and Meiji Japan.* Toronto; Buffalo; London: University of Toronto
Press, 2016.

Kirschner, L. *De tien Geboden der Hygiëne voor de Tropen*. Bandoeng: Drukkerij Maks & v.d. Klits, 192?.

Klein, Jakob.A., and Anne Murcott, eds. *Food Consumption in Global Perspective. Essays in the Anthropology of Food in Honour of Jack Goody*. Basingstoke: Palgrave Macmillan, 2014.

Klift-Snijder, A.G. *Moeder-cursus in Mowewe (z.o. Selebes)*. Zeist: SIMAVI, 1936.

Klinkert, H. Cornelius, and Claas Spat. *Nieuw Nederlandsch-Maleisch Woordenboek*. 3rd ed. Leiden: N.V. Boekhandel en Drukkerij Voorheen E.J. Brill, 1926.

Ko, Kevin E. "The Non-Immanent Frame: Medicine as Ethics in the Islamic Modernist Movement of Late Colonial Indonesia." *History of Religions* 58, no. 4 (2019): 404–431.

Kohlbrugge, J.H.F. "De vragen 94-102 van den Leidraad van het Gewestelijk Onderzoek naar de Oorzaken der Mindere Welvaart van de Inlandsche Bevolking op Java en Madoera." *Verslagen der Algemeene Vergadering van het Indisch Genootschap* (1907): 189–218.

Koloniale School voor Meisjes en Vrouwen (The Hague, Netherlands). *Propagandaboekje van de Koloniale School voor Meisjes en Vrouwen*. The Hague: Koloniale School voor Meisjes en Vrouwen, 1927.

Koven, Seth, and Sonya Michel, eds. *Mothers of a New World: Maternalist Politics and the Origins of Welfare States*. New York, NY: Routledge, 1993.

Kratoska, Paul H. *The Japanese Occupation of Malaya and Singapore, 1941–45: A Social and Economic History*. 2nd ed. Singapore: NUS Press, 2018.

Kurniawati Hastuti, Dewi. "Javanese Women and Islam: Identity Formation Since the Twentieth Century." *Southeast Asian Studies* 1, no. 1 (2012): 109–140.

La Berge, Ann F. *Mission and Method: Early Nineteenth-Century Public Health Movement*. Cambridge, UK: Cambridge University Press, 1992.

Leimena, Johannes. *Membangun Kesehatan Rakjat*. Djakarta: Noordhoff-Kolff, N.V., 1952.

Leimena, Johannes. *Public Health in Indonesia: Problems and Planning*. The Hague: Van Dorp, 1956.

Leong-Salobir, Cecilia, ed. *Routledge Handbook of Food in Asia*. London: Routledge, 2019.

Lewis, Milton James, and Kerrie L. Macpherson, eds. *Public Health in Asia and the Pacific: Historical and Comparative Perspectives*. Abingdon, UK: Routledge, 2007.

Liang, Qizi, and Charlotte Furth, eds. *Health and Hygiene in Chinese East Asia: Policies and Publics in the Long Twentieth Century*. Durham, NC: Duke University Press, 2011.

Lo, Ming-chen Miriam. *Doctors Within Borders: Profession, Ethnicity, and Modernity in Colonial Taiwan*. Berkeley, CA: University of California Press, 2002.

Locher-Scholten, Elsbeth. *Women and the Colonial State: Essays on Gender and Modernity in the Netherlands Indies, 1900–1942*. Amsterdam: Amsterdam University Press, 2000.

Lombard-Salmon, Claudine. "Chinese Women Writers in Indonesia and Their Views of Female Emancipation." *Archipel* (1984): 149–171.

Low, Morris, ed. *Building a Modern Japan: Science, Technology, and Medicine in the Meiji Era and Beyond.* New York, NY: Palgrave Macmillan, 2005.

Mandal, Sumit Kumar. *Becoming Arab: Creole Histories and Modern Identity in the Malay World.* Cambridge, UK: Cambridge University Press, 2018.

Manderson, Lenore. "Health Services and the Legitimation of the Colonial State: British Malaya 1786–1941." *International Journal of Health Services: Planning, Administration, Evaluation* 17, no. 1 (1987): 91–112. DOI: 10.2190/J56K-HPBE-9H1K-XNQQ.

Mark, Ethan. *Japan's Occupation of Java in the Second World War: A Transnational History.* London: Bloomsbury Academic, 2018.

Martyn, Elizabeth. *The Women's Movement in Post-Colonial Indonesia: Gender and Nation in a New Democracy.* London: RoutledgeCurzon, 2005.

Mayer, Tamar. *Gender Ironies of Nationalism: Sexing the Nation.* London: Routledge, 2000.

McArthur, A. Margaret. *Report to the Government of Indonesia on the Central Java Nutrition Project.* FAO CEP Report. Rome, 1962.

McClain, Dani. *We Live for the We: The Political Power of Black Motherhood.* 1st ed. New York, NY: Bold Type Books, 2019.

McClintock, Anne. *Imperial Leather: Race, Gender, and Sexuality in the Colonial Contest.* New York, NY: Routledge, 1995.

McGilvary Theological Seminary Chiangmai, Thailand. *Family Life Education: Outline of a Course of Training for Christian Teachers.* Manila: Philippine Federation of Christian Churches, 1958.

McGilvary Theological Seminary Chiangmai, Thailand, and Philippine Federation of Christian Churches. *Christian Family Life: A Course for Theological Student by Chienmai Delegates to the Study and Training Institute on Marriage Guidance and Family Life Education.* Manila: Philippine Federation of Christian Churches, 1958.

McGregor, Katharine E. *Systemic Silencing: Activism, Memory, and Sexual Violence in Indonesia.* Madison, WI: University of Wisconsin Press, 2023.

Meerwijk, Maurits Bastiaan. *A History of Plague in Java, 1911–1942.* Ithaca, NY: Southeast Asia Program Publications, an imprint of Cornell University Press, 2022.

Menchik, Jeremy. "The Co-Evolution of Sacred and Secular: Islamic Law and Family Planning in Indonesia." *South East Asia Research* 22, no. 3 (2014): 359–378.

Moon, Suzanne M. "Takeoff or Self-Sufficiency? Ideologies of Development in Indonesia, 1957–1961." *Technology and Culture* 39, no. 2 (1998): 187–212.

Moon, Suzanne M. *Technology and Ethical Idealism: A History of Development in the Netherlands East Indies.* Leiden: CNWS Publications, 2007.

Moore, Aaron.S. *Constructing East Asia.* Palo Alto, CA: Stanford University Press, 2015.

Mrázek, Rudolf. *Engineers of Happy Land: Technology and Nationalism in a Colony.* Princeton, NJ: Princeton University Press, 2002.

"A Mohamedan 'fatwa' on Contraception." *Human Fertility* 10, no. 2 (June 1945): 45–46.

Muwardi. *Keséhatan (Tentang Hal Sport)*. Solo: Pembatjaan Ra'jat, 1934.

Nadkarni, Asha. *Eugenic Feminism: Reproductive Nationalism in the United States and India*. Minneapolis, MN: University of Minnesota Press, 2014.

Najmabadi, Afsaneh. "Crafting an Educated Housewife in Iran." In *Remaking Women: Feminism and Modernity in the Middle East*, edited by Lila Abu-Lughod, 91–125. Princeton, NJ: Princeton University Press, 1998.

Nederlandse Rode Kruis Feeding Team. *Report on Nutritional Survey in Netherlands East Indies, Conducted During Oct. 1945 till June 1946*. The Hague: Van Loon, 1948.

Neeb, H.M. *Rede Uitgesproken Ter Gelegenheed van De Opening Der Eerste Hygiëne Tentoonstelling in Nederlandsch-Indië*. Bandoeng: Drukkerij Maks & v.d. Klits, 1927.

Niehof, Anke, and Lubis Firman, eds. *Two Is Enough: Family Planning in Indonesia Under the New Order 1968–1998*. Leiden: KITLV Press, 2003.

Nitisastro, Widjojo. *Population Trends in Indonesia*. Ithaca, NY: Cornell University Press, 1970.

Officieele Catalogus der 8ᵉ Ned.-Ind. Jaarbeurs en -Markt en der Eerste Hygiëne Tentoonstelling in Ned. Indië, 1927.

Oldenziel, Ruth, and Karin Zachmann, eds. *Cold War Kitchen: Americanization, Technology, and European Users*. Cambridge, MA: MIT Press, 2009.

Padmasusastra. *Tata Cara*. Jakarta: Departemen Pendidikan dan Kebudayaan, Proyek Penerbitan Buku Bacaan Sastra Indonesia dan Daerah, 1980 [1907].

Palmer, Steven Paul. *Launching Global Health: The Caribbean Odyssey of the Rockefeller Foundation*. Conversations in Medicine and Society. Ann Arbor, MI: University of Michigan Press, 2010.

Papanek, G.F., and D. Dowsett. "The Cost of Living. 1938–1973." *Economics and Finance in Indonesia*, Faculty of Economics and Business, University of Indonesia, 23 (1975): 181–206.

Peacock, James L. *Muslim Puritans: Reformist Psychology in Southeast Asian Islam*. Berkeley, CA: University of California Press, 1978.

Pengadjaran (Sekolah Rendah dan Sekolah Landjutan) 1954/1955. Djakarta: Biro Pusat Statistik, Statistik Sosial, Kulturil dan Umum, Seksi Pengadjaran, 1958.

Pengadjaran Sekolah Rendah dan Sekolah Landjutan 1954/55–1955/56. Djakarta: Biro Pusat Statistik, Statistik Sosial, Kulturil dan Umum, Seksi Pengadjaran, 1957.

Pengadjaran (Sekolah Rendah dan Sekolah Landjutan) 1956/1957. Djakarta: Biro Pusat Statistik, Statistik Sosial, Kulturil dan Umum, Seksi Pengadjaran, 1959.

Peverelli, Pierre, and F. van Bemmel. *Blyf Gezond!: Platenatlas ten Behoeve van het Onderwijs in de Gezondheidsleer op de Indische Lagere Scholen = Sehatlah Selaloe!: Boekoe Gambar Jang Dipergoenakan Oentoek Mengadjarkan Ilmoe Kesehatan Disekolah Rendah Ditanah Hindia*. Groningen: Wolters, 1933.

Phan, Quang Đán. *Public Health in Indonesia and Principles of Technical Assistance in the Field*. 1953.

Poesponegoro, Marwati Djoened, and Nugroho Notosusanto. *Sejarah Nasional Indonesia*. Vol. VI. Jakarta: Departemen Pendidikan dan Kebudayaan, 1993.

Poeze, Harry A. *Verguisd en Vergeten: Tan Malaka, de Linkse Beweging en de Indonesische Revolutie, 1945–1949.* Leiden: KITLV Uitgeverij, 2007.

Pollard, Lisa. *Nurturing the Nation: The Family Politics of Modernizing, Colonizing and Liberating Egypt (1805/1923).* Berkeley, CA: University of California Press, 2005.

Pols, Hans. "European Physicians and Botanists, Indigenous Herbal Medicine in the Dutch East Indies, and Colonial Networks of Mediation." *East Asian Science, Technology and Society: An International Journal* 3, no. 2 (2009): 173–208.

Pols, Hans. *Nurturing Indonesia: Medicine and Decolonisation in the Dutch East Indies.* Cambridge, UK: Cambridge University Press, 2018.

Pols, Hans, and Warwick Anderson. "The Mestizos of Kisar: An Insular Racial Laboratory in the Malay Archipelago." *Journal of Southeast Asian Studies* 49, no. 3 (2018): 445–463.

Prasdho, A. *Mentjegah Hamil: Mengatur Kelahiran Anak untuk Membina Keluarga Sehat, Ekonomi Kuat.* Surabaja: Marfiah, 1961.

Programma van den Pasar Gambir, Batavia, 1923. Batavia: Vereenigin "Het Pasar Gambir-Comité," 1923.

Protschky, Susie. "The Colonial Table: Food, Culture and Dutch Identity in Colonial Indonesia." *Australian Journal of Politics & History* 54, no. 3 (2008): 346–357.

Protschky, Susie, ed. *Photography, Modernity and the Governed in Late-Colonial Indonesia.* Amsterdam: Amsterdam University Press, 2015.

Protschky, Susie, Tom van den Berge, and Timothy P. Barnard, eds. *Modern Times in Southeast Asia, 1920s–1970s.* Leiden: Brill, 2018.

Raffles, Thomas Stamford. *The History of Java.* London: Oxford University Press, [1830] 1965.

Ram, Kalpana, and Margaret Jolly, eds. *Maternities and Modernities: Colonial and Postcolonial Experiences in Asia and the Pacific.* Cambridge, UK: Cambridge University Press, 1998.

Ramali, Ahmad. *Peraturan² untuk Memelihara Kesehatan dalam Hukum Sjara' Islam: Sumbangan untuk Penerangan Kepada Orang Muslimin tentang Ilmu Kesehatan.* 2nd ed. Djakarta: Balai Pustaka, 1956 [1950].

Rasidjan, Maryani Palupy. "'Kita Habis . . . We Will Be Gone': The Politics of Population, Family Planning and Racialization in West Papua." *Medical Anthropology Quarterly* 38, no. 4 (2024): 407–419.

Ray, Sangeeta. *En-gendering India: Woman and Nation in Colonial and Postcolonial Narratives.* Durham, NC, and London: Duke University Press, 2000.

Reid, Anthony. *Southeast Asia in the Age of Commerce, 1450–1680.* Vol. 1. New Haven, CT: Yale University Press, 1988.

Report of the Technical Meeting on Home Economics for South and East Asia, Tokyo, Japan, 5–12 October 1956. Rome: Food and Agriculture Organization of the United Nations, 1957.

Republik Indonesia: Daerah Istimewa Jogjakarta. Bandung: Kementerian Penerangan, 1952.

Reyes, Raquel A.G. "Modernizing the Manileña: Technologies of Conspicuous Consumption for the Well-to-Do Woman, circa 1880s—1930s." *Modern Asian Studies* 46, no. 1 (2012): 193–220.

Rice, Nicholas M. *Kentucky at Bogor: A Final Report to the United States Agency for International Development*. Institute Pertanian Bogor and University of Kentucky Center for Developmental Change, 1968.

Ricklefs, Merle C. *A History of Modern Indonesia since c. 1200*. Basingstoke: Palgrave Macmillan, 2008.

Ricklefs, Merle C. *Polarizing Javanese Society: Islamic and Other Visions, c. 1830–1930*. Honolulu: University of Hawai'i Press, 2007.

Rijandi, Rahmah. *Membatasi Kelahiran Anak*. 5th ed. Medan: U.P. Segara, 196?.

Robinson, Kathryn May. *Gender, Islam, and Democracy in Indonesia*. New York, NY: Routledge, 2009.

Roces, Mina. "Filipino Elite Women and Public Health in the American Colonial Era, 1906-1940." *Women's History Review* 26, no. 3 (2017): 477–502.

Rogaski, Ruth. *Hygienic Modernity: Meanings of Health and Disease in Treaty-Port China*. Berkeley, CA: University of California Press, 2004.

Rogers, Everett M., J.D. Eveland, and Alden S. Bean, "Extending the Agricultural Extension Model. Preliminary Draft." Stanford, CA: Stanford University, 1976.

Said, Edward W. *Orientalism*. New York, NY: Vintage Books, 2003.

Sand, Jordan. *House and Home in Modern Japan: Reforming Everyday Life 1880–1930*. Cambridge, MA: Harvard University Press, 2005.

Sangkanningrat. *Iets over Hygiëne: in Verband met Adat, Geloof en Bijgeloof van het Soendaneesche Volk*. Bandoeng: Nix, n.d.

Sardjito and R.A. Wongsosewojo. *Dari Hal Mentjari Kesehatan*. Batavia: Balai Poestaka, 1930.

Satō, Shigeru. *War, Nationalism, and Peasants: Java Under the Japanese Occupation, 1942–1945*. Armonk, NY: M.E. Sharpe, 1994.

Satrio. *Revolusi Makanan Rakjat*. Djakarta: Dept. Kesehatan, 1965.

Schama, Simon. *The Embarrassment of Riches: An Interpretation of Dutch Culture in the Golden Age*. New York, NY: Knopf, 1987.

Scheffler, Frauke. "Producing Citizens: Infant Health Programs in the Philippines, 1900–1930." PhD dissertation, University of Cologne, 2019.

Schneider, Helen M. *Keeping the Nation's House: Domestic Management and the Making of Modern China*. Contemporary Chinese Studies Series. Vancouver: UBC Press, 2011.

Schulte Nordholt, Henk. "Modernity and Cultural Citizenship in the Netherlands Indies: An Illustrated Hypothesis." *Journal of Southeast Asian Studies* 42, no. 3 (2011): 435–457.

Schulte Nordholt, Henk, ed. *Outward Appearances: Dressing State and Society in Indonesia*. Leiden: KITLV Press, 1997.

Sears, Laurie J. *Fantasizing the Feminine in Indonesia*. New York, NY: Duke University Press, 2020.

Sears, Laurie J. *Shadows of Empire: Colonial Discourse and Javanese Tales*. Durham, NC: Duke University Press, 1996.

Seng, Guo-Quan. *Strangers in the Family: Gender, Patriliny, and the Chinese in Colonial Indonesia*. Ithaca, NY: Southeast Asia Program Publications, an imprint of Cornell University Press, 2023.

Shehabuddin, Elora. *Sisters in the Mirror: A History of Muslim Women and the Global Politics of Feminism*. Oakland, CA: University of California Press, 2021.

Silverberg, Helene. *Gender and American Social Science: The Formative Years*. Princeton, NJ: Princeton University Press, 1998.

Simpson, Bradley R. *Economists with Guns: Authoritarian Development and U.S.-Indonesian Relations, 1960–1968*. Stanford, CA: Stanford University Press, 2008.

Smith, Margaret Charles, and Linda Janet Holmes. *Listen to Me Good: The Life Story of an Alabama Midwife*. Columbus, OH: Ohio State University Press, 1996.

Smith, Susan Lynn. *Sick and Tired of Being Sick and Tired: Black Women's Health Activism in America, 1890–1950*. Philadelphia, PA: University of Pennsylvania Press, 1995.

Soedarmo, Poorwo. *Dapur Indonesia Djaman Baru*. Djakarta: Djambatan, 1952.

Soedarmo, Poorwo. *Pedoman untuk Membuat Menu dan Kumpulan Menu untuk Pelbagai Golongan dan Umur*. The Hague: Van Goor, 1952.

Soedarmo, Poorwo, and Arjatmo Tjokronegoro. *Gizi dan Saya*. Jakarta: Fakultas Kedokteran, Universitas Indonesia, 1995.

Soekarno. *Sarinah: Soal Perempoean, Laki dan Perempoean, dari Goea ke Kota*. T. Tinggi Deli: Tjerdas, 1948.

Soja, Taylor, "Kitchen Window Feminism: Sarah Macnaughtan, Wartime Care and the Authority of Experience in the South African and First World Wars." *Gender & History* 33, no. 3 (October 2021): 668–682.

Sproat, Liberty P. "Nurturing Transitions: Housewife Organizations in (Colonial) Indonesia, 1900–1972." PhD dissertation, Purdue University, 2015.

Statistik Pengadjaran Rendah di Indonesia 1949. Djakarta: Penerbitan Kantor Pusat Statistik, 1951.

Statistik Pengadjaran Rendah di Indonesia 1951. Djakarta: Penerbitan Kantor Pusat Statistik, n.d.

Steedly, Mary Margaret. *Rifle Reports: A Story of Indonesian Independence*. Berkeley, CA: University of California Press, 2013.

Stein, Eric A. "Colonial Theatres of Proof: Representation and Laughter in 1930s Rockefeller Foundation Hygiene Cinema in Java." *Health and History* 8, no. 2 (2006): 14–44.

Stein, Eric A. "Vital Times: Power, Public Health, and Memory in Rural Java." PhD thesis, University of Michigan, Ann Arbor, 2005.

Stokvis-Cohen Stuart, N., and H. Subandrio. *Sang Baji Datang: Sebuah Buku untuk Para Istri dan Ibu Muda*. Djakarta: Djambatan, 1950.

Stoler, Ann Laura. *Carnal Knowledge and Imperial Power: Race and the Intimate in Colonial Rule*. Berkeley, CA: University of California Press, 2010.

Stoler, Ann Laura. *Race and the Education of Desire: Foucault's History of Sexuality and the Colonial Order of Things*. Durham, NC: Duke University Press, 1995.

Stoler, Ann Laura. "A Sentimental Education: Native Servants and the Cultivation of European Children in the Netherlands Indies." In *Fantasizing the Feminine in Indonesia*, edited by Laurie J. Sears, 71–91. New York, NY: Duke University Press, 2020.

Strassler, Karen. *Refracted Visions: Popular Photography and National Modernity in Java*. Durham, NC: Duke University Press, 2010.

Sudarmo, Poorwo, *Perbaikan Makanan di Indonesia*. Djakarta: Kementerian Penerangan, 1958.

Sukarno. *Sarinah: Kewadjiban Wanita dalam Perdjoangan Republik Indonesia*. Jakarta: Panitya Penerbit Buku-buku Karangan Presiden Sukarno, 1963 [1947].

Sullivan, Charles, "Years of Dressing Dangerously: Modern Women, National Identity and Moral Crisis in Sukarno's Indonesia, 1945–1966." PhD dissertation, University of Michigan, Ann Arbor, 2020.

Suryakusuma, Julia I. *State Ibuism: The Social Construction of Womanhood in New Order Indonesia = Ibuisme Negara: Konstruksi Sosial Keperempuanan Orde Baru*. Jakarta, Depok: Komunitas Bambu, 2011.

Suwardjo. *BPMD (Balai Pendidikan Masjarakat Desa—Village Educational Center)*. Djakarta: Pusat Djawatan Pertanian Rakjat, 1953.

Suwardjo. *Menudju ke Kemakmuran Desa*. Djakarta: Kementerian Pertanian, 1950?.

Suwignyo, Agus. "The Breach in the Dike: Regime Change and the Standardization of Public Primary-School Teacher Training in Indonesia (1893–1969)." PhD dissertation, University of Leiden, 2012.

Swellengrebel, N.H., *Documenta Neerlandica et Indonesica de Morbis Tropicis (Quarterly Journal of Tropical Medicine and Hygiene)* 1, no. 3 (September 1949).

Taha, Mai, and Sara Salem, "Social Reproduction and Empire in an Egyptian Century." *Radical Philosophy* 204, (Spring 2019): 47–54.

Tan, Michael L. *Pembatasan Penduduk dan Pengendalian Kelahiran I*. Kediri: Interstar, 195?.

Taylor, Jean Gelman. "The Sewing-Machine in Colonial-Era Photographs: A Record from Dutch Indonesia." *Modern Asian Studies* 46, no. 1 (2012): 71–95.

Taylor, Jean Gelman. *The Social World of Batavia: Europeans and Eurasians in Colonial Indonesia*. 2nd ed. Madison, WI: University of Wisconsin Press, 2009.

Taylor, Jean Gelman, ed., *Women Creating Indonesia: The First Fifty Years*. Clayton, Australia: Monash Asia Institute, 1997.

Teeuw, Andries. "The Impact of Balai Pustaka on Modern Indonesian Literature," *Bulletin of the School of Oriental and African Studies, University of London* 35, no. 1 (1972): 111–127.

The Keywords Feminist Editorial Collective, ed., *Keywords for Gender and Sexuality Studies*. New York, NY: New York University Press, 2021.

The Population Council. "Country Profiles: Indonesia." The Population Council, April 1971.

Thomson, Gerald E. "'A Baby Show Means Work in the Hardest Sense': The Better Baby Contests of the Vancouver and New Westminster Local Councils of Women, 1913–1929." *BC Studies* 128 (2000): 5–36.

Tillema, Hendrik F. *"Kromoblanda": Over 't Vraagstuk van "het Wonen" in Kromo's Groote Land*. The Hague: H. Uden Masman, 1915.

Tillman Margaret M. "Measuring Up: Better Baby Contests in China, 1917–45." *Modern Asian Studies* 54, no. 6 (2020):1749–1786.

To, Kelvin K.W., and KwokYung Yuen. "In Memory of Patrick Manson, Founding Father of Tropical Medicine and the Discovery of Vector-Borne Infections." *Emerging Microbes & Infections* 1, 10 (2012): 1–7.

Tomes, Nancy. *The Gospel of Germs: Men, Women, and the Microbe in American Life*. Cambridge, MA: Harvard University Press, 1998.

Treviño, A. Javier, and Helmut Staubmann, eds. *The Routledge International Handbook of Talcott Parsons Studies*. Abingdon, UK: Routledge, 2022.

United Nations Women. *A Short History of the Commission on the Status of Women*. New York, NY: United Nations, 2019.

United States. *National Wartime Nutrition Guide*. Washington, DC: United States Department of Agriculture, War Food Administration, Nutrition and Food Conservation Branch, 1943.

Van den Akker, W. "Over de Taak van den Veterinair-hygiënist bij de Indische Gemeente." *Nederlandsch-Indische Bladen voor Diergeneeskunde* no. 41 (1929): 201–215.

Van der Meer, Arnout. *Performing Power: Cultural Hegemony, Identity, and Resistance in Colonial Indonesia*. Ithaca, NY: Cornell University Press, 2020.

Van Dijk, Kees, and Jean Gelman Taylor, eds. *Cleanliness and Culture: Indonesian Histories*. Leiden: KITLV Press, 2011.

Van Nederveen Meerkerk, Elise. *Women, Work and Colonialism in the Netherlands and Java: Comparisons, Contrasts, and Connections, 1830–1940*. Cham: Springer International Publishing, 2019.

Van Veen, André. "Nutrition Studies in Indonesia 1850–1950." *Documenta Neerlandica et Indonesica de Morbis Tropicis* 2, no. 4 (1950).

Verslag der Eerste Hygiëne-Tentoonstelling in Nederlandsch Indië. Bandoeng: Vereeniging tot Bevordering der Hygiëne in Nederlandsch-Indië, 1927.

Von Römer, L.A.S.M. *Over Baringen: Een Boekje voor de Doekoen-doekoen Beranak = Pemimpin Doekoen Beranak*. Weltevreden: Balai Poestaka, 1922.

Wal, S.L. van der. *Het Onderwijsbeleid in Nederlands-Indië, 1900–1940: Een Bronnenpublikatie = Education Policy in the Netherlands-Indies, 1900–1940*. Groningen: J.B. Wolters, 1963.

Weinbaum, Alys Eve, and Modern Girl Around the World Research Group. *The Modern Girl around the World: Consumption, Modernity, and Globalization*. Durham, NC: Duke University Press, 2008.

Welter, Barbara. "The Cult of True Womanhood: 1820–1860." *American Quarterly* 18, no. 2 (1966): 151–174.

White, Sally Jane. "Reformist Islam, Gender and Marriage in Late Colonial Dutch East Indies, 1900–1942." PhD dissertation, Australian National University, 2004.

Wieringa, Saskia. *Sexual Politics in Indonesia.* Basingstoke: Palgrave Macmillan, 2002.

Williams, Doone, and Greer Williams. *Every Child a Wanted Child: Clarence James Gamble, M.D. and His Work in the Birth Control Movement,* edited by Emily Flint. Boston, MA: Harvard University Press, 1978.

Wyndham, Hugh Archibald. *Native Education: Ceylon, Java, Formosa, the Philippines, French Indo-China, and British Malaya.* London: Oxford University Press, 1933.

Yacob, Shakila. "Model of Welfare Capitalism? The United States Rubber Company in Southeast Asia, 1910–1942." *Enterprise and Society* 8, no. 1 (2007): 136–174.

Yamamoto, Nobuto. "Print Power and Censorship in Colonial Indonesia, 1914–1942." PhD dissertation, Cornell University, 2011.

Index

Note: Page numbers in *italics* indicate figures.

The authorized representative in the EU for product safety and compliance is:
Mare Nostrum Group
B.V Doelen 72
4831 GR Breda
The Netherlands

www.ingramcontent.com/pod-product-compliance
Lightning Source LLC
Chambersburg PA
CBHW020511270326
41926CB00008B/834